James Harrison Rigg

A Comparative View of Church Organisations, Primitive and Protestant

With a Supplement on Methodist Successions and Methodist Union. Third Edition

James Harrison Rigg

A Comparative View of Church Organisations, Primitive and Protestant
With a Supplement on Methodist Successions and Methodist Union. Third Edition

ISBN/EAN: 9783337162641

Printed in Europe, USA, Canada, Australia, Japan

Cover: Foto ©ninafisch / pixelio.de

More available books at **www.hansebooks.com**

A COMPARATIVE VIEW

OF

CHURCH ORGANISATIONS,

PRIMITIVE AND PROTESTANT.

WITH A SUPPLEMENT ON

METHODIST SECESSIONS AND METHODIST UNION.

BY

JAMES H. RIGG, D.D.,

Author of "The Living Wesley," "The Churchmanship of John Wesley," etc.

THIRD EDITION. REVISED AND ENLARGED.

London:

CHARLES H. KELLY,

2, CASTLE STREET, CITY ROAD, E.C.; AND 66, PATERNOSTER ROW, E.C.

1897

PREFACE.

THE demand for a third edition of this volume brings with it for the Author fresh opportunity, and also special responsibility.

I have been enabled to publish in the Appendix to this edition condensed historical *résumés*, showing, in something like completeness of outline, the organic development in detail of Wesleyan Methodism, in two chief respects. First, a view is given of the rise and growth of the system of Connexional government by means of District Meetings, now called District Synods, by which unity and detailed efficiency of administration were secured after Wesley's death, and have been maintained ever since, during a century of wonderful growth and development. Secondly, a distinct, and in all essential points, I believe, a complete history is given, in outline, of the not less interesting or vitally important subject of Circuit development in Methodism.

I have felt, now that I have passed into the second

half of my eighth decade of years in life, that it was my special duty to make this, which I must regard as my final edition of a work to which has been conceded a place in the standard literature of my Church, as accurate and complete throughout as it was possible for me to make it. In handling subjects more or less controversial, also, I have done my best so to say what seemed necessary to be said, as to avoid all possible occasion for offence on the part of reasonable persons. At the same time, I have added several pages, and made a few verbal corrections, in regard to points of leading importance, in what I have written on the subject of Anglicanism.

How far I have succeeded in my aims, others will judge. To do my utmost has been for me a happy labour and study

It may not be improper here to note that, while this volume has been passing through the press, some of the subjects dealt with in the chapters on Anglicanism have been under discussion at the Church Congress held lately at Shrewsbury. The parallelism of the line of discussion and suggestion on the subject of "The Laity and Church Government" with the course of argument in this volume, as to the present and pressing needs of the Church of England in the way of reorganisation and disciplinary reform, was marked and notable. Yet more striking, perhaps, is the evidently unconscious parallelism with another argument in this volume of Lord Halifax's earnest and pathetic defence of the orders and spiritual legitimacy of his Church against the Pope's Bull on the subject of Anglican Orders and Sacraments—a deliverance claiming the attribute of infallibility, which would go to unchurch our National Establishment, and which pronounces its Sacraments to be destitute of Divine character and authority. The argument in this volume to which I refer is that employed (at pp. 76-79) in defending orthodox Nonconformist Churches against the sentence pronounced on them by Anglo-Catholics like Lord Halifax, who deny the authority and spiritual efficacy of their sacred ministrations, and assert that they are debarred from the fountains of sacramental life in Christ. The pleading of Lord Halifax against the sentence of the Pope may well move Nonconformist readers to compassion. Forty years ago, Cardinal Manning rebuked the Anglican exclusiveness of Dr. Pusey, comparing his pretensions as an Anglican unfavourably with the merits of such Dissenters as the saintly Richard Baxter and other eminent Nonconformists; now, the Pope disallows and reproves the intolerant and exclusive claims of Lord Halifax and the Church Union. It remains to be seen whether Lord Halifax and his followers, more wise in their time than their teacher was forty years ago, will learn from the Pope the lesson which Dr. Pusey would not learn from Cardinal Manning, and, abandoning the road to Rome, take their stand on the Reformed Evangelical platform.

It has been a great satisfaction to find that in other Churches than my own a candid and kindly reception has been accorded to the two former editions of this late "fruit of an old tree," and I am encouraged to hope that the present edition will receive an equally kind and candid reception.

I have to acknowledge with special thanks the valuable help of Mr. W. A. Parsonson, of the Wesleyan Conference Office, in reading the proof sheets of this edition, and the kind service rendered by the Rev. J. Edward Harlow, of Ross, in preparing the Index.

JAMES H. RIGG.

November 5, 1896.

PREFACE TO THE SECOND EDITION.

THE reception given to the first edition of this book has been very gratifying. I have to thank my critics of various denominations for recognising so frankly, and reciprocating so fully and kindly, my own sincere endeavour to write throughout in a candid and catholic spirit. So far as I know, no journal representing any one of the great denominations, whose principles and whose practical influence, as illustrated by their history, I undertook to review, showed any resentment at my criticism, while leading and representative journals, notwithstanding the frankness, here and there, of my strictures, gave ungrudging praise. Nor, with one exception, did the organs of the smaller Methodist bodies show anything like irritation. Their general tone of comment was generously appreciative.

Unfortunately, in a few instances, I had, in the closing pages of the volume, written under great pressure, fallen into statistical errors—not indeed of a serious character, but still to be regretted. These I have corrected in this edition. They were not such as materially to affect any point in my argument.

A new chapter, relating to American Methodism, will, I hope, make the volume, as it now appears, more complete and valuable than the first edition. I have also, in an Appendix, added a cardinal document, issued a few years ago by the Wesleyan Conference, which shows how closely and strictly modern Methodism adheres to the primary and central principles and provisions of early Methodism, so far as regards its spiritual character and discipline.

JAMES H. RIGG.

June 1, 1891.

PREFACE TO THE FIRST EDITION.

THE papers of which the following pages contain the substance were written at the request of my friend Dr. Gregory, the late editor of the *Wesleyan Methodist Magazine*, and were published in that journal during the years 1885 and 1886. They appear in the present form at the unanimous request of the Wesleyan Book Committee. In compliance with the earnest request also of the same Committee, whose urgency under the circumstances had force to overcome a great degree of reluctance on my part, I have added two chapters, one almost entirely, the other entirely, new, the latter of these being a "supplementary chapter" on "Methodist Secessions and Methodist Union."[1] I had supposed myself to have done more than thirty years before with most of the subjects with which, especially in the last two chapters, I have been led to deal in this volume; but I have felt it to be a duty to respond to the call of my brethren, and do what is in my power to define and defend the position of Wesleyan Methodism, not only in relation to the other great Churches of the country, but also in relation to other Methodist bodies in England. I may add that the earlier chapters have all been carefully revised, and that considerable additions have been made, chiefly in the way of notes, but also partly in the text.

During the last twenty years several series of lectures have been delivered in which, from the point of view respectively of all the great British Christian denominations, the Churches of the country, including Wesleyan Methodism, have been subjected to criticism, always fair in spirit and intent, if not always well informed. In the present volume, last of all, an analogous critical and comparative survey of the Churches has been undertaken from the point of view of Wesleyan Methodism, the basis of all the criticism and of the whole comparison being sought in the fellowship of the primitive Church and in the motives and principles of Church organisation and

[1] The former of the two chapters referred to is that on "The Distinctive Ecclesiastical Principles of Wesleyan Methodism," pp. 235-261 in the present edition (1897).

discipline, so far as these may be probably inferred from the Scriptures of the New Testament and from the other Christian writings of the first century of the Church's history. I have endeavoured in my writing to imitate the Christian courtesy as well as the frankness of those critics of other Churches to whose works I have referred. No one will deny that the time had come for a Wesleyan representative to explain and defend the position and principles of his own Church. If I have offended against justice or charity, I shall be liable to judgment. I can hardly hope that I have escaped all fault of prejudice any more than all error of statement. But I am conscious that I have at least striven to be fair, and taken pains that I might be accurate.

JAMES H. RIGG.

February 10, 1887.

CONTENTS.

I.

The Primitive Church.

CHAPTER I.

THE FELLOWSHIP OF THE PRIMITIVE CHURCH . 3

CHAPTER II.

ORGANISATION OF THE PRIMITIVE CHURCH (30–130 A.D.) 24

II.

Anglicanism.

CHAPTER I.

WHAT THE REFORMATION MEANT FOR THE CHURCH OF ENGLAND, AND WHAT IT ACCOMPLISHED— ANGLICANISM DURING THE TUDOR PERIOD . . 49

CHAPTER II.

THE MODERN CHURCH OF ENGLAND—THE WANT OF A LAY FELLOWSHIP—THE DILEMMA OF THE ENGLISH CHURCH   67

CHAPTER III.

PRESENT QUESTIONS FOR THE CHURCH OF ENGLAND—THE CONTROVERSY ON CHURCH REFORM . . 87

III.

Presbyterianism.

CHAPTER I.

FIRST PRINCIPLES AND EARLY CHARACTER AND INFLUENCE OF PRESBYTERIANISM . . . 117

CHAPTER II.

THE CHARACTER AND INFLUENCE OF PRESBYTERIANISM AS MODIFIED IN LATER TIMES 138

IV.

Congregationalism.

CHAPTER I.

AN HISTORICAL STUDY OF THE PRINCIPLES AND WORKING OF INDEPENDENCY TILL RECENT YEARS . . 153

CHAPTER II.

AN EXAMINATION OF THE PRINCIPLES OF CONGREGATIONAL INDEPENDENCY 170

CHAPTER III.

EXAMINATION OF THE PRINCIPLES OF CONGREGATIONAL INDEPENDENCY—*continued* 183

V.
Wesleyan Methodism.

CHAPTER I.

THE METHODISM OF THE WESLEYS—THE DOCTRINE AND THE FELLOWSHIP OF WESLEYAN METHODISM—THE SPREAD OF WESLEYAN DOCTRINE—THE MUTUAL RELATIONS OF DOCTRINE AND FELLOWSHIP—THE SPECIAL CHARACTERISTICS OF METHODIST PREACHING 207

CHAPTER II.

OUTLINE OF THE ECCLESIASTICAL ORGANISATION OF WESLEYAN METHODISM 221

CHAPTER III.

THE DISTINCTIVE ECCLESIASTICAL PRINCIPLES OF WESLEYAN METHODISM—COMPARISON WITH "REGULAR" PRESBYTERIAN CHURCHES—WESLEYAN METHODISM AND METHODIST SECESSIONS 235

CHAPTER IV.

AMERICAN EPISCOPAL METHODISM . . 262

VI.
Supplementary.

METHODIST SECESSIONS AND METHODIST UNION . . 305

Appendices.

A. THE CLASS-MEETING IN WESLEYAN METHODISM . 345
B. THE DISTRICT SYNOD IN METHODISM, ITS DEVELOPMENT AND PRESENT FUNCTIONS: AN HISTORICAL SKETCH 355
C. THE CIRCUIT DEVELOPMENT OF METHODISM . . 377

I.

THE PRIMITIVE CHURCH.

CHAPTER I.

THE FELLOWSHIP OF THE PRIMITIVE CHURCH.

IN order to gain a comparative view of the various leading forms and organisations of Christian activity, or, in other words, of the different Churches which undertake to represent and to diffuse the kingdom of Christ, it is necessary, in the first instance, to understand from what living root of organisation Christianity began to live and grow and spread. A clear understanding as to this point will serve, at least, to show what are the essential attributes of Church life, *i.e.* of Christian life in organised fellowship. It may also serve to indicate what was the initial bias given to the development of the Church, and in what manner its life began to unfold. Hence may possibly be suggested some laws or conditions of development which are of permanent application and authority, and also some conclusions as to what points of organisation or development are non-essential and subordinate.

The appeal of Anglican High Churchmen is chiefly to the example and authority of the Church of the first four centuries. If the appeal were made to the really primitive Church at Jerusalem, they would be cast at every point; if to the apostolic Churches among the Gentiles, their discomfiture might be somewhat less complete, but would be signal still. The appeal of their contradictory opposites, the "Brethren," in their different and conflicting sections, is specifically to the primitive Church in its earliest form, which, however, when its life and character are truly understood, lends no sanction to their peculiar principles; while, if the appeal were carried to the apostolic Churches as their organisation is disclosed in the Acts and the Epistles, the views of the "Brethren" would be found in direct conflict with apostolic principles and precedents. The Presbyterians, again, make their appeal to apostolic precedents and instructions as contained in the Acts and Epistles, and they find much to support their theory. But they fail to observe that their claim to stereotype the Church according to their form, and to fix its limit and liberty of adaptation and development according to their theory, is contrary to the precedents of the primitive Church and to the spirit which governed its development; and, moreover, that their economy fixes as the necessary and universal law of the Church some points of usage which, so far as they obtained in the apostolic age, were occasional and accidental.

The Congregationalists, once more, contend that their principles of Church government and discipline, and theirs only, are in accordance with primitive usage and apostolic teaching, and should be maintained as the model for all ages and stages of the Church's advancement: whereas the apostolic history and letters prove that the Congregational form represents, not an ideal model, but particular cases arising out of circumstances; that its limits and its special features represent, not perfection of form and full development, but defect of opportunity, and arrest of influence and extension arising from such defect; and that its fundamental principles of negation, erected as they are into dogmas of limitation, are in contradiction to the spirit and vital tendency of Church development in the apostolic age.

Such being some of the leading questions which are raised when we seek to gain a comparative view of the various forms and theories of Church organisation and government which divide the allegiance of Christians,—leaving Romanism out of account,—it is evident that we cannot fairly start upon our way without, in the first instance, entering upon an enquiry as to the earliest form, and the bias and laws of the earliest development, of the primitive and apostolic Church, both at the beginning in Jerusalem and afterwards among the Gentiles. Whether the views which have already been stated in outline and by anticipation, will be established by the investigation on which we are entering, my readers will judge. If they should be, larger conclusions will follow.

The form of the Church at Jerusalem in its earliest phase of existence is very clearly set before us in the early chapters of the Acts of the Apostles. The penitents having professed their faith in Jesus Christ, and having been baptized in His name, were admitted into a "fellowship" founded on the "apostles' teaching," sealed and renewed continually by the "breaking of bread," and manifested in a loving and generous care for the poor (Acts ii. 37–47; iv. 32–35; v. 42). They had—as yet they could have —no collective assemblies for worship in sanctuaries of their own. So far as public worship was concerned, at this earliest period they were of necessity restricted to the use of the Temple services—the "prayers" spoken of in Acts ii. 42. In attendance on these Temple prayers they

were assiduous, following the example of the apostles
(Acts iii. 1; v. 42). But the special character of this
primitive believing multitude was that of a very numerous,
but more or less private, "Society." They "brake bread
from house to house, eating their meat with gladness and
singleness of heart." Their own proper fellowship meetings
were at once social and sacred. They met not collectively,
but distributively; they could not meet collectively; they
were counted by thousands, and they had no synagogues of
their own. They met to take the evening meal at each
other's houses, but each meal was made sacramental; they
ate "with gladness," and they "brake bread" eucharistically
with religious solemnity. These evening gatherings were
also the ordinary opportunities for hearing the "apostles'
teaching," which, it cannot be doubted, was often given
by those who, although original disciples, were not apostles,
but belonged to the company of the "hundred and twenty"
(Acts l. 15). The central and more select meetings of the
apostles and the elder disciples, some of the most worthy
and distinguished of whom were afterwards to become in an
official sense "elders," we may presume to have been held
in the sacred upper room where the tongues of fire
appeared, crowning that blessed original company. Thus
they continued steadfastly in the "apostles' teaching and in
the fellowship, in the breaking of bread, and in the [public]
prayers" at the Temple. Thus they ceased not "daily with
one accord" to worship "in the Temple," and also to "break
bread from house to house." Thus "daily in the Temple,
and in every house, they ceased not to teach and preach
Jesus Christ." After a time the apostles, in part through the
fame of their miracles, were able to make the Temple courts
places for habitual preaching, not merely to the "disciples"

or "brethren" who gathered there, but to the unconverted people, as Peter had preached on the day of Pentecost.

To this first phase and shape of organisation in the Christian Church some of the "Brethren" have been accustomed to appeal. But even they have not attempted literally to conform to this pattern anywhere for any length of time. They have not held all their strict fellowship meetings from house to house, nor made the evening meal, being the principal meal of the day and partaken of from house to house, a necessary part of their devotional fellowship, combining with it the eucharistic "breaking of bread." Of late years, indeed, I believe there has been less pretence than formerly that the fellowship of the "Brethren" has been strictly modelled, or that any Christian fellowship can be modelled, upon the type of the Jerusalem Church in its earliest period. It needs no formal argument to convince one who really thinks about the matter, at that period the primitive Church was, in relation to the more mature type that was to be developed,— to the full grown "man in Christ Jesus," to apply St. Paul's metaphor in its just sense (Eph. iv. 13),—as the new-born infant to the adult. From the sacred history itself we gain some knowledge of the stages by which, before the destruction of the Temple and the Jewish commonwealth, the Church was developed within Judæa. Further still, and what is of essential importance, we learn how the apostolic Churches outside Palestine, Gentile Churches or partly Jew and partly Gentile, were developed with greater independence and a larger reach of movement and of liberty, out of sight, as they were, of the Temple at Jerusalem, and many of them out of sight also of the synagogue, with its special organisation, its rules and prescriptions.

Although the earliest fellowship at Jerusalem affords no model of organic perfection in a Church, but rather of organic imperfection, it does furnish a living instance, and therefore a test, of what is essential to the vital play, the fresh and true experience, of the regenerate soul. In the sub-Pentecostal Church at Jerusalem we see the experimental life of the Christian believer, in the genuineness and simplicity of his "first love," nakedly shown in its individuality, apart, as far as possible, from organisation, or at least in combination with a minimum of form. Accordingly we see this essential life, and its pure and simple play, more distinctly and in more bare and absolute truth of presentation here than elsewhere. It is as though we could look straight into the inner heart of the Christian fellowship, and see its vital elements, its beat, its circulation, its action and reaction.

Let us ask ourselves, then, what, as shown by this palmary example, are the essentials of Christian life and fellowship, as distinguished from the proprieties or conveniences or helpful instruments and ordinances of a matured Church organisation. Here are the elements as we find them in the history :

1. For each individual believer, Repentance and Faith (Acts ii. 37–41); then Baptism, the public and solemn confession of the Triune God, and of Christ the Saviour, Son of God and Son of man, this confession being made under the influence of the Holy Spirit, and attended by special spiritual power and blessing (Acts ii. 38, 41 ; Matt. xxviii. 19).

2. An actual loving, social fellowship of the converts, carried on from house to house, carried out in large and noble beneficence towards all that were in poverty and

distress, and sealed continually by the Eucharist, crowning the social and common meals of the brotherhood as partaken of "from house to house."

Two other things are also to be noted:

3. The "apostles' teaching" was the staple and never-exhausted subject of instruction at all the meetings of the believing converts, who were not only brethren, but "disciples" of the risen Lord, followers of His life and doctrine as taught by the apostles and original disciples.

4. The public worship of God was strictly and sedulously observed by regular attendance at the Temple, at the hours of prayer and sacrifice, twice daily. Of their own properly and specially Christian worship, collective and public, as yet there was none. But the Jewish worship was for them illuminated with a Christian meaning. Moreover, in the courts of the Temple the merely ritual psalmody and prayer-service was supplemented by gospel teaching. Whatever was still deficient was made up by the instruction so zealously and unintermittingly given from house to house, and by the free spiritual fellowship of their homely, social gatherings.

The primitive fellowship, accordingly,—that which shows us simply and precisely in what Christian life and fellowship essentially consist,—was a fellowship founded on "the apostles' teaching," "as the truth is in Jesus" (Eph. iv. 21); a fellowship inspired and animated by conscious life in Christ —the new life of the believers through repentance and faith, attended by a happy sense of the Divine acceptance; a fellowship expressed and sustained by new and special means of spiritual sympathy and intercourse, and by special developments of mutual care and beneficence; a fellowship sealed by the Sacraments which our Lord had instituted—Baptism and the "breaking of bread"; a fellowship maintained in harmony with the appointed ordinances of public worship, as established in the Temple services.

Here, then, we see what are the essential doctrines of evangelical orthodoxy: *repentance, faith,* and *regeneration,* which implies, as its continuation and completion, *sanctification.* These lie at the root of all teaching; these are before rites or sacraments; these doctrines, however learnt, by whatsoever channel received, are the living truths which, through the Holy Spirit, are effectual for the salvation of men.

Here, again, we learn what are the proper and necessary sacraments, which, though not the primary source of spiritual life or salvation, are yet its divinely appointed accompaniments, its signs and its seals: Baptism, as the solemn rite of admission into the holy fellowship; the Lord's Supper, as the sacred seal of recognition by which believers continually renew their covenant relations with God in Christ and with each other. And here, inmost mystery of all, is the pulsing life itself, as it manifested itself in that "hour of prime," that dawn of the Church's everlasting glory, the life into which believers are introduced through the Christian doctrine, spiritually apprehended and received, and which cannot but remain one and the same life in all true believers from age to age, and cannot but reproduce in those who receive it the spiritual experience of the primitive believers.

As to the mode and form of the fellowship, it is not easy, in looking upon the picture of the primitive Church at Jerusalem, to discriminate between that which is essential and that which was only accidental. It is evident that neither as to the manner of meeting together from house to house, nor as to the occasions and mode of "breaking bread," any more than as to their manner of public worship, is it possible for Christians to-day to follow the example of the Church at Jerusalem. The provisions for public worship, for hearing and learning the "apostles' teaching," for the administration of the sacraments, for ministering to the needy, and for close spiritual fellowship in true interchange of sympathy, soul with soul, must widely differ to-day from what the sacred history shows to have existed then. They must differ according to various conditions of time, place, and circumstance. So much as this, however, we are warranted to say: that unless a Christian Church in some effective manner makes provision for real individual fellowship,—fellowship which joins into one living brotherhood the general society of believers, so that each believer may have actual spiritual comradeship with some company of other believers, and be linked to the whole body in vital and organic connexion, and so that all may have an opportunity of using their spiritual faculties and gifts,—that Church is essentially defective.

At Jerusalem the fellowship was a true and equal brotherhood under the general direction of the apostles. It is impossible to read the account given in Acts iv. 23–31 with attention and an open mind, without perceiving that "their own company," to which Peter and John, with the healed cripple, returned after their dismissal from before the Sanhedrim, were not only "all filled with the Holy Ghost," but all "spake the word of God with boldness." As on the day of Pentecost, so afterwards, in that Church the spirit of testimony rested on all the believers, without regard to office or ordination. Thus when persecution broke out, and the disciples were "all scattered abroad," they "went about preaching the word" (Acts viii. 1–4). In strict agreement and consecutive consistency with this statement, we further read (xi. 19, 20) that of those "scattered abroad" in this "persecution," and who travelled from Jerusalem as far as to Antioch, "speaking the word to the Jews," some, who "were men of Cyprus and Cyrene," when they came to Antioch, "spake unto the Greeks [1] also, preaching the Lord Jesus." These men were neither apostles nor yet prophets, for we read a few verses later of the first arrival of "prophets" at Antioch from Jerusalem; they were merely disciples, destitute of any official character whatever. But they spoke freely the truth they had received, and used "the gift that was in" them. With such facts before us, it is unreasonable to doubt that in all meetings of the primitive Church where there was discourse as to the doctrines and duties of the gospel faith and life, there was free scope for any to speak who were moved to speak. They spoke with simple freedom their experience, they used whatever gifts they possessed, they were full of a new life, and "the Spirit of life in Christ Jesus"—of this new life—"gave them utterance."

So it was in the Church at Jerusalem, and so it continued to be in the apostolic Churches. St. Paul lays down the very principle which sanctions such freedom of mutual intercourse, such interchange of ideas and feelings, such family simplicity of communion and fellowship, when, in the fourth chapter of his Epistle to the Ephesians, he says that Christ's body, the Church, is to increase "through that which every joint supplieth, according to the working in due measure of each several part," all "speaking the truth in love," and thus all growing up together "in all things into

[1] The right reading, as in the Revised Version.

Christ the Head." Nor is it possible to read the twelfth chapter of the Epistle to the Romans (vers. 3-13), or those graphic chapters of the first Epistle to the Corinthians (xi., xii., xiv.), where the apostle depicts the interior scenes of disorderly Church life occasioned by a too exuberant and various energy and excitement, in which spurious impulses and influences combined with the spring and outflow of the new life in Christ Jesus, without recognising the fact that a broad freedom of Christian speech and intercourse prevailed in the primitive period of the apostolic Churches. True, there was abuse and excess, but the abuse was a perversion of the use, and an evidence of its existence and its rights, according to the ancient legal maxim, "Abusus non tollit usum." The excess was a thing to be corrected and guarded against; when it arose out of a liberty identified with the very life of the Christian faith and fellowship in its first awakening, its remedy was not to be sought in quenching, but in regulating, that liberty. When we remember that if Peter and John were the chief teachers at Jerusalem, Paul had "planted, Apollos watered, and God gave the increase" at Corinth, we shall understand that the bright and beautiful picture at Jerusalem and the disorderly developments at Corinth teach the same lesson,—that "where the Spirit of the Lord is, there is liberty," and that to "each one" was given "the manifestation of the Spirit to profit withal," whether it were "a psalm, a teaching, a revelation, a tongue, or an interpretation"; that "all" were at liberty to "prophesy one by one, that all might learn, and all might be comforted," although, at the same time, it was needful to remember what at Corinth some forgot, that all things needed to be done decently and without confusion. The possession of supernatural gifts by many of the primitive believers heightened and diversified the effects of the new life as manifested in the Church assemblies; but at the foundation of all these gifts, and spreading far beyond them in range, was the experimental witness-bearing and the mutual edification and exhortation which formed the staple of the uttered fellowship of those first believers. The prophets were not under miraculous inspiration, although doubtless they were under supernatural influence, when in the public assembly they spake " unto edification, and exhortation, and comfort " (1 Cor. xiv. 3). Those " prophets," as we learn from the *Teaching of the Apostles*, were teachers, often itinerant preachers, found everywhere in the Churches, and recognised as having a place in the Church economy; but they were not ordained pastors or rulers of the Church. Indeed, not only prophets, evangelists, gifted brethren— sometimes gifted sisters—bore their part in witnessing " as the Spirit gave them utterance," but brethren, as we have seen, who were absolutely undistinguished, simple units in the primitive fellowship, " went about preaching the word." So free was that earliest Christian fellowship; so spontaneous, so simply mutual, was the frank intercommunion flowing from heart to heart and lip to lip.

How far, then, from conformity to primitive Christianity are those Christian communities in which no provision is made, no opportunity offered, for such fellowship, such intercommunion, as that which has now been described! Where the members of the fellowship are all merely passive, where no one teaches or speaks or offers vocal prayer but the priest, pastor, or minister, there is no trace left of likeness to the original fellowship of Christian believers as it existed in the apostolic age. Unfortunately there are Protestant

Churches maintaining, in form and general statement at least, the doctrines of apostolic Christianity, which not merely have made no attempt to realise the spiritual and mutual fellowship of the primitive Church, but, indeed, appear to ignore it altogether. Such are the politico-ecclesiastical forms of Church organisation that have been established on the Continent since the rise of Luther, whether known as Lutheran or Reformed "communions." Voluntary organisations, indeed, within these Churches— "Pietistic" communities—have at times afforded something like a reproduction of the early fellowship, with its experimental savour and its simple spontaneousness; but these have commonly been regarded with disfavour by the authorities; they have formed no part or appendage of the recognised Church organisation. This failure on the part of the Continental Protestant Churches has been one main cause of their stagnancy, of their rationalism, of their dead halt in the midst of the conflict with Rome, and their sterility for centuries past. This defect and the rigidity of State control which has fettered them—kindred and allied evils —have smitten Continental Protestantism with spiritual barrenness, forcing at the same time the highest energies of the Churches into the field of merely intellectual comment and criticism, such as, when orthodox, has too often assumed forms of unprofitable subtlety, and such as, in a large proportion of instances, has rioted in heterodox speculation of altogether pernicious and antichristian tendency. Having lost consciousness of the great end of all Christian doctrine and organisation, which, as St. Paul teaches, is " love out of a pure heart and a good conscience and faith unfeigned," they have wasted their strength on questions that minister strife " rather than godly edifying," and are as ill-adapted to the furtherance of true religion and godliness as the "endless genealogies" of which the apostle speaks in the context of the passage just quoted (1 Tim. i. 5).

In England, national liberty—a sort and degree of liberty, even in that age, with all its forms of legal violence, altogether unknown on the Continent—saved our Christianity in the sixteenth and seventeenth centuries from suffering from a similar blight. The spirit of English liberty so far prevailed against State authority and ecclesiastical prescription, even in the Church of which the sovereign was the constitutional head, as to leave scope for Puritanism. In connexion with Puritanism, for the space of a century, spiritual liberty—liberty of witness-bearing and of homely and experimental fellowship—maintained itself, although often in ways accounted "irregular," and sometimes against canons, rubrics, and Star Chamber inquisition and oppression. When Puritanism was cast out of the Church of England, the national life in all senses was declining; and only partially and for a time did the Nonconformists maintain the spiritual liberty and the living fellowship that had distinguished Puritanism in its highest forms and its best times. When Methodism arose, the Church life of England had fallen lower than among the Protestant Churches of the Continent, where such men as Bengel and Francke, Pietists of the noblest type, upheld the standard of primitive doctrine and experience, and where the Moravians had, in not a few respects, reproduced, in its essential features, the life of the primitive fellowship.

The fatal defect of which I have spoken has placed the Protestant Churches of the Continent in some respects at a disadvantage as compared even with the Church of Rome.

That Church had lost the primitive fellowship,—had, indeed gradually perverted and destroyed it; but in the process it had developed, for certain purposes and in certain respects, a sort of substitute, though by no means an equivalent. The two institutions by which Rome replaced the primitive fellowship were monasticism and the confessional. By the former it made provision for enthusiastic or deeply impressionable spirits, longing for a religious vocation and consecration, although not seeking the priesthood. By the latter it brought every heart when under the influence of religious emotion into direct relation with the Church and its ministry, and gave a voice to every burdened spirit. Truly it was a terrible and blasphemous perversion which enforced confession to the priest and pretended to invest him with the power of absolution. But yet it gave the Church a hold, by the way of the conscience and heart, on every member: on the man, above all on the woman, and even on the tender minds of boys and girls; whereas Continental Protestantism was a mere mechanism of congregational rites, freezingly cold and impersonal, without a touch or movement or faintest breath in them of individual emotion or mutual fellowship, linked to a provision of dogmatic instruction administered by the public officials. What wonder if, under such conditions, Romanism won back not a little of the ground in which Protestantism had at one time taken root! What wonder that Romish superstition took a stronger hold of human hearts than Protestant rationalism! But for the disparaged Pietists and for the mystics of the better side, however obscure might be some of their teaching, and however tinged with enthusiasm, Continental Protestantism, before the end of the eighteenth century, would have been nothing but the dry stubble of dead forms, showing only that once there had been life and growth. Whatever improvement there has been during the course of the present century has been mainly due in part to a powerful and profound recoil from the abysmal darkness and horrors of the great French Revolution, and in part to the influence of Methodism, carried over in various ways to the Continent, since the downfall of the first Napoleon, from England, and, especially of recent years, from America.

And if the want of a genuine fellowship, vivid, spiritual, and truly mutual, has been the blight of Continental Protestantism, the blessing of such a fellowship, as reproduced in Wesleyan Methodism, has been the secret of strength, of propagandist power, of vitality, plasticity, ease of movement, and facility of development, for the various Churches of the great Methodist family—a family of Churches which is now manifestly in the ascendant among the forces of Protestantism throughout the world.

How far it may be possible for the other Protestant Churches to introduce into their systems provisions equivalent to those which have given such powerful vitality to Methodism, remains to be seen. Can the Established Church within her loose folds allow a liberty, and even encourage influences and developments, which may, for all that are touched with earnest feeling as to their souls and eternity, afford the opportunity of real spiritual fellowship, living and sympathetic? If she can and does, it will be for her prosperity and for the lengthening of her tranquillity. If she cannot, and if, failing to do this, she takes the only alternative possible in this urgent age, and turns the earnestness of her members into the channel of the confessional, of the secluded sisterhood under priestly tutelage, and the priest-guided guild, such a recurrence to mediæval forms of discipline and devotion, such a return to abject spiritual bondage,—not free spiritual service of God, but degrading subjection of mind and will to men "of like passions," "compassed with infirmity,"—can only result in disaster to that Church and dishonour to the Christian faith and name. There is at this moment a conflict within the Established Church between the two tendencies. Both are powerful. On the result of this conflict how much depends! Is the confessional, is the conventual and sacramentarian tendency, to win? or is the free evangelical movement to prevail? and will that evangelical movement lead to such a practical and customary modification of Church arrangements as to make adequate provision for Christian fellowship in true primitive simplicity and in free variety of testimony and of personal activity?

The like questions arise in regard to other Church organisations. The want of organised provision for free and simple experimental fellowship within the Presbyterian Churches of Scotland has been a vital defect in the past. Hence the rule of "Moderatism," which, if it meant spiritual apathy, meant not the less Presbyterianism unimpeachable in form and safe in all its arrangements. In connexion with any and every outburst of new life, violence had to be done to the regular forms and approved precedents of administration and discipline. And the influences which brought in the new life seldom, if ever, sprang up among the regular Presbyterian Churches themselves; they were derived from foreign sources, or came down from remainders of olden liberty and life, from "schismatic" survivals. These revival movements have conquered for themselves a certain recognised place among the Presbyterian Churches of our times. But what provision is there in the different branches of Presbyterianism for their continuance, their maintenance and reproduction ? Are they not still in the nature of " irregularities," rather than part of the normal life of the Churches ? are they yet regarded as essential to the integrity and vitality of true apostolic Presbyterianism ?

Similar questions might be asked as to the Congregationalist bodies, both Baptist and Pædobaptist. For, in fact, even more than mere soundness of doctrinal forms, the organised provision of free and mutual spiritual fellowship is a vital condition of prosperity for every Christian Church, and may be regarded as a working test *stantis aut cadentis Ecclesiæ*—of a living or declining Church.

For a short time after the period of the Commonwealth, as I have already intimated, the Nonconformist Churches of England maintained, in a greater or less degree, the spiritual freedom and the living fellowship which had distinguished Puritanism in its highest forms and in its best times. Before the middle of the eighteenth century English Dissent had fallen to the level of that decorous but materialistic age. Nor did it begin to revive till the influence of Methodism had touched the Churches. In the early part of the present century this revival was beginning visibly to spread. From this time for many years the Church meetings partook increasingly of the nature of fellowship meetings, and there was often much " unction " in the Church prayer-meetings. For some years past, however, the Congregational Churches generally have been undeniably losing ground in this respect. The spiritual declension among the Baptists, indeed, has been more than arrested during the same period, very largely, it cannot be doubted, through the influence of the late Mr. Spurgeon. Apart from this special and personal influence, the question must be asked, as to the English Nonconformity of to-day, whether in the majority of existing Churches the savour of experimental fellowship gives freshness and life to the Church meetings, or power and variety to the regular prayer-meetings?

If there is substantial truth in the considerations which have been advanced in the foregoing pages, there can be no difficulty in understanding the growth and spread, especially in neighbourhoods where Methodism is weak, of the "Plymouth Brethren"—or, as they prefer to be called, the "Brethren"—in one or other of their varieties. For the "Brethren" represent the principle of free fellowship and equal brotherhood among Christian people, as opposed to the various systems which maintain—practically, at least—a close monopoly of spiritual functions for the minister, whether he be called priest, or elder, or pastor. The fellowship principle, in some form or other, is destined to win. The very success of the extreme confessional High Church party is, in fact, due to the charms of this principle, however perverted or misapplied. The success of such special movements among Low Churchmen as those of the late Mr. Pennefather and of Mr. Aitken, as clergymen, is due largely to their taking hold of the same principle. Although it is not recognised by their Church in its organisation, they have collaterally brought it forward and worked upon it. The various undenominational evangelistic societies, the power of which is felt in many directions, are embodiments of the same principle.

The Church of England, in particular, unless its organisation be materially changed, will not fail in the future, as in the past, to furnish a continual supply of recruits to the "Brethren." Men of some degree of culture, of some social pretensions, of much earnestness, and of a specially energetic temperament, men who have been accustomed to active movements and a life of variety, not unnaturally feel as if, by bearing witness to the truth, they could, in a plain and simple fashion, reach some who would never come to church. Hence a multitude of "unattached Churchmen" go to swell the number of "Brethren." Military officers especially are apt to join these irregular companies of volunteers. These men would never join the Methodists, or any organised Nonconformist sect. It suits them to belong to companies where gentlemen as such naturally take the lead, where they can never rank as "privates," seeing that there are no "officers," or else all are officers, and where they pose, not as members of any "sect," but of the primitive Church of the Lord. An organised provision of service and work, with opportunity of free speech and witness-bearing, in the Established Church, would have the effect of retaining most of these unattached Churchmen within that Church, and would, in many ways, be a blessing to the country and the world.

What I have thus far written may, I hope, serve to give a suggestive view in outline of a very large subject, of fundamental importance in its bearing upon the questions of the present hour as to evangelical doctrine and the nature and objects of Church fellowship. It was impossible even to take this preliminary view of the vital characteristics of a true Christian Church, as we look upon its living tissue of fellowship and its earliest outline of organic incipiency, without opening some questions which touch upon the subject of Church organisation in its matured forms. I have, however, barely touched upon them. I propose now to deal more directly with the subject of apostolic Church organisation and discipline, as the forms of organisation are disclosed to us in the New Testament and the earliest remains of Christian antiquity, taking account especially of such additional light as has been brought to us by the welcome discovery of that remarkable document *The Teaching of the Apostles.*

CHAPTER II.

THE ORGANISATION OF THE PRIMITIVE CHURCH (30–130 A.D.).

IT is necessary at this point again to remind my readers that various denominational defenders of their respective Church organisations have not yet ceased to claim a Divine sanction for their diverse models of Church arrangement and government, and for their different schemes of Church principles, on the ground of conformity to the New Testament ideal. It is assumed in their ecclesiastical expositions and manifestoes that there is an ideal of Church organisation and government revealed in the New Testament, and that all Churches are more or less faulty, or at least defective, which do not conform to this ideal. Such a view, however, has not been held by Wesleyan writers on the subject. They have been accustomed to teach that only a few general principles as to the matter of Church organisation and government can be said to have any distinct sanction in the New Testament, and that the particular application of these principles and the details of organisation and arrangement have been left to be determined according to the varieties of human character and of surrounding conditions and relations. They do not believe that any *ideal* is shown in the New Testament. They are of opinion that if the social, moral, and political conditions surrounding the primitive Church had been materially different from what they actually were, the form and development of the Church would have differed correspondingly.

The Church of Rome does not insist on such a claim as I have now spoken of; that Church, on the contrary, has claimed *for itself* Divine direction and authority through all its long line of development. But the Church of England, in order at the same time to claim apostolic authority, to gain sanction for its special organisation and its highly developed ritual, and to mark a line of distinction between itself and the Church of Rome, has been accustomed, as represented by not a few eminent writers, to seek within the limits of the first three or four centuries for the full and authentic development of apostolic principles and ideas in the organisation and administration of what it has been customary to speak of incorrectly as the primitive Church. It is impossible, however, to fix any limit which can be accepted as marking off the legitimate ages of development upon apostolic lines from a following period of unauthoritative development. It cannot be said that the end of the third century, or of the fourth century, or any intermediate date,—for example, the epoch of the Council of Nicæa,—separates between the period of authoritative antiquity and that of unassured and possibly erroneous development. Isaac Taylor's volumes on *Ancient Christianity*, fifty years ago, with a superfluity of learned illustration and argument, completely demolished all show of solidity or plausibility in such a line of Anglican exposition or defence.[1] Besides which, the Anglican appeal to antiquity and apostolic authority, as identified with the ages before the Nicene Council, implies that the higher

[1] The force of Taylor's argument is recognised by Lord Selborne in his *Memorials*, vol. i. p. 210.

the antiquity of any ecclesiastical usage or precedent, the purer and more authoritative, the more certainly apostolic it is in its character. Whence it follows that whatever in the Church development of the first three centuries is inconsistent with the practice and principles of the true apostolic age—which may, without controversy, be limited to the first century after the day of Pentecost—must be held to be illegitimate and unauthoritative. Hence the Church economy of the Anglican Establishment is, by its own pretensions, brought within the range of the test of apostolicity as defined by the practice of the first century.

The same test is appealed to by the defenders of Presbyterian and Congregational Church principles, as establishing the scriptural authority of their respective systems.

The view I shall support in this volume is that, except as to a very few first principles, the New Testament affords no authoritative standard of Church organisation or government; that the apostolic Church organisations were themselves variable, according to circumstances; that during the whole of the first century development was going on; that it is most reasonable to hold that successive changes in surrounding social and civil or political conditions and circumstances would justify and render necessary corresponding changes in the polity and discipline of the Church, according to its various provinces or spheres; and that, in modern times, there is the amplest reason and adequate authority for freely adapting Church arrangements to modern conditions, in many respects so different from the conditions which surrounded the earth.

In the Church at Jerusalem immediately after the day of Pentecost, the organisation was of extreme simplicity. There was the homely fellowship of which we have con-

sidered the nature and form, a fellowship without as yet
any settled ritual or any distinct and consecrated centres
of worship, and there were the apostles. The distinct and
definite organisation was all summed up in the apostolic
brotherhood; all authority and discipline centred there.
Whatever was done by others must have been done under
the sanction of those on whom the Lord had breathed, and
to whom He had given the keys of His kingdom. Not
only had they charge of the "word of God," and of the
two sacraments, but, as is implied in the sixth chapter of
the Acts, the "service" also of "tables" was at first a part
of their responsibility, and was regulated under their direct
authority. Here, then, was the primitive form of Church
government; and if the earliest must needs be the best,
if the primitive must indeed be the ideal, then here would
be the ideal form. And yet it would not be more unreasonable to refer back to the tribal rule of nascent
nationalities as the ideal of national government, than to
the primitive organisation of the Church at Jerusalem as
the ideal form of Christianity for modern nations and the
present time. There is a Divine law of development for
the growth and organisation of the Church of Christ, as
there is for the unfolding of all the vital forces and latent
possibilities included in every realm or province of human
growth and progress. The sixth chapter of the Acts marks
the first stage in such organic development in the primitive
Church. Here came in the necessary law of the division
of labour, in its first distinct and formal manifestation
and record. The apostles devolved on a special class of
Church officers the work which they found more or less
incompatible with the happy and effective discharge of
their highest duties as expounders of the "word of God."

"It is not fit," they said, "that we should forsake the word of God, and serve tables"; accordingly, that they might "continue steadfastly in prayer, and in the ministry of the word," they "appointed over the business of the daily ministration" to the widows "seven men," approved by the suffrages of the Church, as "of good report, full of the Spirit and of wisdom."

Here was a development which arose as simply and directly out of circumstances as did John Wesley's first appointment of Stewards in London to take charge of the fund of the Methodist Society, and of Leaders at Bristol to take oversight of the members. There was here no constitution fashioned after a model, or to fulfil an ideal supposed to be taught in the New Testament or discovered in the Mosaic institutions. Doubtless here we have the germ of the diaconate as, under one or other name, found in every Church, at least in its earlier and simpler stages. From this germ it might well be that the diaconal office would itself develop afterwards.

The next stage of which we have a trace in the development of the Church at Jerusalem was the appointment of elders, an order of Church officers doubtless suggested by the organisation of the Jewish synagogue. I am only tracing an authentic history, and lightly illustrating an easy and indeed obvious argument, which, nevertheless, the prepossessed eye is strangely apt to overlook. Therefore I say nothing at this point as to the genesis or the meaning and contents of the office of elder in the early Christian Church. My business here is to note that we learn only incidentally, and by the barest reference, in the eleventh chapter of the Acts, that, by the time Barnabas and Saul had seen the work of the gospel at Antioch well rooted, there was already a body of "elders" in the Church at Jerusalem. This may have been, not improbably, about 43 A.D., thirteen years or more after the day of Pentecost. As at the beginning of the eleventh chapter we read of "the apostles and *the brethren* that were in Judæa," and not, as in the fifteenth chapter, of "the apostles and the *elders*," it may not be improbable that at the period referred to in chapter xi. 1, which cannot well have been much earlier or later than 40 A.D., there was no formally recognised body of elders at Jerusalem. The one point on which I wish to insist is, that this step in organisation, referred to so slightly and altogether incidentally, must have been reached by a natural process, and, so to speak, almost unconsciously, in the course of the Church's growth. If it had been intended by the Head of the Church that the forms of organisation and discipline established in the apostolic Church at Jerusalem should be the Divine pattern after which later Churches were to be modelled, there would have been a solemn and explicit history on the subject in the volume of New Testament revelation. The slight, cursory, and obscure character of the notices relating to the subject actually found in the Acts is quite incompatible with the idea of a divinely prescribed model of Church organisation.

Nor are the uncertainties of the record, so far as relates to the history of the primitive Church at Jerusalem, in any degree compensated by exact and full information respecting the organisation of the Gentile Churches. As to the great Gentile mother-Church of the Syrian Antioch, we have, respecting the point of Church organisation, in reality, no information. As to other Churches, what we learn is exceedingly little, in detail nothing. In the Churches of southern Asia Minor which were founded by

St. Paul, he ordained elders within no great while after his first visiting them, though the period may perhaps have extended over more than one year. Most, if not all, of the towns were small, and among the converts were those who had had the training of Jews or Jewish proselytes : hence it may have been easier to find men of suitable knowledge and of trained character to fill the office than in such large towns as Ephesus or Corinth. At Ephesus, after some years of labour, the apostle had committed the charge of the Church to elders, who are also called bishops ("overseers," Acts xx. 28). At Corinth the Church seems to have been left by him without any complete or regular organisation, at least until the period of his visit immediately preceding his last journey to Jerusalem. If, from the opening of the Epistle to the Philippians, which, some years later, St. Paul wrote from Rome, it should not improbably be inferred that elders—called in that epistle bishops—and also that deacons, had, by the apostle's direction, been appointed comparatively early in the Philippian Church, there is, at any rate, nothing said or intimated on the subject in the Acts. But for the Epistles to Timothy and Titus, written in the latest period of the apostle's life, after the close of the history in the Acts, it would not be known that, about thirty years after the founding of the Church at Jerusalem, it had come to be the rule among the Gentile Churches for elders to be everywhere appointed; nor would it be known that it was a general and growing custom to appoint deacons as helpers to the elders and as servants to the Church, not only as to ministrations of beneficence, but also as to spiritual offices of support and consolation. So little importance would seem to belong to the historical details of these steps of organisation.

As to the nature of the elder's office, little exact or detailed knowledge can be gathered from the Acts or the Epistles. Dr. Hatch suggests that while the office of elder in Judæo-Christian Churches was probably as nearly as possible equivalent, *mutatis mutandis*, to its Jewish original, —was, in fact, the Jewish office in principle, applied and adapted to the conditions of Christian worship and fellowship,—the office of elder in the Gentile Churches was vaguer and more general in scope, in correspondence with the authority belonging to the councils of seniors or senators in Gentile cities and states; that, in fact, the one word had in Jewish-Christian Churches a distinctly Jewish, and in Gentile Churches a Greek or Græco-Roman, colouring, but so as, in either case, to connote government rather than teaching. The suggestion is not only ingenious, but seems to have something more than plausibility in its favour. Nevertheless, if we take the Pastoral Epistles as our guide, it appears singular indeed that any one should have a doubt as to the presbyter-bishop's office in Gentile Churches having, according to ordinary custom and rule, included the function of teaching as well as governing. That there were, however, at least in some Churches, in certain stages of their development, exceptional cases in which an elder, though he took his share in governing, took little part in public and formal teaching in the Church, seems to be a fair, if not an inevitable, inference from the one text on which Presbyterian doctrinaires of the strict Genevan or Scottish school, transforming an exception into a ruling principle, build so much more than can be safely founded on a solitary text which is not in obvious harmony with other texts. (Cf. 1 Tim. iii. 2 ; 2 Tim. ii. 24 ; Titus i. 9 ; 2 Tim. ii. 2 ; 1 Tim. v. 17.)

The one thing which seems to be certain is that there were considerable differences of organisation in the apostolic Churches. There were probably characteristic differences between the Judæo-Christian Churches and all others. There were certainly striking differences between some of the Gentile Churches and others. The Churches in the Pisidian Antioch, in Iconium, and in Lystra and Derbe, were, within a year or two, placed under the government of elders. These, as it has been already intimated, were small Churches, and appear to have included a large proportion of converted Gentile proselytes to Judaism, especially of women. There was no class of converts in the early Churches so widely intelligent and so unsuperstitiously devout as this class of " devout men " and " devout women," who, before they became Paul's converts, had forsaken heathenism and embraced the Jewish faith. Where, in small Churches, this class of converts was in the ascendant, it is not difficult to understand that organisation under the charge of elders might be more easily and speedily effected than when contrasted conditions obtained, as at Corinth.

In St. Paul's first Epistle to the Corinthians, interior views are disclosed of the condition of that Church six years after its founding by the apostle, which show how far it remained, even at that period, from anything like settled organisation. At Ephesus, three or four years after St. Paul's first visit, elders (presbyter-bishops) had been ordained.[1] And yet after six years the Church of Corinth remained in a state hardly more like settled organisation than that of Rome at the date of St. Paul's writing to that Church, which had then received no visit

[1] Acts xx. 17.

from an apostle. In the Epistles to the Corinthians, as well as in that to the Romans, there is no reference to elder or deacon, or any regular Church officer. To the Romans St. Paul says, "Having gifts differing according to the grace that was given to us, whether prophecy, let us prophesy according to the proportion of our faith; or ministry, let us give ourselves to our ministry; or he that teacheth, to his teaching; or he that exhorteth, to his exhorting: he that giveth, let it be in disinterested simplicity; he that ruleth, let it be with diligence; he that showeth mercy, with cheerfulness."[1] Here the reference is to the various gifts, freely exercised in the Church by its members, whereby, especially in the absence of a regular ministry, the Church was built up in faith and knowledge and Christian life. So in respect to Corinth the apostle writes: "God hath set some in the Church, first apostles, secondly prophets, thirdly teachers, then powers, then gifts of healings, helps, governments, divers kinds of tongues. Are all apostles? are all prophets? are all teachers? are all powers? have all gifts of healings? do all speak with tongues? do all interpret?" etc. With which should be collated other passages, such, for example, as the following: "When ye come together, each one hath a psalm, hath a teaching, hath a revelation, hath a tongue, hath an interpretation.... If any man speaketh in a tongue, let it be by two, or at the most three, and in turn; and let one interpret.... And let the prophets speak by two or three, and let the others discern."[2]

From these passages we may surely infer that at the time referred to, there were no ordained ministers in the Corinthian, any more than in the Roman Church.

[1] Rom. xii.   [2] 1 Cor. xii.; xiv.

Apostles visited them; prophets exercised their special gifts among them; itinerant teachers, such as Timothy, Titus, or Apollos, instructed them;—these three classes belonged to "the Church," the collective Church: they visited the Churches;—"*then*" there came the local array of "gifts" which so abounded at Corinth, and by means of which, including "governments," the Corinthian Church, in the absence of the apostle or his commissioned representatives, seems to have carried on its services and maintained its life, though with a grievous lack of discipline. There were no presbyter-bishops. The condition of the Church as revealed in the two epistles precludes the possibility of this. Nor would it be less than absurd to suppose that in such letters, in which the moral and disciplinary condition of the Church is in question throughout, the apostle would have absolutely ignored the existence of the responsible ministers of the Church, if there had been any such in existence. That such a man as Dr. Dale could have adopted an opposite conclusion on this point is a marvellous illustration of what denominational prepossessions as to the Divine right of a special type of Church organisation can bring an able and candid man to maintain. It is, however, in fair harmony with the same writer's contention that the apostolic Churches at Jerusalem and Ephesus consisted of one sole congregation.

It may indeed be said that the Epistle to the Ephesians shows that, even to a Church in which we know that there were presbyter-bishops, St. Paul was capable of addressing a letter in which the ordained ministers of the Church are altogether ignored. The Epistle to the Ephesians, however, was in the nature of a circular letter. This conclusion, which has been held by many of the ablest critics, including Bishop Lightfoot, is sustained by a multitude of cogent considerations. The contents of the epistle are altogether general; it does not contain a local allusion or a personal reference from first to last, except only the reference to Tychicus as the apostle's representative, who was presently to visit the Churches; and this has no specific relation to Ephesus. There are no salutations to individuals. The doctrinal teaching of the epistle is, indeed, peculiarly suitable to the requirements of the Christian believers in and near Proconsular Asia, and is in marked parallelism with the contents of the Epistle to Colossæ, situated within the same region; but it contains nothing that is specifically suitable to the particular circumstances of the Church at Ephesus, nor is there anything like historical reminiscence, although St. Paul's experiences in Ephesus had been peculiarly memorable, and form the groundwork of special reference in his letters to the Corinthians and to Timothy. When all these points are weighed, it will surely appear to be every way probable that this letter was a general epistle, intended for the instruction and confirmation of a circle of Churches, of which Ephesus was the chief. The Ephesian epistle may accordingly be regarded with much probability as the "epistle from Laodicea" which was to be sent to Colossæ.[1] On this understanding all difficulty vanishes in respect to the omission from the epistle of any reference to the elders of the Church.

On the same understanding, the nature of the apostle's references to the Church and to the ministry in the fourth chapter becomes clear, and is seen to be appropriate. The Church of which he speaks[2] is the Church in its largest

[1] Col. iv. 16. [2] Eph. iv. 11-16.

and grandest sense; the ministry is correspondingly described in the most general terms, terms applicable to any contemporary Church. "Apostles, prophets, evangelists," these were ministers of the gospel truth, for the most part itinerant or visiting ministers; "pastors and teachers" is a phrase descriptive of the local servants of the Church, on whom its edification depended, some of whom may have been formally ordained as presbyters. This would be the case in all the older Churches; while others may have been "pastors and teachers" *de facto*, without having been formally ordained to the office of elder.

This incidental but not unimportant discussion affords further illustration of the futility of any attempt to find in the organisation of the apostolic Churches a model for the Churches of after-ages. It becomes more and more evident that there were considerable varieties of organisation among the Churches, and that the law of development obtained throughout the whole field of apostolic Christianity.

Before many years had passed, the Church at Corinth was fully organised, like that of Ephesus. It may be conjectured that St. Paul himself organised the Church and ordained for it presbyter-bishops and deacons on his second visit, recorded in Acts xx. That venerable document of the earliest Christian antiquity, the Epistle of Clement of Rome to the Corinthian Church, is in evidence that towards the end of the first century the Church had long been fully organised. The strict directions which, in the latest years of his life, St. Paul gave to Timothy and Titus, leave no room for doubt that at that period elders were in course of being systematically appointed in every considerable Christian community, in every mother-Church.

But the perspective of variations and developments in the Churches of the apostolic age does not find its limits when the date is reached of the Pastoral Epistles, or of the death of St. Paul. That most interesting and valuable relic, the *Teaching of the Apostles*, admits us to a view of still further variations and of new developments, before the first century had closed.

It is true that the order and usages of which we gain a glimpse in that precious little tract would seem to have been those prevalent among Churches of Judæo-Christian foundation rather than among Gentile Churches of Pauline foundation, and that the region in which the authority of the *Teaching* was recognised is more likely to have been in the neighbourhood of Palestine or of Alexandria than of Asia Minor, Greece, or Italy. Still the tract relates to apostolic times and to Christian Churches as organised before the close of the first century. It may fairly be cited, accordingly, to prove the variety of organisation which prevailed in the primitive Church, and to show how the apostolic Churches followed, not all alike, but all in some form and manner, the law of development.

In some respects the *Teaching* coincides strikingly with passages, already cited from St. Paul's epistles, which relate to Church organisation and government.[1] The varieties of ministry in the Church are recounted as being carried on by apostles, prophets, and teachers, bishops and deacons. Of these the first three are referred to in a manner which shows that they were occasional and special—we might say, extraordinary—while the bishops and deacons are evidently ordinary and permanent ministers. The "apostles" are in no true sense the successors of the "twelve." They are not even

[1] 1 Cor. xii. 28 ; Eph. iv. 11.

the successors of those "apostles," to whom St. Paul refers in the passages lately cited, who were counted among the original founders of the Christian communities before the first great period of gospel-planting had come to an end. They were venerable men, relics of the very earliest believers, who had "seen the Lord," and on that account, in a special sense, they were His witnesses; as such they visited the Churches, observing very strict and primitive rules in their itinerancy. In the *Teaching* the rule is laid down that the apostle should not remain three days in the same place, a rule which, it may be conjectured, served, in the later years of the century, as an effectual—perhaps a necessary— guard against the impositions of "false apostles," who, like some of whom St. Paul had had occasion to speak in his Epistles to the Corinthians, would have burdened the Churches with their maintenance. It is added, "If he ask for money, he is a false prophet."[1] Of the apostle, however, the *Teaching* says very few words, only by a single stroke, as we have seen, intimating his position and the manner of his coming and going. His figure we must picture as that of a rare visitor to the Churches, a worn and aged pilgrim, coming from afar, going on a vast circuit, with his one coat, his wallet, and his staff, and with no money in his pouch. He is a vanishing figure, belonging to the past rather than the present. More is said about the "prophet," who, it is evident, had filled a great place in the life and the mission work of the earliest Churches. The prophet was the inspired preacher of that first age. The itinerant prophet was the revivalist or missioner of the Churches; he designated men to missions; he took a sort of charge for the time being of

---

[1] *Prophet* is used here in its generic sense, to mean messenger from God, or inspired speaker.

the Church services and evangelistic work in any Church where he was welcomed as a prophet indeed. The resident prophet—for there were many cases in which, like Philip at Cæsarea, the prophet abode in the same Church—was recognised as, not for administrative or disciplinary purposes, but for preaching, a divinely ordained power in the Church. In all cases, St. Paul's definition held good: he spake "unto men to edification, and exhortation, and comfort." With the prophet is linked the "teacher," who also is to be duly maintained. He is, however, only named incidentally and but twice, and evidently was a sort of prophet-substitute.[1]

Sometimes there was to be found a Church without a prophet. There was, however, no such thing in fact or in thought as a Church without "bishops and deacons." These were to be "appointed," as a matter of course. "They too render you the service of the prophets and teachers. . . . Do not then despise them, for together with the prophets and teachers are they to be held in honour among you." Nothing is said as to the maintenance to be furnished for the bishops. Perhaps the principle of such maintenance is implied in the passage just quoted, or the right and the duty are taken for granted. It is exceedingly probable that the bishops were provided with

[1] Considering what is the essential and distinctive character of the prophet, as shown throughout the Scriptures, and especially as defined by St. Paul (1 Cor. xiv.), with which the indications in the *Teaching of the Apostles* strictly agree, it argues a desperate case when Principal Gore, in his volume, *The Church and the Ministry*, attempts to find in the prophets of the *Teaching* the links of descent by which the stream of apostolic authority and virtue has come down to the hands of Anglican Bishops. He would make these prophets the successors or equivalents of such evangelists as Timothy and Titus, whereas the prophetic endowment was not disciplinary or administrative, but hortatory and effusive.

maintenance according to their need. It is evident, at any rate, that in regard to these ministers of the Church and their maintenance there was some diversity between the custom and rule in the Churches to which the *Teaching* relates and those to which St. Paul writes. Excepting Paul and Barnabas, the first "apostles" claimed maintenance; and maintenance, in varying degrees, according to their need, was enjoined by St. Paul on behalf of elders; but certainly it does not appear that for prophets as such, any more than for other believers endowed with "gifts," maintenance was claimed or expected among the Churches of which we read in the Acts of the Apostles.

Another notable point is the fact that in this tract we read nothing of "elders," only of "bishops and deacons." This is the more noteworthy, because of the Judæo-Christian character of the tract, the designation *elder* being so peculiarly Jewish. If, however, we accept the suggestion of one of the critics of the *Teaching*, that it was a manual intended for the use of Churches which, though converted by Jewish teachers going forth from Jewish-Christian "synagogues,"[1] consisted chiefly, if not wholly, of Gentiles, it may not be difficult to understand how a term came to be adopted which was equally free from Jewish colouring, and, in the Churches where the *Teaching* ruled, from any politico-social suggestions, such as it might have carried with it in Hellenic or strongly Hellenised communities, a word which was purely and plainly descriptive of the duties of the pastoral office—*episcopos, superintendent*—in luminous correlation with the word *diakonos, deacon, servant.* The two words together would be the very aptest and most

[1] James ii. 2.

intelligible for the conveyance of the ideas needing to be conveyed. According to Dr. Hatch's ingenious and learnedly sustained, but yet, as I venture to think, one-sided theory, the word *episcopos*, in its later and non-apostolic sense of chief minister and director, came into use during the second century, because of the associations connected with its application to officials of high responsibility in Hellenic or Hellenised cities. It can, however, have been owing to no such cause that the word *bishop*, rather than *elder*, appears in the *Teaching*. It is evident that the word is used here in a sense equivalent to that in which St. Paul used it in his address to the Ephesian elders and his Epistles to the Philippians and to Timothy and Titus. In the Acts, the Epistles, and the *Teaching of the Apostles*, we have caught no glimpse of anything like episcopal superiority in the organisation of the Churches; we have only found one order of ordinary pastors—that of the presbyter-bishop; and, besides, the order of the diaconate. In the Apocalypse the "angel of the Church" has been frequently understood as meaning the bishop *par excellence*—the president of the council of presbyters. But this obscure intimation is all the evidence seeming to favour the theory of episcopal superiority over the presbyterial council which can be adduced from Scripture. And, so far as this goes, it is, of course, evidence only in favour of a chief presbytership, not at all of diocesan episcopacy.

The *Teaching of the Apostles*, however, is not the only early Christian writing which furnishes evidence respecting the Church organisation of the first century. The Ignatian Epistles must be dated within the first ten years of the second century, and the organisation which in those epistles is indirectly and by scattered hints disclosed to view must have been for many years the settled order of the Churches to which the epistles relate. The range of these epistles is, therefore, contemporary with that of the *Teaching*. The contrast between the two disclosures, as to the conditions of the Churches respectively referred to, which the student finds in these two authorities, is very striking, especially as regards the subject of episcopacy.

The *Teaching* had for its local sphere of reference, in all likelihood, the region that skirted the south-east angle of the Mediterranean, including Alexandria as one of its *foci*; what I may speak of as the Ignatian range of local reference—leaving Rome just now quite apart—comprehended the Pauline regions of Asia, mainly on the opposite side of the Mediterranean, but extending from Syrian Antioch north-westward to Troas. In this district of country was included the Christian province of "Syria and Cilicia," repeatedly referred to, but never described, in the Acts, of which region Antioch was to the apostle or evangelist the natural base, a region where St. Paul seems to have bestowed, more than anywhere else, his "more abundant" earliest labours. This was the earliest field of the apostle's labours after his first visit to Peter at Jerusalem; and to the Churches in these parts was addressed, in the first instance, the letter from "the apostles and elders" at Jerusalem in regard to the terms of agreement with the Gentile Christians. In the Ignatian region were also included those parts of Asia Minor of which Ephesus was the centre, which had been evangelized by St. Paul; these were afterwards for some time under the special charge of Timothy, and still later came under the paramount influence of St. John. This great section of Christian mission territory had thus received very early the gospel message ; the Churches had been early organised, they had developed under vigilant and powerful care and authority, and had received, it must be presumed, their final shaping from the teaching and influence of St. John. The epistles of Ignatius were addressed to Churches scattered throughout the area which I have described, and lying along one of the beaten routes towards Rome, to which city the martyr was taking his way. And these epistles afford conclusive evidence that, whereas in the Churches to which the *Teaching* belonged there were only " bishops and deacons," in those addressed by Ignatius the established order was for each Church to have a bishop, presbyters, and deacons, the bishop having an acknowledged superiority over the presbyters, being a kind of monarch in each Church. The subject is fully discussed by Bishop Lightfoot in what he has written on St. Ignatius and his epistles.[1]

The conclusions of the bishop on the subject are thus stated :

" The New Testament itself contains no direct and indisputable notices of a localised episcopate in the Gentile Churches, as distinguished from the movable episcopate exercised by Timothy in Ephesus, and by Titus in Crete ; yet there is satisfactory evidence of its development in the later years of the apostolic age ; this development was not simultaneous and equal in all parts of Christendom ; it was more especially connected with the name of St. John; and in the early years of the second century the episcopate " [not, however, a diocesan episcopacy] " was widely spread, and had taken free root, more especially in Asia Minor and in Syria."

[1] *Apostolic Fathers*, part ii., vol. i.

Meantime, at this very period, there was as yet in Rome, in that staunchly Roman colony Philippi, and also in Corinth, no episcopal president and superior of the presbyters. The presbyters were themselves bishops, as in apostolic days. Before long, however, in large Churches, and where much business needed to be promptly and energetically dealt with, there must have been a natural tendency to invest with distinct precedence and presidential authority the ablest and most experienced of the presbyters. This tendency may well have combined in Greek cities with the secular associations of administrative authority belonging to the word *episcopos*, so as to fix this title in a special sense on one among the elders. The usage grew into universality during the second century, whilst at the same time administrative necessity or convenience was developing episcopacy into a diocesan character.

Thus the law of adaptation and development worked everywhere with a powerful progressiveness throughout the history of the apostolic Church. Thus the right of adaptation and development according to circumstances was established for the Christian Church throughout its whole history. The same law must also have prevailed as to ritual; and there are not wanting traces that it did prevail, especially in regard to the Lord's Supper and the Agape. It is evident that the variation was great between the manner of the primitive "breaking of bread" at Jerusalem and the sacramental feasts which were so grossly abused at Corinth. It is further evident that the apostle's remonstrance, rebuke, and sharp question in regard to this subject in his first Epistle to the Corinthians imply a suggestion of that separation between the Church feast (or Agape) and the Supper which appears to have been carried out early in the second century, and warrant adaptations and varieties in the mode of administration, so long as the original mandate of the Lord Jesus is truly observed.[1]

I have been compelled to omit reference to several interesting points. Nor can I do more than mention here a point to which I shall hereafter have occasion to direct special attention, a point as to which all candid students of the New Testament and the earliest Christian documents are, I think, agreed: that, in organisation and discipline, the apostles and their representatives had supreme authority; that the chief authority in the appointment of ministers was placed in the hands, next to the apostles, of the apostolic representatives, such as Timothy and Titus, and afterwards, and with permanent local responsibility, of the elders. Such was at least the established order during the apostolic and sub-apostolic age.

Imperfect as the preceding investigation has been, it will serve as a convenient basis and introduction in view of the discussions which are to follow, and of which the first will deal with the position and claims, legitimate and illegitimate, of the Established Church of England, regarded on its own merits as a Church organisation.

[1] Cor. xi. 22.

II.
ANGLICANISM.

CHAPTER I.

WHAT THE REFORMATION MEANT FOR THE CHURCH OF ENGLAND, AND WHAT IT ACCOMPLISHED—ANGLICANISM DURING THE TUDOR PERIOD.

THE claim of the Church of England, as set forth by the majority of her standard divines, and in particular by such High Churchmen as Canon Curteis and Canon Liddon, is to be accepted as a primitive and apostolic Church. The English Catholic Church, it is maintained, was at its root and beginning an offshoot from the Western Catholic Church in the seventh century; and, after struggling bravely, and yet, on the whole, in vain, during several centuries, to preserve its national identity and autonomy unimpaired, was by a modest and needful reformation, a reformation truly, though not in formal aspect, national, and of which Henry VIII. was only in part—only in certain respects—the instrument, restored in the sixteenth century to its rightful position, to its national integrity as the true and ancient Church of England. The breach of unity with the Roman Catholic Church is by these writers laid at the door of the Papacy, which refused to concede the reasonable demands of the English Church and nation. It is maintained, accordingly, that the Church of England holds a position co-ordinate with the Church of Rome, and even superior to it, as having, unlike that Church, returned to the primitive truth and purity when these had been departed from, and after having been wrongfully and oppressively treated by that Church. It is held, moreover, that the English Church must rank on a level with the Greek Catholic Church. The three so-called catholic Churches are held to be each and all vitalised and legitimated, whatever may be their incidental errors and imperfections, by the life-giving succession of apostolic bishops, through whose hands has flowed down the stream of Divine authority and influence from the Lord Jesus Christ, the Divine Head of the Church. Canon Curteis, in his Bampton Lectures, divides Christendom into three Church families: the Greek, the Latin, and the Teutonic; and claims for the Church of England that it is the natural head of Teutonic Christianity, and that all the communions which call themselves Churches, whether in England or on the Continent, and which are of Teutonic nationality, ought by right to coalesce into one grand Christian Church in organic union and identity with the Church of England.

There is no alternative between some such highly imaginative and unhistorical hypothesis as that which I have thus sketched and a much humbler matter-of-fact statement of the case, such as, in its lowest and least pretentious—and I must add least spiritual—form, has been set forth by the late Dean Stanley, and in a more stately and impressive, and much more spiritual, but yet a strictly historical and not too ambitious form, by the late Archdeacon Hare. As agreeing, in the main, with the historical views and tone of Archdeacon Hare, so far as they traverse the same ground, I may refer to the writings of the late Dr. Jacob, which deserve to be much better known than they appear to be.[1] Unfortunately the mythical

[1] *Ecclesiastical Polity of the New Testament.*

and mystical theory has taken such hold of the modern Church of England as to pervade and influence all its intercourse with other Christian communions which do not profess to be Catholic and Episcopal, whether in Great Britain, on the Continent, or elsewhere, communions which few Anglican spokesmen of to-day will admit to be in any real sense Churches. Conversely, such Anglican views as I have described cannot but influence these slighted Churches in their views and tone in regard to the Church of England. If the Church of England might be taken simply for what it is and has been historically, with all its defects and faults, a veritable English Church, alike in its strength and in its weakness, in its good and in its evil, there would be few, even of those outside its pale, who would not yield it due respect; whilst very many, not of its sons, remembering the difficulties which have surrounded it through all its course and the imperfection of all human instruments, would deal gently with its failings or even misdeeds, and, for the sake of its saints and godly heroes and its splendid galaxy of learned and profound divines, of eloquent and impressive preachers, would render it sincere reverence, as being, not indeed in theory, but in concrete fact, and notwithstanding too many unsightly blemishes, the grandest national Church in Christendom. It is the infatuation of its High Church doctrinaire ecclesiastics, with their misleading claim of continuity, visibility, and organic unity for the Catholic Church, and for the Church of England as a primary branch of that Church, which compels me to say that, theoretically, ideally, even historically, no Church stands more in need of apology than the Church of England. Let its imperfections and errors be excused on the ground that it could not but retain much of the character and quality of the corrupt communion from which it was separated, and that, from age to age, it has found the way to effectual and progressive reformation beset with difficulties, and it will be admitted that the apology has much force, and that, in despite of all, the Church can show a great history—a history, perhaps, on the whole, never so great since the sixteenth century came to its close, and yet never so full of perilous movement and controversy, as during the last fifty years. But to those who maintain its supremacy as a Church, and its sole and absolute legitimacy, at least in England, as primitive and apostolic, we must speak in a very different tone. To them it were folly and unfaithfulness to "prophesy smooth things."

The leading feature of the ecclesiastical revolution by which the English Church ceased to be part and parcel of the mediæval Romish Church, and vindicated its national integrity and independence, was that the sovereign of the realm took the place of the Roman pontiff in regard to ecclesiastical supremacy and government, and became in effect *summus episcopus*—primate of primates—within the Church. This momentous change was a great national deliverance, in so far as it shut out the Pope from our country, as it did effectually for ages; and it may be defended on the ground that, as it was necessary at a stroke to expel the Pope, so it was necessary, if the wheels of the ecclesiastical machinery were still to revolve, if all things were not to be brought to a standstill, that the place of central supremacy, hitherto filled by the Pope, should be immediately filled up by a force and authority adequate to the burden and strain of wielding so great an organisation. Hence there was no alternative but to accept the king, being the head of the nation, as also the head of the Church. It is true that

Henry's character was the reverse of saintly, but it was noble and exemplary in comparison with that of the pontiffs who, before Clement VII., had for many years governed the Roman see. In Henry's person, too, as monarch of the realm, the laity and the law of England seemed, in a sort, to be represented—the English laity and the English law as against the lordly caste of priests, who, prompted and protected in this respect by successive popes, had held themselves not only far above the laity, but above the law of England. For the time being this defence might serve. But for the monarch thereafter still to remain sovereign head on earth of the Church, whilst the national laity were, in fact, to be as much ignored as under the Papacy, were never to be recognised as entitled to any vital share in the Church's active spiritual service and fellowship, or as possessing any rights in regard to its administration and legislation, was to leave the Church and the nation still suffering under some of the worst evils of Popery. In principle, moreover, the permanent headship of the monarch over the Church would seem to be still more incongruous and indefensible than the headship of the Pope, although in practice, the Pope himself being the temporal ruler of a corrupt and inferior kingdom, and no true spiritual superior, being a foreign potentate surrounded by selfish parasites, the headship of the sovereign was likely to work far better for the Church and the nation. The truth of the matter is that the Reformation was never carried far enough, and scarcely seems at any time to have been projected on true lines, at least by those who were in chief authority. The English Reformation, though it had its real roots in national feeling and convictions, began as a practical public movement with the sovereign, and has always been carried forward or arrested in accordance with the ideas and requirements of State policy. Statecraft and human device have governed where the laws and motives of the "kingdom of heaven" should alone have ruled.

In a passage which Dr. Arnold has prefixed to the preface to his *Sermons on Christian Life*, Coleridge lays it down that the great prevailing error and corruption in the history of the Church of Christ is, not so much the usurpation of the Papacy, as that the rights and privileges of the Church have been narrowed and restricted to the clergy. And in the preface itself Dr. Arnold affirms that "that discipline, which is one of the greatest of the blessings belonging to Christ's Church, never can, and indeed never ought to, be restored till the Church [by which he means the lay communicants of the Church] resumes its lawful authority, and puts an end to the usurpation of its powers by the clergy." These passages bring us towards the root of the matter, and help us to understand the disabilities under which the Church of England has suffered since its partial reformation, and suffers still. But only towards the root. The real source and seat of all the evil lies deeper still: in the gradual decay and the final extinction of the primitive individual and mutual fellowship, such as existed in the Church at Jerusalem and in all the apostolic Churches. Within, alas! but a few centuries after Christ, this free, mutual fellowship had died out, having been gradually displaced in part by the growing superstition and bondage of confession to the priest, and in part by the growth of the secluded monastic fellowship. The Church had no longer a manifest body of living believers, had no longer an available laity accustomed to the unostentatious exercise of spiritual gifts, from amongst whom deacons and elders might easily be chosen, their gifts and their character having been tested, trained, and ascertained, and amongst whom, and with whose cognisance and moral support, a godly discipline might and would have been demanded and maintained, as we have evidence that it was maintained in the earliest ages of the Church. When a lay member of the Church, if not a brother under monastic vow, had come to mean nothing more than one who, after confession to the priest, was allowed to receive the Eucharist, how could there be any longer a living laity, or a godly Church discipline, sustained by the opinion and feeling of a godly laity? Where could believing, gifted, manly Churchmen be found to unite with a body of clergy, and where a body of clergy worthy to unite with such godly laymen, in presbyteries, or synods, or councils, provincial or general? Even before the confusion and heathenish corruption of the nominally Christian community, as we see it in the later years of the Western Roman empire, had been made "worse confounded," and more manifestly and grossly heathenish, by the wholesale admission, after the dissolution of the empire, of "baptized" myriads of heathenish nominal converts to the Church, the upgrowth of the confessional, and, together with that, of hierarchical prerogative, had, as we have noted, destroyed the lay element in the Church as an element of any power or independent intelligence. The clergy became the Church; the laity were reduced to a condition of absolute bondage, they became abject slaves. From such a laity it was not possible to keep up a fit supply of able and godly clergy. Only a scholar, here and there, by sheer intellectual force, joined to a strong and free personality, lifted up a voice now and again on behalf of Divine truth and Christian liberty.

Sometimes the scholar was also a divine, like Grosseteste or Wiclif; and then seed of truth and stirring thought was sown which was to bring forth fruit in after-days.

Such, apart from the papal despotism which fitly crowned the whole growth and fabric of spiritual superstition, was the condition of mediæval Christianity which came as an inheritance to the Church of England, and which such reformation as came to that Church in Tudor and Stuart times did little to remedy. It has not, indeed, been remedied to this day; and it will be our next business to enquire what are the causes which have kept the Church of England in a false position, and prevented an effective evangelical renewal of its body and spirit, or any organised endeavours after such an enlightened re-formation, such an amount of wise and godly reconstruction, as would seem now to be pressingly necessary if the Church of England is to maintain a successful resistance to the organised attacks which have so long been maintained against it.

It has been shown how the lay element—the element of a godly lay fellowship—died out of the Church within not many centuries after Christ. So early as the time of Augustine, as is plain from the whole scope of his controversy with the Donatists,[1] it had entirely disappeared. The Bishop of Hippo assumes, as one of the settled premises in his argument, that there was no organised body of godly communicants, but that the great majority of the members of the Church were notoriously men of ungodly character and evil lives. Similarly, two or three centuries later, Gregory the Great of Rome maintained that "the ungodly are the largest number in the Church."[2] This continued

---

[1] See Dr. Gregory's *Fernley Lecture*, pp. 263-275, first edition.
[2] *Ibid.*, p. 280, first edition.

to be the recognised—this was allowed and even defended as the normal—condition of things until the era of the Reformation. Private brotherhoods, indeed, brotherhoods of earnest souls, who in modern writings have, for the most part, been spoken of as mystics, though some of them have been described and commemorated as " Reformers before the Reformation," kept up to some extent among the laity the tradition of devotional and godly living, and, though dimly, the idea of a true spiritual Church of Christ ; but these brotherhoods were scarcely recognised as orthodox, were regarded as irregular, and sometimes—nor in every instance without reason—were treated as heretical. The broad facts as to the Church's condition, the established ideas as to its nature and organisation, the laws and customs of its administration and government, were not affected by the existence of these brotherhoods. The Church everywhere was a Church without a godly lay fellowship, a Church with no laity but the world at large, a Church which, indeed, claimed the whole world as its laity. The professedly devout left the world, and sought retirement in monastic institutions. Hence, I may note in passing, the dissolution of monastic institutions by Henry VIII. was, in a sense of which he never thought, a step towards the reformation of the Church and the world. Though it let loose on the world many worthless monks, it also sent out into society some godly men and women, who could find no foreign monastery in which to take refuge ; and it prevented the godly men and women of after times in England from abandoning the world, of which they were to be the " salt," and leaving it to become increasingly and more and more hopelessly corrupt.

It was, accordingly, a Church without a living Christian

laity, without any godly lay fellowship existing as an organic part of it, which had to be reformed in the sixteenth century. In the midst of such a Church even Henry VIII. appears scarcely to occupy an anomalous position when he poses as Reformer. He who not many years before had been crowned with the papal laurel as " Defender of the Faith," being at least somewhat of a theologian, albeit he was not only layman and warrior-knight, but the stalwart king of an unpolished people, might, amid such conditions of Church and State as then prevailed, take upon himself the rôle of a Reformer without any sense of incongruity. The nation he ruled and represented was full of reforming ideas, ideas which, if not always pious, were not godless, and were honest, manly, and national. In the steps of reformation which he took, he gave more or less effect to those ideas. It is true that he had quarrelled with the Pope in his own cause. Not the less, in the steps which he took in reformation, was the king doing the people's will, so far as his reformation tended to restore to the country, in matters of religion, self-government,—to exclude foreign prelates from English sees, so that such a prelate as Cardinal Campeggio should never again be forced upon the Church of England, as a few years before he had been forced on the see of Salisbury,— and to put an end to papal domination and to the swarming nuisance of monkery. The writings of Wiclif and the influence of the Lollards had done much to prepare Englishmen to welcome such measures. Nor had the writings and influence of Erasmus, or the words and deeds of Luther, the object formerly of the king's theological assault-at-arms, been without effect in preparing for these measures. The actual Reformation, however, as a series of ecclesiastical changes, effected by public law, was, on the part of the king, a movement prompted mainly by personal motives, and on the part of his able counsellors and instruments, was largely a political movement; while it was to take effect—it could only take effect—on a Church that was still to remain without any other or more select body of laity than the people of England at large.

Consequently the new settlement, the reformation of the Church in England, could not but be either Erastian [1] or high ecclesiastical in its character, unless it were at once Erastian and high ecclesiastical. It could not be an evangelical reform. It could not be a reform which proceeded on the basis of a godly lay fellowship, such as might co-operate with and balance the influence of the clergy. All through the course of our English Reformation, alike in Tudor and in Stuart times, this disability affected its character, and prevented it from being scripturally complete or truly evangelical. The reformation had to be made by the sovereign,—with whom, but always under whom, were the secular statesmen of the royal council,—and by the clergy, *i.e.* practically by the bishops. The sovereign in Privy Council, and the bishops, either apart and alone in their own Council, or in Convocation, where they were always supreme, had all the work of reformation to do from first to last. Whatever Parliament eventually sanctioned was prepared and proposed by them. And, from first to last, they all agreed in suppressing whatever might have tended to bring forth a godly lay fellowship, competent to take part in the discipline and government of the Church.

---

[1] Erastianism treats the Church as merely a department of the State for the moral education of the people, "a branch of the civil service." See the dictionaries on Erastus.

Much of the controversy between the queen (or bishops) and the Puritans under Elizabeth, and between the bishops and the Independent divines under the Stuarts, hinged on this point; it related to the "liberty of prophesying," or the questions about ministers and ruling elders. Some of the Presbyterians, indeed, were in form and theory little, if at all, more advanced towards the evangelical and primitive platform than the Episcopalians. Nevertheless in their Church system the lay or ruling eldership had the effect of bringing into connexion with their clergy tested and for the most part godly men, who were only theoretically of the clerical order, who practically were leading laymen from among the congregation.

For any national reformation, however, in the sixteenth or seventeenth centuries, carried out by public authority and law, the alternative was always, and indeed, until after the evangelical revival of the last century, the only visible alternative still remained, that either Erastianism or such High Churchmanship as ignored the rights of the laity must supply the governing principle, or else the two views must be combined in some sort of compromise. In all established Churches, indeed, except that of Scotland in very recent years, the same alternative has ruled till the present time. Erastianism has been the curse of Lutheranism, which knows as little of true evangelical fellowship principles in its Church organisation and government as the Church of England. Erastianism governed absolutely in Genevan Calvinism, and has blighted it to the core. In Scotland, as in English Presbyterianism during the Commonwealth, the provision of the ruling eldership, to which I have already referred, operated powerfully towards the development of something like a lay fellowship, which was often, more or less, of a godly sort.

It also enabled the Presbyterian Church to establish and maintain an effective moral discipline. The living leaven, thus subsisting in the national Church of Scotland, was, indeed, too powerful to be confined within established and statutory limits. Secession after secession stirred up more and more deeply and widely the spirit of godly zeal and strict evangelical fellowship. These reacted in revivals within the pale of the Scotch Establishment itself, until finally the great Free Church movement gathered power and found for itself a separate sphere. The result has been a development within the separated Churches of increasingly free fellowship, with some vital growths of much promise, supplementary to the mere eldership in its various combinations, and, in the Established Church, the destruction of lay patronage and of Erastianism, except in mere shadow, the Lord High Commissioner being now the shadow of dethroned Erastianism.

Erastianism and the official clerical element as represented by the bishops were, as we have seen, the two factors which in their combination and interaction gave guidance and form to the English Reformation. Of these two the less variable element with the Tudor sovereigns was Erastianism, or the influence and will of the sovereign; the more variable was the influence of the bishops and their council of divines. In the persons of the Tudor father and daughter, Henry and Elizabeth, Erastianism was resolute and inflexible, and was governed by a settled policy. Under the Stuarts, as we shall presently see, the will and purpose of the sovereign was largely swayed by the episcopal mind and will.

The fluctuations of proportion and relation between the force and efficiency of the two factors during the period of ecclesiastical reconstruction are not difficult to discern or describe. Henry's will was very resolute. Indeed, the bishops were too divided to have any effective policy of their own. Gardiner and Bonner remained essentially Romanists, as was afterwards shown under Mary. Cranmer, who led the Reforming section, was a cautious, not to say timid, Protestant. Under the young Edward VI. the balance of forces was materially altered. The Protector and those who surrounded the king had a decided Protestant bias. Continental Protestantism had taken strong hold of the most energetic classes of the people. The counsels of Cranmer and the Protestant bishops were now firm and decided. Accordingly much was done in this reign towards doctrinally reforming the Church. Private masses and image-worship were abolished, the Prayer-Book was revised, confession to a priest was made to be merely voluntary, the cup was given to the laity in the Lord's Supper, the use of Latin in worship was done away, and the Forty-two (not as yet Thirty-nine) Articles of Religion were adopted, thus laying what was virtually a Protestant basis for the theology and faith of the Church. As to ritual, however, the Reforming advance was slow and cautious. The Reformation itself was not always thorough in principle, and the new regulations were not strictly carried out. In fact, although leading theologians and many energetic religionists might have adopted Reforming opinions, the great body of the country squires, nearly all the country clergy, and almost the whole of the rural population, still remained more or less "Catholic" at heart. Meantime, the Reforming bias which prevailed among the bishops and at court was largely imbued with Genevan or Zwinglian ideas and tendencies. High Episcopalian views were at this time in suspense, so far as the Protestant section of the bishops was concerned.

After the dark interval of Mary's reign, a stronger reaction than ever set in against the Papacy. The Reforming bishops were now more distinctly Genevan or Zwinglian than before; the hearts of the Protestant people of the land, many of whom, or their relatives, had found a refuge from persecution among foreign Protestants, both Lutheran and Reformed, went out towards their Protestant brethren on the Continent. Besides which, Catholicism was identified with disloyal and rebellious designs against Elizabeth. There was accordingly a strong tendency towards carrying out the Reformation more fully in a sense favourable to Presbyterianism. At this period, indeed, Presbyterianism was frankly recognised by many of the bishops of the Church of England as a sister form of Protestantism, and some Presbyterian ministers were received, as duly in orders, into the English Church. Not till the end of Elizabeth's reign was the Anglo-Catholic theory of orders set up first by Bancroft. Between strongly enforced Erastianism—for Elizabeth was a strong-willed head of the Church—and the Presbyterian bias of the Reforming bishops, Anglo-Catholicism, in the public policy of the earlier part of Elizabeth's reign, found no place. Throughout this period, however, in her own special services and in her private influence, Elizabeth maintained an attitude inclining towards high ritualistic ideas and principles. Hence the Reformation in the Protestant direction made comparatively little progress. All this while also the services in country churches often remained much as they had been in Mary's time. All along, indeed, the reform of the Liturgy and the daily ritual, even on paper, had, in character and spirit, lagged behind the reform of the Articles, which, early in Elizabeth's reign, had been reduced in number, and finally defined as the thirty-nine we know. Still, during the earlier period of Elizabeth's reign, the Reformation in England was on the whole well sustained.

An event happened, however, in the year 1588, which, though it might have been expected to settle and seal the English Reformation, in effect arrested it. This event was the destruction of the Spanish Armada. Strange to say, that wondrous stroke of Providence changed England from a country of growing Puritanical Protestantism into a largely Anglo-Catholic country. Paradoxical as it may seem to affirm this, Mr. Froude has decisively shown that so it was. Up to the time of this event, it seemed more than possible, especially to the sanguine hopes of Elizabeth's enemies, including all the Catholics and Anglo-Catholics of the country, that Spain and the Roman Catholic confederacy might succeed in the league against Elizabeth and English Protestantism, and that the rule of the Papacy might once more be restored in the land. But the complete destruction of the Armada quenched all these hopes, both at home and abroad. One result was that the country gentlemen and the country clergy threw up the game of disloyalty and intrigue they had played for so many years. Mary of Scotland, indeed, so long the centre of their disloyal hopes, had been done to death shortly before the invasion of the Grand Armada. And now, all hope being finally gone of any foreign help for the old Catholic clique and interest which was identified with the Papacy, it only remained for them to give in their submission, at once politically and ecclesiastically, to Elizabeth. They became members of the "Reformed Church of England"; but they brought with them their essentially Popish predilections, and thus infused Popery or semi-Popery into the administration and ordinary life of the Church of England throughout a great breadth of the country.

By the same event, Elizabeth, who had learnt to associate Continental Protestantism with uncourtly ways, with petty ecclesiastical scruples and cavils, and with republican independence of tone and spirit, was relieved from any necessity to court or keep in favour with foreign Protestants. She was now at liberty to favour the High Church tone and ritual which she personally preferred. Of her bishops, those of most considerable weight—including, it would seem, even Archbishop Parker, whom she compelled to be her representative and instrument—had, in the earlier part of her reign, disapproved the ritualistic tendencies of the queen. But hers was not the will to bend, and now in Archbishop Whitgift she found a willing servant. Hence the latter part of her reign showed a resolute bias towards ritualistic Churchmanship, and by her strongly enforced Act of Uniformity and her high-handed and unsparing use of her Privy Council prerogatives, the Puritan ministers were ejected from the churches, and silenced as public teachers. Here opened the first chapter in the great Puritan controversy in the Church of England, which for a century was to work such woe in the country.

From this time High Churchmanship was to assert itself more and more in the Church of England. Let it be observed, however, that even when the movement in favour of Reform had, under Elizabeth, reached its highest point, nothing had been done towards creating a lay fellowship. Neither the Erastianism of the sovereign, who claimed and exercised a power of direction or of veto as to all that was done, nor the counsels of the bishops and clergy, with whom often rested the practical initiative in the way of reform, had so much as recognised this fundamental need of a Christian Church.

Had Presbyterianism superseded the traditional customs and rules of the Church of England, some sort of initial provision, as I have already indicated, would have been made for this need of the congregation. The Puritan section of the Church of England, after a distinct breach had been made with the High Church majority, recognised with growing distinctness the need of some equivalent provision. For a time, under the Commonwealth, when Presbyterianism enjoyed its brief triumph in England, lay elders were appointed; and their gifts were largely exercised. But England would not give up its Liturgy; the Genevan discipline was not congenial to the people:— I, for one, cannot bring myself to think that it ought to have been nationally accepted. Nevertheless, for want of accepting somewhat of its spirit, or some better equivalent for it, and of more thoroughly carrying out the reformation of the Church, that Church remains to-day unevangelical in its organisation, and always likely, so long as its form is unchanged, to be dominated by the ultra-High Church spirit.

CHAPTER II.

THE MODERN CHURCH OF ENGLAND—THE WANT OF A LAY
FELLOWSHIP—THE DILEMMA OF THE ENGLISH CHURCH.

IN the last chapter I showed how, during the Tudor period of the Reformation in England, the Erastian and the hierarchical forces combined in working out a revolution in the condition and government of the Church of England. This revolution, as we have seen, proceeded on no fixed principles, except indeed the exclusion of the Pope's authority. It represented, on the one hand, the will and counsel of the monarch, sometimes with and sometimes without the Parliament, and, on the other hand, the will and counsel of the bishops—these two forces operating in concert or in mutual compromise and balance. But it did not represent in any manner or degree a national fellowship of believers, or the mind and will of a real Church laity. We pass now to the Stuart period of Anglicanism.

Under the Stuarts, the Erastian factor in the guidance and regulation of the Church coalesced almost completely with the episcopal factor. A close union of Church and State appeared, under a form altogether different from that identity of Church and State which was one of the features of the early history of England. The divine right of kings was a tenet which would have been abhorrent alike to barons and people, and even to the clergy, in the England of the Plantagenets; but it became part and parcel of the Church teaching of the Restoration, and for Charles II., as John Wesley somewhere caustically remarks, was invented that phrase in one of the petitions of the Church's Common Prayer-Book which speaks of "our most religious and gracious" king (or queen). After the epoch from which dates the formal commencement of the Puritan schism in the Church under Elizabeth, the theology of the Church was to become more and more distinctly High Anglo-Catholic, until the Stuart period was over, and any hope of further reformation seemed to have been left far behind.

During the following century of earthly and level common sense, the eighteenth century, High Church politics and principles went out with the Jacobites and non-jurors, High Church devotion went out with William Law, being quenched in his mysticism, and Erastianism slumbered secure and undisturbed on its leaden throne. Latitudinarianism reigned in the English Church, as Moderatism ruled in the Scotch Establishment. Nor was it until the present century had come in, that, following in the wake of the Methodist Revival, evangelical religion began visibly to revive in the Church of England, taking forms as little Anglican as possible, negligent of the ritual properly characteristic of the English Church, and making all the worship as little unlike, as much like, the service in a Presbyterian or Dissenting place of worship as possible. Next came— more than fifty years ago — the High Church awakening, which could not but follow the Low Church revival, and which has grown higher and higher, till we are set back again, so far as High Church teaching and pretensions go, into the days of Laud and Juxon, while the ritual is not only Romanised in every possible way, but is decked with show and splendour, and is celebrated with form and ceremony, of almost more than Romish gorgeousness and brilliancy. Pretensions are set up on behalf of the bishops and clergy such as were never known, nor would have been tolerated, in Tudor times. And the position is claimed for the Church of England which I have described as set forth by Canon Curteis.[1] It is as though, like the Stuarts, High Churchmen had forgotten nothing and learnt nothing. Yet it must be granted that, if Erastianism is to be disallowed, and we are to hold that the Church should be guided, governed, and administered from within itself, and if there is no such thing as a lay fellowship, a spiritual fellowship of godly laymen, recognised as the body and basis of the Church, then government by the clergy alone, and the descent of authority and grace through the line of the ordaining succession of clergy,— *i.e.* the bishops,—is the only available Church theory. It is a most unreasonable and unevangelical theory; it is nothing less than a monstrous theory—a theory "all compact" of usurpation and superstition; but if there is no provision whatever for evangelical lay fellowship, and if Erastianism such as the Lutheran Erastianism or Dean Stanley's unevangelical Broad Churchmanship is to be disallowed, then, I repeat, this monstrous High Church theory which Canon Curteis and Canon Liddon teach is for the Church of England as it stands the only possible Church theory. The inference is, that the Church of

[1] Page 50.

England stands very greatly in need of a deep and evangelical reform; such a reform, indeed, is necessary, not only to bring forth into light and into due development and power the element of a godly lay fellowship, but to deliver the Church from the sceptical latitudinarianism which has long been gathering power within its pale, and which gives tone and character to the Erastianism of to-day.

The general and preliminary historical discussion contained in my last chapter will have helped to clear the ground for a view of the actual problem of the English Church to-day, both as it presents itself to the earnest anti-Erastian Churchman, and as it is likely to present itself to a dispassionate evangelical Christian who criticises it from an independent point of view. The Church of England, even although "Reformed," has always been a Church without an organised lay fellowship. Its individual churches have their clergy and their communicants. But the communicants are such, not as duly tested and duly accepted members of a godly mutual fellowship, but either because they assume the position of communicants merely as attendants at the public service of the church, or because, where there is some revival of a sense of responsibility alike in them and in the minister of the church, they have been confirmed, and have had private religious conversation with the minister as a preparation for communion. In no case is there any Church assembly, whether of the communicants generally or of their representatives religiously regarded, by means of which discipline may be exercised, or common counsel taken as to the Church, or suitable persons for office as deacons or pastors of the Church discerned and singled out. Nor are there any regularly organised and officially recognised assemblies, larger or smaller, similar to those of the primitive Church, in which close mutual fellowship may be enjoyed, and spiritual gifts freely exercised. In short, the laity as such are, so far as the law and constitution of the Church are concerned, mere ciphers: they are allowed to receive the Lord's Supper; that is all. They do this either by their own mere will, or at the mere will of the "priest," who, in that case, is absolute. There is no brotherhood that knows of them, or takes any cognisance of their position or rights as communicants.

Now, on what theory can such a Church system be defended, unless it be either a Broad Church Erastianism, which absolutely identifies the Church and the world, and which accounts the clergy as only one branch of the national civil service, or else a theory of Churchmanship which makes the clergy everything in the organisation of the Church, and the laity nothing? The clergyman who rejects the former alternative must needs hold to the latter, if he undertakes to defend his Church and its organisation. He has to justify a Church which ignores the rights and status of the laity in all matters of organisation; which, in matters of discipline, either leaves them utterly alone, to live as they list, and to receive or neglect the Holy Sacrament as they list, or assumes the right to admit or exclude them at the mere pleasure of "the priest," ignoring them in every other organic Church function or relation. It is evident that the High Churchman who is determined to uphold the proper Church principles (if he can find them out) of the Church of England as such, and to maintain its proper authority, to maintain its own intrinsic status and claims, has no alternative but to embrace and uphold a theory which limits Church rights, and all office and responsibility in the Church, to the clergy. In fact, he must maintain that the clergy are the only vital element in the Church, that all authority and power belong to them, that the maintenance and continuance of the Church, its guidance and its perpetuation, belong absolutely to them. The clergy are the Church.

Further, inasmuch as, where there is no commonwealth or constitutional organisation in any community, the actual government can only be either monarchical or oligarchical, and must needs be exclusive and absolute, so, under such conditions as I have indicated, the government of the Church must either be with pope or patriarch, or it must be shared among a council of bishops. It must in any case be strictly hierarchical and exclusive. It is under such conditions that earnest men whose souls revolt from the mere Erastianism of Dean Stanley are led to maintain such views as those expounded by Canon Curteis in his Bampton Lectures and by the late Canon Liddon in his ordination sermon, entitled " A Father in Christ." If Canon Liddon had but illustrated his sermon from the lives and works of the bishops of his own Church, taken impartially, or the bishops of Rome, to whom, on his own hypothesis, the teachings of his sermon must apply at least as justly as to English bishops, the result would surely have been instructive. With able and estimable men of such Church sympathies and predilections, the doctrine of apostolical succession and episcopal spiritual power and authority is a necessity. It is a matter of faith, which no historical questions can be allowed to shake. Assuredly it is held in defiance of all historical evidence and of all evangelical principles of theology. One might almost be tempted to think that they adopt the maxim, " Credo, quia impossibile."

However incredible, this ecclesiastical doctrine is necessary if the claims of Anglo-Catholics are to be upheld, necessary if it is to be maintained that a Church without a lay fellowship is Christ's one Church, instituted as such—and alone instituted—that it might be the means and instrument of salvation for the world. Hence Dr. Hook was bold enough to maintain the "fable," as John Wesley called it, that "the clergy of the Church of England can trace their connexion with the apostles by links, not one of which is wanting, from the times of St. Paul and St. Peter to our own." This fable Macaulay, and many besides Macaulay, as, for instance, the learned Methodist writer, Thomas Powell, have teased and torn into contemptible shreds and tatters ; but it is necessary to the Anglo - Catholic theory, and therefore it must be maintained. How much wiser would it have been to leave the " succession " to be a " dogma," a " mystery," an " article of faith," than, like Dr. Hook, gravely to assert its demonstrable historical verity! This " fable " being laid down as the historical foundation, Canon Liddon proceeds to build upon it the spiritual postulate which is necessary to the exclusive theory of his Church, and lays it down that, as " the apostles had the power to transmit the ministry," so " the episcopate is not only necessary to the *bene esse* of the Church, but to its *esse* "— necessary not only to the well-being, but to the very existence, of a Christian Church.[1] If the clergy are indeed

---

[1] Similarly, Canon Gore concludes that "a ministry not episcopally received is invalid, that is to say, falls outside the conditions of covenanted security, and cannot justify its existence in terms of the covenant."—*The Church and the Ministry*, p. 345.

the Church, and if councils or companies of presbyter-bishops, spreading out in all directions in a way inconsistent with hierarchical subordination, or with "Catholic unity" in any compact form or organic visibility, are not to be accepted as legitimate, then the prerogative of ordination must, for Anglo-Catholic ends and purposes, and to meet fully the claims of the English Church, be limited exclusively to the bishops. Especially must this be rigidly maintained if the English Church is to hold its position on the same plane with the Western Catholic and the Greek Catholic Churches, in which the right of ordination had, long ages before the time of the Reformation, come to be confined to the episcopal order. Exclusive Church claims as maintained on behalf of the Church of England are, in fact, inconsistent with any other hypothesis than that of the apostolico-episcopal succession.

The necessity, however, for formulating this theory was not discovered till half a century had passed since the separation from Rome of the Reformed Church of England. It had not been maintained or defined in any ecclesiastical decree or *corpus theologicum* of the Church of Rome. It was, as formulated, an invention of the Church of England to meet its controversial necessities when pressed hard by the zealous champions of the Puritan party. These insisted on the Divine right of their Presbyterian platform as opposed to prelatic episcopacy. By a notable coincidence, in the very same year, the year of the Armada, to which I have already referred as marking the date when the Reformed Church of England became, by a sudden and sweeping change, Anglo-Catholic, Dr. Bancroft, afterwards archbishop, preaching at Paul's Cross, suggested rather than asserted the Divine right of bishops in the

Church of England, thus claiming to make good its position against the "Divine right" asserted by Rome on the one hand and claimed for the Puritan "discipline" on the other. This was, at the time, an entirely novel suggestion, and involved a desertion of the ground hitherto held by Jewell, Whitgift, and Hooker, and, to quote Mr. Child's language, "appeared to have been enunciated simply, as one may say, to overtrump" the great Puritan controversialist "Cartwright's trick."[1] Shortly afterwards, this view was elaborately set forth and maintained by Dr. Bilson, afterwards Bishop of Winchester. It was, however, a startling and very notable change of position for Churchmen to take up in Elizabeth's reign. Indeed, Bilson's argument was not only opposed to the views of Whitgift and Hooker before him, but of Andrewes after him, of whose character and authority so much is made by modern Churchmen. A distinguished High Church ecclesiastical scholar, Dr. N. Pocock, writing in the *Guardian* in 1892 (Nov. 23), says roundly that "the belief in an apostolical succession in the episcopate is not to be found in any of the writings of the Elizabethan bishops," and that "probably not a single bishop was to be found who believed in his own Divine commission or in the efficacy of the sacraments."

As the power, the pertinacity, the Divine right assumptions of the Puritan party, however, grew more and more formidable, during the reigns of the first two Stuart kings of England, the High Church controversialists took more and more to this novel argument. The school of Laud made much of it. After the Restoration, High Anglicanism

[1] *Church and State under the Tudors*, by Gilbert W. Child, M.A., p. 238.

started with it. But Puritanism almost from the date of the Restoration began to decay; with the Nonjurors also, in the beginning of the eighteenth century, High Churchmanship of the Laudian school died away. "Latitudinarianism," to use an unfriendly name for the school of Stillingfleet, occupied the field. So the argument from the Divine apostolicity of orders was lost sight of for nearly a century. The growth of Dissent, and along with this the revival of High Church claims, zeal, and aggressiveness under Newman's lead at Oxford, led to the rehabilitation of the "Stuart-Reformation" claims of the Church of England.

For the reasons now explained, this incredible hypothesis has been felt to be necessary as a ground of argument by High Anglican Episcopalians. But, also, it is otherwise an extremely serviceable and convenient assumption; convenient, indeed, precisely in proportion to its incredibility. The more incredible are the claims of the clergy, the more convenient is this theory. What Anglo-Catholic exclusiveness has to maintain is, that other communions in England besides the Church of England are precluded from being the channels of salvation, whereas, as Canon Gore says, "where the apostolic organisation abides," there is "the covenanted fulness of the gift of the Spirit." Now, judged by every available test, by every test of fruit, or life, or spiritual experience, or effect and influence on society, this is a simply incredible assertion, a claim too ridiculous for serious refutation. The lives of the saints, such as Baxter, or Howe, or Henry, father and son, or Doddridge, or Watts, or Robert Hall, or Joseph Benson, or Richard Watson, or John Angell James; the writings as well as the lives of these saints, and many more such; the effect of these men's lives and writings on the generations among whom they lived, and generations following;—all combine to stamp this exclusive claim of the Anglo-Catholic school with incredibility. Above all, when with the lives, the writings, the influence of such men, we compare the lives and the influence of such "fathers in Christ" as the Catholic Churches have shown, of scandalous popes, of worldly patriarchs, of lordly, greedy, dissolute prelates, such as have been too common in all these Churches, nay, of worldling bishops in the Reformed Church of England itself, it becomes more and more amazing that it should be maintained that the "gift of the Spirit" did indeed pass into and through the hands of these popes, patriarchs, and prelates of unsanctified hearts and ungodly lives, and that by their means and agency the "covenanted fulness" of the Spirit's grace and blessing came into the possession of those whom they in their turn ordained, and of those to whom these ministered the sacraments, while the other teachers and preachers, men of holy lives and teachers of the "truth as it is in Jesus," were no true "ministers of Christ" to any. Episcopally ordained and ordaining men of unholy hearts and ungodly lives showed no Christian example, used no moral means to influence others for their good, made no attempt, like the true Apostle Paul, "by manifestation of the truth" to "commend themselves to every man's conscience in the sight of God"; they exercised no salutary or truly Christian personal influence; nevertheless, through their manual movements and murmured, broken sentences, often unheard, the power of the Spirit flowed to others. By "digital contact" they became channels of the highest spiritual gift and prerogative from Christ. Whilst, on the other hand, men who preached Christ's truth and gospel in substance and spirit, as St.

Peter preached it at Jerusalem, as St. Paul preached it on his missions and wrote it in his epistles, and as the first unofficial and unordained disciples, who went everywhere forth from Jerusalem "preaching the word," taught and enforced it, to the salvation of those that heard it; men, too, who by their lives "adorned the doctrine of God their Saviour"—these men in their ministrations, which proved so effectual to the conversion of sinners and the transformation of character, had no covenanted help of the Spirit, and were the means of conveying no blessing of true renewal and sanctification to any of those who received their word as from God. In the one case, there was undeniable wickedness, often frank and flagrant; but with and under this was the Spirit of God, the "covenanted fulness" of grace and blessing. In the other case, there was moral excellence which none could gainsay, manifest saintliness, influence for good, devout reverence for God, and lowly faith (not indeed in the Church, but) in Christ; yet there was in all this no fruit of the indwelling Spirit of holiness promised by Christ to His disciples.

These are the contradictions which the Anglo-Catholic claim on behalf of the Episcopal Church, as the exclusive inheritor in England of Christ's covenanted grace, His only Church, requires us to believe. In order to maintain such claims as these, it is necessary to hold that the grace of the Spirit of Christ Jesus is shut up in bond under the seal of the Episcopal Church, and can only be opened by the key of the lineally successive episcopally ordained priesthood; that it flows from bishop to priest exclusively through the "digital contact" effected by the bishop, and from priest to people exclusively through the hands that dispense the consecrated elements. Only on such a theory could such claims as the Anglo-Catholic conceives himself bound to make for his Church be sustained; only thus can good, when necessary, be denied all tincture of Christian quality or character, and evil be made the fountain of Divine goodness and grace. The more incredible the claims of the Church are, the more convenient, as I have said, the more necessary, is this hypothesis.

Such an hypothesis would be violent, and, when regarded with true intelligence, really incredible anywhere, in any country. But it is especially monstrous in England, with its history of Presbyterian, and Independent, and Baptist, and Methodist, and other Nonconformity, with its national record of Nonconformist virtue and godliness, with its memories of Nonconformist saints. It is now also more monstrous than ever before, since the roll and record of Nonconformist Christianity has been growing in volume and in impressiveness down to the present hour. And yet now is the time chosen for insisting on these irrational, I had almost said insane, pretensions. The original Reformers held views as to the realities of Popish evil, and of gospel grace and truth, inconsistent with such Romish-like pretensions as these. But they were still hoping that there might be some way found for gaining evangelical liberty for the people of the Lord, and, in some form or other, a true lay fellowship; they did not regard all prospect of a further and deeper reformation as cut off. Since the Stuart-Restoration period all such hope seems to have come to an end; and, rather than accept mere Erastianism, this is the theory which High Churchmen embrace.

But all the difficulties connected with this hypothesis are not yet enumerated. In endeavouring to find a position, such as they may claim and hold, consistent with the relations of the Church to the State and to Nonconformist communions, Anglo-Catholics fix themselves in a dilemma, with regard to the Roman Catholic and the Greek Churches, from which extrication is impossible. They cannot pretend to deny that the Roman Church, of which for so long the English Church was part and parcel, is itself a branch, and a leading branch, of the Catholic Church. They cannot dare to repudiate, as withered and dead branches of the great world-vine of the Church of which they speak and think, according to their "one and the same visible Church" theory, those sister national Churches with which the Church of England was once co-incorporated as fellow members of the great Western Catholic Church. Nor can they dare to deny the catholicity of the "orthodox" Greek Church. All that they can pretend to is, that the Church of England shall be admitted as parallel and correlated with the Western and the Eastern Catholic Churches, as, like them, an aboriginal offshoot from the pure and primitive one Church of Christ. It is a pretence that lies very open to critical doubt and objection. But I have no intention to criticise it in detail, or except as to one particular. I desire only to point out the incongruity of the claim thus made on behalf of the Church of England. This Church claims to be a sister Catholic Church with that of Rome, both being true apostolic and episcopal Churches. And yet the English Church violently and permanently broke away from the Western Catholic unity, with its Roman centre; while in return the Roman Catholic Church has excommunicated, and does excommunicate, the Church of England. The same Church has excommunicated the Greek Catholic Church. On the other hand, the Greek Church excommunicates the Roman Church, and holds the English Church to be schismatical, if not also heretical. Surely it is evident that the claim of co-catholicity with the Roman and Greek Churches, as against the "non-Catholic" Reformed and Nonconformist Churches, which is put forth by Canon Curteis and by Anglo-Catholics generally, is one which cannot be logically or consistently maintained. The threefold complication of dilemmas is such as no Anglo-Catholic has been able to resolve.

But, in fact, this dilemma, and the whole tangle of difficulties in which the Anglo-Catholic externalist finds himself, point to a fundamental error, which is common to the Anglo-Catholic High Church theory and every form of (so-called) Catholic externalism, and is an inheritance from mediæval Christianity. I have dealt at some length with the error which, ignoring lay fellowship as the foundation of the Church's organisation, identifies the Church with the clergy. A twin error is that which regards the Christian Church as a visible organisation, one and the same from age to age, spreading through the nations, and destined to be co-extensive with the world. This is the grand root-fallacy of externalism. No truly spiritual view of the nature of the Christian Church, or of the Divine laws of Church organisation and development, will be attained by any one until he has settled aright his views as to the unity of the Church, as to the relation of the Church to Christ as its Head, and as to the law of vitality and continuity which belongs to its character and history.

There are three ways of explaining the unity and historic continuity of the Christian Church. One of these, that which English High Churchmen maintain, the only one which can be maintained by those who identify the Church with the clergy, finds the unity and continuity of the Church in the perpetuation of its orders, and of the organisation of which the clergy are the necessary substratum as well as the controlling directorate—finds it in an external and officially organised Church identity. That way, whatever English High Churchmen may try to persuade themselves, leads from Canterbury straight to Rome. Another way finds the unity and continuity of the Church in the continued existence of Christendom, as manifested generally by national confessions, as realised in what is spoken of as a common Christian consciousness, and as distributively set forth and expressed by various Christian communions and organisations. This is the Broad Church view. It is in the common acceptance of this view that the definition of Broad Churchmanship must be found. It was in this respect only that Mr. Maurice, the subtle Platonical theosophist, and Dean Stanley, the vague latitudinarian, who eschewed not only all theosophy and mysticism, but philosophy in any form, agreed as Broad Churchmen, being in all else the strongest possible contrasts. This is the view which best agrees with Erastianism, and which was in effect held and taught by the able latitudinarian and Erastian school of eighteenth century divines, the only school with which, as thinkers and reasoners, Dean Stanley was really in sympathy. The third way of understanding the unity and continuity of the Christian Church is that which identifies the Church with Christ's "body" of true believers, distributed among the various professedly Christian communions, and of whom some inidviduals may even conceivably be apart from any organised Christian community, but who all by living faith and the true sanctification of the Holy Ghost, are joined in one spirit to Christ Jesus, their living Head. This is the evangelical view. Although rejected or ignored by Anglican Churchmen of the high type, or possibly never entering into their thoughts, never dawning upon their conception, it is yet the only spiritual view of the nature of the Christian Church. This is the view held not only by evangelical Nonconformists, but, for the most part, by thoroughly evangelical Churchmen. It is the view that has been held by Continental divines of the most profound spiritual intelligence and insight, such, for instance, as Vinet. Among the mediæval Catholics, it was taught by the mystics of the better side, and it was the doctrine of the saintly French Catholic mystics of the eighteenth century. In the midst of the worst times of Protestant Erastianism on the Continent, it was maintained by a succession of holy men, who were identified with those Pietist communities which kept alive the traditions, at once contemplative and practical, of primitive and experimental Christianity; and it is the only view to be maintained by those who are neither prepared to follow the way of hierarchical externalism to Rome, nor to embrace the universalising Broad Church theory, which regards the self-same aggregate of individuals as either Church or world according as " the light which lighteth each man," or the darkness and confusion which also belong to each, may happen to be thought of.

From the formularies of the Church of England, as would naturally be expected, no clear light is to be obtained on this critical point. The Nineteenth Article evades the question altogether, in a convenient, but yet a curious fashion. It teaches that "*the* visible Church of Christ is *a* congregation of faithful men, in the which the pure word of God is preached, and the sacraments be duly ministered," the Latin original lending itself to such vagueness of expression. From such a form of words I know not what is to be learnt, at least as to the point in hand. In the Collect for all Conditions of Men, the "Catholic Church" might seem to be indirectly identified with "all who profess and call themselves Christians." This, of course, would be Erastianism. And yet it might be fairly argued, from the clauses which follow, that by "the Catholic Church" should be understood those professed Christians who are "led into the way of truth, and hold the faith in unity of spirit, in the bond of peace, and in righteousness of life," an interpretation which would agree perfectly with the spiritual view and definition of the Christian or "Catholic Church."[1]

The result of the discussion in this chapter is to bring us back to the position already marked out as that which independent but not unfriendly Protestant critics of the Church of England are compelled to occupy. By our detailed examination of the claims and pretensions of Anglo-Catholic High Churchmen, we have but added an outwork and a line of defence to our position. On the exclusive theory of Anglo-Catholicism, we have now seen that the claims of the Church of England are unworthy of any respect, are, in fact,

[1] See, for a really Catholic definition of the "true Church," the Homily for Whitsunday (Oxford University Edition, 1844, p. 413); and, as to the whole subject dealt with above, see Dr. Gregory's Fernley Lecture on *The Holy Catholic Church, The Communion of Saints.* I have pleasure also in referring to the Fernley Lecture for 1885, by the Rev. W. F. Slater, *Methodism in the Light of the Early Church*, the exact and wide learning shown in which is not less remarkable than the ability of the argument.

intolerable. On any evangelical or spiritual ground her organisation is exceedingly defective, defective because the Church, as organised, is devoid of a godly lay fellowship. For this the one apology is, that she inherited the defects and disabilities, in a spiritual sense, of the mediæval Church, and that her reformation, owing, at least in part, to the hand of the State lying heavy upon her, has never been properly completed. The Church of England stands very greatly in need of a deep and evangelical reform.

In the foregoing argument I have made no reference to the moral and social effect of the High Anglican theory and claims as set up by the clergy of the Established Church. A great gulf is fixed between them and all other Christian ministers in the country, except, indeed, the Romish priests. They regard all these ministers as in effect usurpers; they proclaim that they are " blind leaders of the blind," that they and their flocks are cut off from the fountains of covenanted grace, that they are in a condition of schism. John Keble, the loving poet, in the preface to a volume of his sermons, classed all Nonconformists as "heretics." He distinguished mankind, in respect of religion, into three classes : " Christians properly so called, *i.e.* Catholics ; Jews, Mohammedans, and Heretics ; and heathens and unbelievers." Thus the High Church, maintaining a theory which has been shown to be unevangelical, unspiritual, unprimitive, at the same time assumes a position the most grievous and alienating which it is possible to assume in regard to much more than one-half, and surely not the less earnest or Christian part, of the people of Great Britain, including of course the Scotch Presbyterians, who, though some of them may be members of an established Church, are all, no less than

English Nonconformists, unchurched and cast off as heretics, or at least schismatics. Equally in England, in the colonies, and even in the United States, the like effect of a monstrous and unchristian theory is found. High Church bigotry abounds and asserts itself in all these countries, and everywhere clears around itself an intermediate space of inhospitable desert, the outlying fringe of its own uncharitable pale. It is not the fact that it is established which makes High Anglicanism thus fatally exclusive. In the United States the same result follows; whereas in Scotland, with a Presbyterian Established Church, and a small and poor Episcopal Church, nothing like it is to be found. The will, indeed, may often not be wanting; but feebleness and poverty make any affectation of social or public exclusiveness too futile to be attempted. In its whole character, and in all its effect and influence, the High Church theory which we have been reviewing is a system of claims and pretensions equally irrational and pernicious.

CHAPTER III.

PRESENT QUESTIONS FOR THE CHURCH OF ENGLAND—THE CONTROVERSY ON CHURCH REFORM.

IT can be no vital objection to any Church that her ordained ministers consist of three classes: bishops, presbyters or priests, and deacons. I am not just now speaking of *diocesan* episcopacy in particular. The earliest post-apostolic Christianity furnished many examples of a not materially dissimilar threefold ministry in the Churches, and, as we have seen, there is reason to believe that even before the first century was completed, not improbably before the death of the Apostle John, and under his personal cognisance, three nearly correspondent distinctions were definitely established in the Churches of Asia, and the precedence and authority of the bishops strongly defined. Nor, to go a step further, is it any valid objection to the Church of England that her bishops have diocesan authority. Canon Liddon's argument on this point, drawn from the cases of Timothy and Titus, if duly limited, ought not to be regarded as singular or novel. Since the time of Hooker, at any rate, the special commission and authority bestowed upon Timothy and Titus have been by many ecclesiastical writers regarded as conferring jurisdiction not unlike that of a diocesan bishop and administrator. It is many years since my own views were defined in this sense. The work and jurisdiction committed to

Timothy and Titus, I have been accustomed to regard as an example and precedent for such official appointments as those of "general superintendent" in the provinces of the mission field, or as Methodist bishop in America. Where Canon Liddon goes astray in this matter is in his maintaining that the power of ordination and of jurisdiction over the presbyters (or clergy) was given exclusively to such representatives of apostolic authority as Timothy or Titus, and has descended exclusively to their successors, the diocesan bishops; that the presbyter-bishops had no power of appointing their successors, and no right of discipline over each other, but only over the laity. If that had been so, what would have been the condition of the Churches to which the *Teaching of the Apostles* had reference, in connexion with which there is no appearance whatever of diocesan bishops or any equivalent dignitaries, but only of stationary "bishops and deacons"? Indeed, the Ignatian Epistles, as may be seen by a study of Bishop Lightfoot's great work, though they magnify the office of the bishops of local Churches, disclose no evidence of the existence of diocesan bishops. Such "evangelists" as Timothy and Titus were called to be, under special circumstances of swift evangelisation attendant on the ministry of the great missionary apostle, afforded an anticipation of a sort of episcopal office and jurisdiction—the "diocesan"—which in after ages would be found convenient for purposes of organisation, either through extensive provinces where mission work needed powerful and unifying direction and oversight, or over large areas where Churches were crowded thickly together, which it was necessary to maintain in close union with each other and with other provinces of Churches belonging to the same Christian communion.

But there seems no reason to believe that Timothy and Titus were the first links in an order or chain of diocesan bishops to whom, and to whom exclusively, was committed, in succession and inheritance from the apostles, nothing less than apostolic authority and prerogative. This contention of Canon Liddon's appears to be merely a bold hypothesis, an hypothesis altogether destitute of historical evidence or probability. One thing it shows: that Canon Liddon gives up the attempt to trace the descent of apostolic authority and prerogative through the successions of presbyter-bishops. There, at all events, is something learnt. But in forsaking one untenable ground of argument for high episcopal claims, he has betaken himself to another quite as untenable. For half a century after the death of St. John, where is there any trace of *diocesan* episcopacy? Where in the West is there any trace of it before the end of the second century? He has also needlessly lowered the position of the primitive presbyter-bishops, who, there can be no doubt, were invested both with the power of ordaining their fellows or successors, and with that of discipline at once over the Church, in concurrence with the brethren of the common fellowship, or their competent representatives, and over each other.

We do not object, then, I repeat, to the three distinctions among the clergy. The deacons of the earliest Church did not always or of necessity only "serve tables," as the Pastoral Epistles show. That there should not be any permanent lay diaconate in the Church of England is, indeed, a serious defect, part of the general defect of lay fellowship; but that the probationary stage of the ministry should be counted as a form of the diaconate is not inconsistent with the teaching and implications either of the Acts or of the Epistles. Many of the primitive deacons, doubtless, having by their good service in the diaconate earned for themselves "a good degree, and great boldness in the faith," did pass forward to the office of presbyter or bishop. Nor need we at all object to the word *bishop*, as a specific official designation, which had already undergone one change and advancement in its meaning when it passed from the level of the presbytery to the pre-eminence of the one sole chief presbyter or president of the presbytery, being further transferred to the diocesan superintendent, *the* bishop of bishops, the bishop *par excellence*. Before this last transfer of application had taken effect, an intermediate episcopal title, to which I have not as yet referred, had already naturally, indeed necessarily, come into use. When the rural interspaces between the large towns came to be occupied by village Churches or Churches in smaller towns, in each of which there was at least one presbyter, and which were all gathered together under the general charge of one superintendent minister, one bishop, that bishop was called *chorepiscopus*, the bishop of a "circuit," as Wesleyans might say, of a country region, of a rural district. Similarly, therefore, it was very natural that the general superintendent of a province of Churches should be called the bishop of that province. We take no objection, accordingly, to the distinction of the clergy into bishops, presbyters or priests, and deacons. Our objection, that which lies at the bottom of all the rest, is that the Church in which the clergy are distinguished into bishops, priests, and deacons, knows nothing either of any such lay diaconate as the primitive Church knew, or, what is more and worse, of any such fellowship of believers as that which was the very life tissue of the apostolic Church.

The first effect of this deficiency is that there is no provision, or indeed opportunity, in the Church for spiritual persons, true members not only of the visible Church on earth, but of Christ's mystical Church and body, to exercise their gifts in mutual prayer and exhortation, and in testifying of the grace of God. There is no Church assembly except the great meeting for public worship, and in that worship the "priest" alone appears. The consequence is, too commonly, formalism. It must often be difficult to avoid falling into this evil.

There is nothing belonging to the Church of England in the least resembling the primitive meetings for fellowship of the first Christians at Jerusalem and elsewhere. Very much of the New Testament is without any relevance to the Christian worship of to-day in our parish churches and to our modern episcopal Church organisation. No lay deacon, like Philip, is at liberty to go and open a mission in a new field.[1] No unordained Apollos, having been instructed and quickened in Christian faith and knowledge by the agency of a godly pair of private believers, is at liberty to go forth and "water" the field of gospel-planting in succession to a pioneer bishop or even a "mission priest." No migrant or emigrant "disciples," not even though they were driven from their homes by persecution, would, if they were strict and loyal members of the Church of England, go "about preaching the word." No great mother Church, like that of the Syrian Antioch, would, according to the principles and prescriptions of the Anglican hierarchy, be founded by the public preaching of travelling lay brethren. There can, on High Anglican principles, be no Church gathered and clustered in a house, such as those of which we

[1] Acts viii.

read in the Acts and Epistles, unless an "apostolic bishop" should be resident in the house; no such Church as that which nestled in the home of Aquila and Priscilla, whether at Corinth or Ephesus or Rome, or as that in Philemon's house at Colossæ. No missionary advance can be made without an apostolic and diocesan bishop to lead. In short, to use Canon Liddon's words, a "bishop is necessary not only to the well-being, but to the very being, of a Church."

This unevangelical and unprimitive condition of things in what High Anglicans speak of as the "primitive and apostolic Church of England" is the direct result of the want of a spiritual and truly mutual lay fellowship in that communion. Almost every other disability and evil under which the Church suffers arises from the same cause. There can be no regular and effective Church discipline where there is no evangelical lay fellowship. There can be no primitive lay diaconate; for churchwardens and sidesmen, whether elected by the ratepayers or nominated by the incumbent of the parish, are but a parody—sometimes a grotesque parody—on such a diaconate. Except by the mere private will and permission of the "priest," there can be no eliciting, no training and development, no testing, of spiritual gifts, and therefore there can be no true or proper "schools of the prophets," from which might proceed, with fit guards and after the needful education, "workmen needing not to be ashamed," able and well-furnished ministers of Christ and of His Church. Till of late years, indeed, no layman exercised spiritual functions of any sort or to any extent, even under episcopal or clerical permission. There is therefore no standing and disciplined body of Church laity who in presbyteries, in ruri-decanal chapters, in synods, might take their place by the side of the clergy, thus meeting one of the most generally acknowledged needs in the way of Church reform. There can, under such conditions, be no proper substitute for that unseemly custom and rule of crude and unregulated lay patronage, with its natural but yet scandalous consequences, the sale of advowsons and next presentations, which now usurps the place that ought to be filled by a duly ascertained and regulated concurrence of the parish laity with the bishop in the appointment of an incumbent to a vacant church.

At present, according to Church and State law, the concurrence of the laity with the clergy in the Church of England is represented by the churchwarden element, by lay patronage, and by Parliament. All other arrangements for uniting the clergy and laity are recent and merely voluntary—are amateur arrangements. How unbefitting and how unreal this state of things is, everybody must feel. The one cause of it all is the absence of a true spiritual lay fellowship. Possibly, indeed, for measures of organic reform or development in the Church—seeing that it is the established and nationally endowed Church—the consent of Parliament would still be necessary, even though there were a living lay body and fellowship. But the consent of Parliament to measures prepared by a representative organisation, which consisted not only of clergymen, but also in due co-ordination as well as subordination of laymen, would be little more than a legal formality. Whereas now a lay Parliament is tempted to dissent from a clerical Convocation. Such a merely clerical Convocation can have no national character and very little weight for purposes of Church reform. A Church assembly which included an adequate lay element, representative of a true and national lay fellowship, would be recognised as the legitimate national representation of the Church of England. To say that our Parliament to-day is such a representation is a mere mockery.

Canon Curteis seems to be well enough content with a merely clerical government of the Church; to be, at all events, not profoundly dissatisfied with things as they are. In fact, his Lectures undertake to show cause why all the denominations of England, from the Roman Catholics at the one extreme to the Unitarians at the other, should be content to merge themselves in the Church of England, even as at present organised. He offers no argument, and hazards no proposals, for reform. He seems to regard the Bishops' Council as well and rightfully competent to govern the Church of England. At the same time, he gravely tells us that "according to the theory of the Church of England"—to which in all things he holds—"the LEGISLATIVE POWER *is lodged in the whole body of the 'fideles' scattered throughout Christendom.*"

The late Archdeacon Hare was a man of different calibre and of other views. Cramped and hampered though he was by the conflicting theories and the actual condition of his Church, he could not but indicate his own sense of the deep and paramount needs of the Church. He speaks, in one of his Charges, first of the "jealous policy" of the Church of Rome, "which has always laboured to keep its lay members in abject spiritual subjection," and then of some of the "rules laid down by our own Church in the sixteenth and seventeenth centuries, which bear the marks of emanating from a like system." He goes on to speak of the results of such a system: "On the one hand, the laity, being almost precluded from taking part in the godly works of the Church, grew to deem that their vocation was altogether secular"; and, as a consequence, many of them lapsed into practical, if not speculative, infidelity, "the evil of which was rather increased than diminished by its combination with a nominal outward conformity. On the other hand, the clergy became outwardly weak, and, in a grievous number of cases, inwardly hollow: weak from the want of that help which they ought to have sought, but had rather repelled; hollow as we are apt to grow when we are destitute of the interchange and reciprocation of our feelings, and are more tenacious of our rights than of our duties." He proceeds earnestly to deprecate any attempt "to prolong a usurpation the only excuse for which lay in the condition of the age when it arose."[1] In the same spirit, in another Charge, he speaks of "the decay of godly discipline deplored by our Church in her Commination Service, where she declares that its restoration is much to be wished." "In the best ages of the Church," he says, "although the power of the gospel brought home to the heart was acknowledged to be the only source of true Christian holiness, it was felt that something more was needed in order to contend against the evil propensities of mankind; and to this end the Church was wont to exercise a godly discipline. But unhappily in the course of ages this godly discipline fell into decay. The world gained power, first within the Church, and then against her, so that the Church scarcely dared any longer to condemn beyond the capricious measure of the world's censure." In a note (A) to the same Charge,[2] after quoting Dr. Arnold to the effect that

[1] Charge on *The Duty of the Church in Times of Trial*, 1848.
[2] *Privileges imply Duties*, 1841.

"to revive Christ's Church is to restore its disfranchised members, the laity, to the discharge of their proper duties in it," and that till this is done Church discipline can never be restored, he proceeds himself to enlarge on the same theme. He asserts that "the decay and extinction of godly discipline in the Church has been mainly owing to this primary corruption, whereby the functions which ought to have been exercised by the whole Church were exercised almost exclusively by the clergy. This gave a partial character to all measures of discipline. . . . Nor assuredly will any measures be effectual to restore a vigorous discipline until the laity regain their full Christian franchise in the Church." And again, in note (J) to his Charge on *The Means of Unity*, he enlarges on the necessity of the laity being united with the clergy in the formal and organised councils of the Church. In particular, he says respecting Convocation: "This is the great defect in the constitution of our Convocation; it represents the conscience and will, and expresses the voice, of the clergy, not of the Church. This was suited to its original function of imposing taxes on the clergy, but unfits it for being the legislative council of the whole Church."

So far I had written, when, towards the end of November, 1885, the question of Church Reform was raised in the public press, with an emphasis and energy that roused attention deep and wide, and produced an impression, I might almost say a shock, of which the effect, the vibrations, were still—when, after an interval of many weeks, I was able to return to the subject—felt by all who took an interest in the Church of England, or, I may say, in national Christianity. The University

Addresses delivered the first heavy stroke. After their appearance, the newspapers, especially the Church papers and the *Times*, and of the Church papers particularly the *Guardian*, continued for weeks together to teem with letters on the subject. Indeed, the overflow of correspondence had not come to an end with the close of the year. Mr. Bosworth Smith's letters, which appeared earlier than the University Addresses, were, indeed, brilliant effusions relating to the general subject of the Church of England, but they were, in their occasion and essential character, really political appeals. They referred to the reform of the Church incidentally rather than primarily, regarding it as necessarily involved in her preservation as a national Church, if she is to be preserved, as Mr. Bosworth Smith desires and hopes—a point to which I must by-and-by advert. It is not to those letters that I wish here particularly to refer, but to some from eminent clergymen, the coincidence of which with the general line of historical exposition and argument in the pages preceding, and with my statements as to the past and present condition of the Church of England, is too remarkable not to be noted.

In the *Guardian* of December 23, 1885, a letter appeared from the Rev. Joseph Foxwell, Vicar of Market Weighton and Rural Dean, from which I make the following extracts:

" The Church of England, which Henry VIII. said was sufficient to settle questions of divinity without external interference, consisted of the clergy only. And to this day, ' going into the Church ' is a phrase which, however objectionable in one sense, is, in the sense of the Church as by law established, perfectly correct. The Church of

England as by law established consists of certain officers, chiefly clergy, who hold in trust certain fabrics and other property for the purpose of offering certain religious ministrations to the inhabitants of certain localities, free of cost. But these inhabitants are in no proper legal sense members of the ecclesiastical institutions which have been planted in their midst, any more than persons who are in hospitals or other charitable institutions are necessarily 'members' of those institutions. Dr. Trevor, being a canon of York, is a 'member' of the cathedral and metropolitical church of York. But the inhabitants of the diocese of York are no more members of that church in any legal sense than if they lived in America. . . . A baptized person has certain personal and individual rights in the public and private ministrations of the vicar over and above the rights of an unbaptized parishioner. But they are not corporate rights. The only corporate rights which a parishioner has in his parish church are those which he exercises through the parish meeting; and these are independent, not only of baptism, but of all and every ordinance and article of Christianity. They are rights, too, not of the parishioners, but of the ratepayers. . . . There is therefore no legal recognition of the laity as such in regard to membership in the Church of England. And I doubt whether there ever was a time when every adult inhabitant of England considered himself a willing or *bona fide* member of the English Church. No doubt the Legislature makes laws which the clergy, church-wardens, sextons, and other 'members' of the legal Church are obliged to obey. But a Parliament which represents Scotland and Ireland, as well as England, can hardly be said to be the laity of the Church of England by representation. It would be as reasonable to say that the Parliament of the United Kingdom is the Great Northern Railway Company by representation, because it makes laws for that company. . . . Corporate Church life—the life of Church membership—recognised by law, ecclesiastical or temporal, there is none. *The members of the body of Christ resident within any parish have certain recognised relationships to the parish priest, but none at all to one another. They are members of the pastor's flock, but not members with him of an organised body. They are sheep, but not brethren.* Hence the weakness of the Church. All other Societies in England, religious and irreligious, are safe. *The Church is in danger because it is not properly a Society at all.* This the Cambridge reformers ask the bishops to rectify. *I need not quote Scripture to show how the absence of recognised membership—recognised, that is, by ecclesiastical law—is the absence of a primary feature of Christ's institution—I mean, fellowship.* But Dr. Trevor thinks this feature cannot be restored in England without obliterating what he calls the national laity. I have tried to show that the 'national laity' have no corporate place in the Church as it is; for their only representatives are the ratepaying laity, and these, with regard to the Church, are 'vanishing away.'"

The passages I have printed in italics are especially noteworthy; and as a Methodist reads them, he cannot at first but feel that Mr. Foxwell is about to strike the vein of primitive Church principles, that he is coming very near to the "kingdom of heaven." How grievous accordingly is the disappointment when, as we follow the rural dean's sentences while he goes on to complete his paragraph, it turns out that all he means by creating a Church fellowship is that every baptized person— baptized and confirmed, it might be supposed he means, but he gives no hint to that effect — should "sign a declaration" that he is a "*bonâ fide* member" of the Church of England. This, he says, would be to define the Church laity in accordance with the principle already embodied in the Public Worship Regulation Act. This plan, he further says, "would amount to a practical application of the Church Catechism. We have taught them that they are members of Christ. Something more than words is needed to make them believe it." Thus, then, it appears, all baptized persons are "members of Christ," though, it seems, very few "believe it." There is no spiritual experience, no spiritual consciousness, involved in the matter. The way to make them believe it is to encourage them to sign a declaration of *bonâ fide* Church membership, and give them after such declaration the right by vote, as members of the Church, or, if thereto chosen and appointed, by official character and action, to represent and act on behalf of the Church of England. " Oh, most lame and impotent conclusion!" Can bathos fall lower than this ? Can spiritual unconsciousness be more complete ? This, forsooth, the equivalent of primitive "fellowship," that "primary feature of Christ's institution" ! It is a pity that Mr. Foxwell did not try what light "quoting Scripture " on this point would have thrown upon the subject. Alas for dead words, deceitful phrases, which, used in a way of unconscious dissimulation, after seeming to light the path to truth and life, turn suddenly aside and lead the misguided "sheep" to a chamber of technical controversy, to a stony pen where there is no pasture, to an election room or a council meeting, as if all their life and hope, their covenant privileges, according to the Catechism, as " members of Christ " and " inheritors of the kingdom of heaven " were centred there!

Let us turn now from the Vicar of Market Weighton to the Dean of Chichester.[1] That redoubtable controversialist could not but have something to say on the question of Church reform. He accordingly contributed to the *Guardian* (December 23, 1885) a long letter of admonition on the subject. He is, as might be expected, offended at the University Addresses, and warns his brethren earnestly against looking to Parliament for Church reforms. He urges that the bishops and clergy have the most important reforms—those, for example, in regard to the traffic in livings and to " criminous clerks "—in their own hands, if they will only rouse themselves to carry them through; he intimates that but for " the dishonest attempt of certain of the clergy to assimilate our English ritual to that of Rome," there would have been comparatively little of the present " reasonable impatience on the part of the laity "; he exhorts his brethren to " catechise the young in an edifying and interesting manner, read Scripture before the congregation with a vast deal more intelligence than they do at present, and leave off preaching such miserably weak sermons "; and he entreats them, " tide what tide, to beware of inviting the interference of an unfriendly House of Commons." In short, Dean Burgon is true to himself. For the Revised Version of the Scriptures he had " flouts, and gibes, and jeers "; for any proposal to reform the organisation of the Church of England, nothing but dissent and censure was to be expected from him. The history of the Church since the Reformation has suggested

[1] The late Dean Burgon.

to him no necessity for organic improvement or adaptation; let the clergy be the Church still as heretofore, let the bishops and clergy be all in all, and the laity nothing; let the constitution of the Church be an iron framework, leaving no scope or opening for the upgrowth and organisation of a lay fellowship of brethren of the common Christian life; Dean Burgon admits, he is conscious of, no constitutional defect, no organic disability. He has his own view of the place of the laity, his own prescription for putting and keeping them in their place, and for duly training them. "I take leave," he says, "to point out that there is plenty of work for the faithful laity to do without either setting Church order at defiance or introducing discord into parishes. Let pious laymen assist the clergyman in teaching the ignorant, reading to the sick and aged, investigating cases of distress. Above all, let them relieve him of the secular duties which he is constrained to undertake, and which are at once distracting and onerous."

So much, indeed, must be conceded to Dean Burgon and to other clerical correspondents (not a few) of the *Guardian*; namely, that if the only, or even the main ordinary, function of the Church laity were legislative and administrative, if the great governing object and purpose of the reorganisation of the Church throughout all its departments were merely, to adopt the language of one of the University Addresses, the admission of "laymen of all classes to a substantial share in the control of Church affairs," there would be not a little reason for hesitation as to the whole movement. In truth, the movement needs to be better defined. The object should be broader and deeper than as thus stated. The scope should not be merely ecclesiastico-political. If the lay representatives of the Church, whether elected from ratepayers or even from the much more restricted and conservative class of "*bonâ fide* communicants," are elected for no other purpose than that of business discussion and ecclesiastical administration or legislation, within the sphere of the parish, the rural deanery, the archdeaconry, the diocese, or the Church at large, there can be no security that the right godly and reverential spirit will prevail in the different assemblies ; there will be grave peril lest the spiritual affairs of the Church should be handled and settled after the temper and spirit of a vestry meeting or a town council, and after the manner of party politics. The body of the Church laity should live continually in true mutual fellowship, according to the spirit of primitive Christianity. Business administration and Church politics should be the *occasional* care and responsibility of chosen men, men, as far as possible, of the spirit of the Seven Deacons, "full of the Holy Ghost and of wisdom." It is strange and sad indeed to observe that all Churchmen who write on this subject, and profess zeal to see the Church of England furnished with a living body of laity, enjoying their proper recognition and rights, seem to be agreed in at least one thing—the only thing in which all agree—that is, in ignoring the *spiritual* rights, the *rights* of spiritual fellowship, which are the primary and fundamental rights of believing brethren ; in ignoring these as *rights*, and as rights to which the avenue and access should lie invitingly open to *all* the brethren ; in ignoring the need of providing free opportunity and scope for all godly and gifted laymen to exercise their spiritual faculties and gifts for the good of their brethren and the spread of gospel truth and power. Ignoring all this, one and another clergyman asks, not unnaturally, what the representative laity, under ordinary circumstances, will have to do in a country parish; adding that, when they find something in which to intermeddle, their action on such rare occasions of discovering that they possess some power, will be unintelligent, inconsiderate, injurious. Such would not be the case if they had been trained in spiritual work, and if the representatives for special work and special occasions had, as assistants to the clergy in their spiritual work and in co-operation with them, proved their fitness for office and trust, and acquired familiarity with the affairs and interests of the Church.

One is thankful, indeed, for the movements initiated of recent years which appear to be tending in the direction of supplying this greatest and deepest need of the Church. The movement of "guilds," in particular, would be one to excite great thankfulness and hope if it were not so widely tainted with confessional superstition, if it were not, speaking generally, one of the signs of ritualising High Churchmanship. It is, at all events, encouraging to know that earnest evangelical Churchmen, forgetting the Calvinistic peculiarities of their section of the Church, sometimes add the fellowship meeting to the Bible-class, or make a happy combination of the two in one meeting.

Some twenty years ago, at a clerical meeting to which I had the privilege of being introduced by Dean Stanley, an active and able High Church London clergyman pressed a Wesleyan minister present, evidently with the deepest earnestness, to give the company information as to the organisation and management of "Wesleyan class-meetings." On the moment, and in that somewhat miscellaneous company, the minister appealed to did not feel at liberty to respond to the request, which was suggested by some remarks made by him, from the Wesleyan point of view, on the subject of Church fellowship and organisation. That clergyman has for many years been an active and influential member of the Episcopal Bench; and has made it a chief point of his policy energetically to promote the guild movement.

There are, it cannot be doubted, large and increasing numbers of men and women in the Established Church who are longing to enjoy the "communion of saints" in a form more direct and earnest and intimate, and more adapted to the actual needs of the soul in the midst of life's duties and conflicts, than they can know at present, at least under ordinary circumstances. Private fellowship, in special cases, is sometimes now enjoyed by twos and threes. But the organisation of the Church should provide for this craving of the earnest and spiritual Christian believer. In connexion with such provision, prayer-meetings and testimony meetings would of necessity be organised. Of course all this implies converted and spiritual ministers. But such organisations as I have been speaking of, created wherever possible by such ministers, would presently and largely increase the supply of ministers like-minded; and such complaints as to the utter unfitness and incapacity of the majority of the clergy for real spiritual and pastoral work as "S. G. O." uttered in the *Times*,[1] could no longer be made. By degrees a change, full of life and hope, would spread over the entire Church. At the centre, as the vital nucleus, of the whole Church-wide company of *bonâ fide* communicants, would be this aggregate of godly people living in actual evangelical fellowship—a fellowship of devotion, of ex-

[1] January 4, 1886.

perience, of philanthropy.[1] In every parish, under such conditions, periodical meetings might be organised of the whole company of professed and actual communicants, at which the parish clergy might fulfil their pastoral functions, by means of suitable addresses and suitable devotional exercises, with the truths and obligations belonging to their Christian profession continually in view of themselves and of the members of their fellowship present with them. Representatives for business meetings, chosen by and from such communicants as these, might safely be trusted. Nay, even if the election were *by* ratepayers as such, provided it were always *from* such communicants, the danger attending such an arrangement, which, in the case of a national and established Church, open as it may be to grave objections, has yet powerful considerations in its favour, would be rendered comparatively small.

The Church of England, under its ecclesiastical guides of the sixteenth, seventeenth, and eighteenth centuries, relieved itself of its godly laity. A large Christian wisdom, a ruling evangelical spirit, would have retained the best, at any rate, and the most influential of the Puritans within the Church of England; would have prevented, in great part, the Nonconformist separation; and would have held Methodism in connexion with the Church. But now what should have been the godly laity of the Church of England is separated from that Church, on this side and on that, by deep chasms which the Church itself—that is, the clergy —took a great and leading part in digging, and which have been rendered more formidable and forbidding by

[1] Canon Gore's address at the late Church Congress (1896), is in striking harmony with the foregoing argument.

fortifications which the Church herself has raised, and by proclamations which her leaders have from time to time fulminated. Now is the crisis, the period of straits and of difficulty, for the fortressed Church herself, long anticipated by all men of foresight. Her friends are many and powerful, her forces are mighty, but nevertheless her difficulties are threatening and apparently insoluble. All is confusion and divided counsels within her borders. The one possession which would be effectual for the relief of her difficulties is wanting—that of a living laity. For want of this, organised representative government and administration, in which the laity may take their proper place and share, seems to be an impossibility. The mixed world cannot be regarded and treated as the Church's laity exercising a politico-ecclesiastical franchise. And yet some organised union of the laity with the clergy seems to be imperatively demanded. What appears to be needed, and needed at once, is parliamentary action in the way of removing Church abuses and effecting an initial reform of its constitution, opening the way to further reforms in due time. But how can Parliament undertake such a task? If indeed the bishops and clergy and the leading laymen were agreed as to what should be done, perhaps Parliament might even make a beginning at this great work. But at present all is discord.

The alternative, many would say, and most naturally, is to disestablish the Church. But does this also mean to disendow and cut suddenly adrift?

Many questions of equity and of practical wisdom arise here. When the American States, one after another, disestablished their respective State Churches, they touched neither Church fabric nor Church property. They did away only with the direct taxation towards the support of the parish ministers and the provision of meeting-houses, of which taxation in this country there is none. But our national Parliament has lent its authority in the past centuries to the shaping and fashioning of the constitution of the Church into its present form of embodied wrong,—the clergy being the Church, and the laity (except the Parliament and the sovereign) ignored, and Church discipline (except in extreme cases over the clergy) something less than a dead letter, and gross abuses such as are involved in lay patronage and the sale of livings being part and parcel of the Church organisation. The question therefore arises: If Parliament is now to disestablish the Church, is it simply to cut it loose, with all these sins of organisation on its head, with all these abuses incorporated in its system, bearing evil fruit of spiritual bondage, of superstition, of formalism and irreligion, and of consequent profanity and infidelity, to cut it loose without the check and influence of Parliament to restrain or guide it—of Parliament, which at present contains at least some potent elements of a national lay representation, however crude and ill-balanced? Many of us would tremble to think what might be the development of Church affairs, if the Church, as she now is, were cast loose to take what form her clergy and "Church Unions" might determine.

No analogy helps us in the outlook. The case of the unendowed Episcopal Church of the United States is widely different, and, so far as there is any parallelism, is not encouraging. It is amazing how strongly semi-Popish principles and ritualistic practices have taken hold of that Church during the last thirty years, albeit the Church is voluntary and free in the midst of a great democratic and middle-class republic.[1] The case of Ireland, again, is essentially different. In partially disendowing that Church, which had always been an exotic, never a really national Church, Parliament also initially reformed it—providing it with power to create a new organisation, and taking care that place should be found for an organised lay element. Besides which, since disestablishment, that Church, even under its reformed constitution, and notwithstanding the concurrence of the laity, and the intense Low Church Protestantism of Irish Protestants, has become continually more High Church.

In view of all that is involved in the case, how difficult it is for a candid man to form any distinct and final judgment as to the course Parliament ought to take in regard to the Church of England, is indicated by the fact

[1] There is a persistent and almost invincible impression—what I may call a politico-ecclesiastical prepossession—rooted in the minds of most Nonconformists (at least, of the extreme democratic school), that in the atmosphere of American liberty, and in a republic where disestablishment has long been complete, the Anglo-American Episcopal Church, in particular, never at any time occupying the position of a national Establishment, no such exclusive views as those held by Anglicans in this country could maintain an existence, or, if for a season here and there they lived as exotics, could escape from inevitable discredit and speedy extinction. To show how completely erroneous is such an impression, and to justify what I have said in the text, I will here quote a few sentences from the *Methodist Review* for January, 1887, which came into my hands as the first edition of this book was passing through the press. The "Editorial Miscellany," dealing with the subject of "The Protestant Episcopal Church and Christian Unity" in relation to the proceedings of the Triennial Convention of that Church held a little while before at Chicago, contains the following sentences :

"It is well known that the Episcopal Church has never offered—and, according to its principles, it never can—to be united with any other ecclesiastical body. . . . Why then should the subject of Christian unity be spoken of unless it is clearly understood that it means

that a leading Nonconformist minister like the Rev. W. M. Statham,[1] and such a Unitarian as Dr. James Martineau, have both pronounced against Disestablishment. At the same time, there can be no doubt that a large proportion of English Nonconformists, including many Wesleyan Methodists, have come to some such conclusion as this: *The Church of England must be either mended or ended.* As little can it be doubted that it is the awful prevalence not only of essentially Popish principles as to confession and the sacraments, but also of a rationalism which it is too often hard to distinguish from absolute infidelity, that has brought so many Methodists to this

the extinction of any other Christian body with which it may unite? That such a proposition should be made by courteous Christian people, without any sense of insolence on their part, shows to what a degree excessive self-appreciation may blunt the soul's best sentiments."
"No administrator of the laws of the Protestant Episcopal Church would for a moment recognise any of the (by them) so-called 'sects' as valid ecclesiastical bodies." "The Church of Rome offers as liberal terms to all men—heathens, Jews, and Protestants—as the would be American Church offers to their confessed fellow Christians; and yet it seems to be expected that the 'Dissenting' dogs will be thankful for such crumbs."

The last sentence glances at the fact that a proposition was before the Convention to change the name of their Church from "The Protestant Episcopal Church" to either "*The* American Church" or "The American *Catholic* Church," for which proposition two-fifths of those present voted. It is not wonderful that the largest collective Church in the States—I mean the Methodist Episcopal Church—should, in the person of the editor of its official *Review*, resent the pretensions of the comparatively small, but not the less pretentious and exclusive, Anglo-American Episcopal Church. Following the lines of American Church life carefully from week to week, I have discovered during the last ten years no signs of any change for the better. Dr. Phillips Brooks indeed was a standard-bearer in the cause of genuine Christian catholicity; but Phillips Brooks has left no successor.

[1] Mr. Statham, soon after the text was first printed, joined the Church of England.

crude but strong conclusion, and has confirmed and hardened Dissenters in their anti-State-Church views.

The lesson of the later political elections [1] does not seem to have been fully understood, after all that has been written about it. In the rural districts especially, the electoral conflict raged more keenly round the standard of the Church of England than anywhere else. There the attack was fiercest, and there the defenders concentrated their forces. It was on that controversy mainly that victory in so many of the counties was finally, and in not a few cases beyond calculation, gained for those whose programme included Disestablishment as one of its terms. The reason has been missed by many. Undoubtedly the new voters, the villagers and countryfolk, turned the scale of conflict. For the first time these were able to make their votes tell. The scale was turned against the Church precisely where the feeling against Anglican assumptions and Anglican ritual is most religiously intense. It was a long-delayed retribution. Prejudices which had taken deep root alike in Suffolk and the west country during the days of Nonconformist proscription and disability two centuries ago, found vent at last in a political struggle. The active intolerance of the clergy, also, as exercised against the Methodists in former generations, their too frequent contempt and arrogance, their pronounced intolerance of spirit, shown in many instances down to the present time, met with natural retribution in the west, the midlands, and the north. I could mention the names of notorious clergymen in Cornwall, for instance, who, up to the present time, and notwithstanding the better spirit and wiser policy of their bishops, have by their conduct in their parishes and their

[1] In 1885.

letters in the newspapers done all in their power to exasperate the Methodists against the Church, and to fill up the cup of bitterness, which could not fail, when the opportunity came, to be wrung out for them to drink. I mention these things because the truth should be told, and not because I myself cherish any bitterness towards the Church of England. The aged Lord Sydney Godolphin Osborne (" S. G. O.") knew the rural parts of England better perhaps than almost any other clergyman; he knew especially well the whole west country. His letter to the *Times* on this subject has been thought to be discoloured by undue severity. One thing is certain—it represents a true side of the case. In his old age the veteran social reformer and philanthropist was aroused to resume his once famous but long-neglected pen, that he might tell his brethren unpalatable truth on this subject.[1]

[1] " S. G. O.'s " letter to the *Times* of January 4, 1886, referred to in the text, is a bold and searching indictment of the existing organisation of the Church of England. The system of Church patronage he stigmatises in the strongest terms. He is very severe on the character and qualifications of a large proportion of the clergy, and on the nature of their selection and appointment to their work. Some charges he insinuates as to the question of pastoral fidelity which a Nonconformist would have been reluctant to bring forward. I can only, however, quote from his long letter the following passage as bearing closely upon some of the questions raised in the foregoing pages:

"No Church can claim apostolic character which is not aggressive. It cannot sit still and urge, 'Here is our ministry, here our temples; here, open to all, are the means of affording to all participation in devotional exercises; here are our ministers, ready to teach all alike the gospel truths which make wise unto salvation, to warn all alike against the sinful life which leads to destruction. Thousands may hear the toll of the inviting bell, and yet how few will come in! Where does the Church possess existing forces to go forth into the high- and by-ways to seek lovingly to persuade them to enter? It can scarcely be expected of the clergy; for, with all the services of tables, pulpit preparation, frequency of serving, and the time and attention

Upon any consideration of the details of needed Church reform I can make no attempt to enter. I may, however, remark, in passing, that public writers again and again recommend methods of reform which would amount to introducing into the Church of England features of Methodist organisation and arrangement, some arrangements, indeed, which certain Methodists, inexperienced in the evils and difficulties that beset other communions, would unwisely like to see altered. Perhaps, even if it were not beyond my proper scope, it would be premature to offer any

to keep these up after modern requirement, and beg the means to do so, let alone the claims made on their ministry among the sick, it is out of all reason to expect they can find the time. I am forced to add, occupied as most of the Churches now are, if the outside stream of the hitherto absentees did flow churchward, where could they find room ? or, if found, would the nature of high-class service be adapted to beget their devotion ?

"What is wanted is an outside guerilla force of earnest, pious men, who would devote themselves to the task of mission work among that class whose habits of life and rearing have been such as to make them naturally little disposed to profit by a ministry working in a groove altogether foreign to their position and condition in life. We want places of worship of simple structure, plainly furnished, in which the officiating teachers and preachers should be earnest, pious laymen, capable of leading short services and such congregational singing of hymns as might be well in accord with a congregation of ordinary working-men, the preaching to be the bold enunciation of those gospel truths which are within the comprehension of such men, in language and with the illustration which would attract and leave a mark on their attention. Even if these preachers, being laymen, were themselves of the working class, or raised but little above it, if encouraged and sympathised with in their work by the clergy, they would be the means, not only of Christianising a great many who are now heathens, but by this irregular Church force very many would eventually be led to come into direct Church association."

One of the most striking parts of the letter is a paragraph in which the writer praises the work done by such labourers as the Primitive Methodist preachers, work which in earlier life he exceedingly disliked.

suggestion on the subject. The day of detailed reform in the Church of England by statute of the realm may be farther off than many seem to think. Enough has been said in these chapters to show how greatly the Church stands in need, and always has stood in need, of reform, and how essentially erroneous is her ecclesiastical position and basis. Of her revived zeal, of her magnificent voluntary activity, of the spiritual forces within her which are disengaging themselves and combining into a fresh growth of organised spiritual faculty and fellowship, at present insecure and only partial, but which may some day have become part of her necessary and legally recognised framework, it would be very pleasant to speak at length; but to dwell on these things is hardly the truth that at present needs to be insisted on. Happen what may, the Church of England will live on, live as the ancient historic Church of the realm, live as the wealthiest, most powerful, and most famous Protestant Church of the world. Her growth during the last fifty years—her spontaneous growth, associated with unexampled generosity and devotion on the part of her people—has been one of the most marvellous chapters of history. If the deep-seated evils of which I have spoken were only removed, what limit could be set to the blessed potency of her influence?[1]

[1] It is discouraging to hopes of any speedy removal of these evils, to note one of the more recent signs on this subject. I refer to the late Bishop (Browne) of Winchester's correspondence with Canon Wilberfórce with respect to the canon's having preached in a Dissenting chapel. In his first letter of admonition to the canon the bishop speaks of the Church of England "as one with the Church of the New Testament and the primitive ages," and "as reformed on the exact model of the primitive body" (*Times*, January 27, 1887). He goes on to deny the Church character of all the "sects," excepting, it must be supposed, the Roman and other "Catholic" Churches.

III.
PRESBYTERIANISM

CHAPTER I.

FIRST PRINCIPLES AND EARLY CHARACTER AND INFLUENCE OF PRESBYTERIANISM.

NOTWITHSTANDING the Genevan proclivities of some of Elizabeth's Reforming bishops, Presbyterianism was from the beginning, in most respects, a strong contrast to Anglicanism. Like Anglicanism, however, although not to the same extent, it failed to recognise those primary rights and privileges of the fellowship of Christian believers which have been kept in view throughout this volume. Presbyterianism was intended to be the antithesis of Romanism in respect of all the corruptions and usurpations included in that wonderful amalgam of truth and error, of Christianity and heathenism. But whilst in most other points it was a complete reaction from that system, and a radical reform, in one respect Presbyterianism, especially the Presbyterianism of Calvin, and of the strictest and highest Scotch school, claimed a position in relation to the State analogous to that occupied and held fast by ultramontane Popery. At the same time, contradictory as at first sight it may appear, Presbyterianism failed to make good its escape from that opposite evil of Erastianism which it agrees with Ultramontanism in denouncing, which, indeed, in Scotland has always been the especial horror of strict old-school Presbyterianism, and with which Scotland has been accustomed for three centuries contemptuously to reproach Anglican England. Just here Presbyterianism stands in contrast with Congregational Independency, which, at least in this country, has placed itself in irreconcilable antagonism at once with Popery and Erastianism by strictly separating the spheres of Church and State. Presbyterianism maintained, alike in Geneva, in Scotland, in England and New England, and in Holland, that the State was to be a Christian State and the Church to be a State Church, a national Church in the strictest legal sense, maintained and sustained by the State. It claimed also as its subject laity the entire people, all the citizens of the State. Like ultramontane Popery, it further maintained—and in this it seemed to itself to contradict Erastianism—that the State was bound to obey in all things the behests of the Church, and carry out its discipline as to matters of faith, worship, and morals ; the Church owning no king but Christ, and no law but its own, founded on Divine revelation and authority. Here Romanism and Presbyterianism touched each other in somewhat ominous accord, however opposed at other points. Calvin at Geneva was as absolutely supreme in matters of faith, morals, and Church discipline—and how vast a scope of authority as to all life and citizenship is directly or indirectly included in such supremacy !—as ever was pope at Rome. And if Knox and Melville in Scotland wielded no such authority as Calvin at Geneva, the reason was that they had to deal, not with the magistrates of Geneva, but with the most stubborn and uncontrollable nobility in Europe, rather than that their ideas and pretensions as to spiritual authority were less wide or exacting than those of Calvin.

But yet, in fact, the essential vice of Erastianism clung fast to Presbyterianism, notwithstanding its transcendental

Church claims. In the case of the Roman Catholic Church, the spiritual power which claimed supremacy over the State was separate from it; the Pope, from his independent ecclesiastical centre, claimed to control the sovereign or the State operating from the national centre. In the case of Presbyterianism, whether at Geneva or in its palmy days of complete development and power in Scotland or America, the Church and the State were inextricably blended. Not only were all the citizens expected to be communicants; the citizens, *as such*, formed the basis and substratum of Church organisation, and therefore, in reality, of Church authority. The Church indeed required the State to obey its behests. But the Church which made the demand was not a really spiritual community, was not an independent organisation; it was merely the State in another form. The State in its Church aspect, and under its Church code and its Church form of administration, relating to matters of faith and morals, claimed to govern and give law to the State in its ordinary civil character and administration. This, however, is not really to escape Erastianism. The Church, after all, on this basis, is not a spiritual power, and is not free from State intermixture and secular influence; State and Church are amalgamated. The essential character of Erastianism clung to the Genevan settlement of Church and State. Its canker and its blight have been a " cleaving curse" in the city of Calvin. While Calvin lived, indeed, the spiritual ideas and forces of the Church, embodied as they were in his transcendent personality, governed the policy and the administrative action of the State. But after his death the Church presently came under the ordinary ideas and influences that governed the civil society of Geneva, all citizens of the State being also members of the Church, and the civil magistrates being as such high Church officials. The like happened also in Scotland. Knox and Melville were able, with much authority and more or less success, to enforce their ideas upon the State when dealing with questions of faith, morals, and worship, and even public policy. But not even the Scottish Church could furnish a continuous succession of such men, especially when the tyranny of the nobles was broken and the times grew tame. The Church accordingly in Scotland, as in Geneva, settled down to the level of the State, and came under the sway of the ideas and influences of general society. For generations Moderatism and Erastianism held dominion in Church and State. Nor would the Veto law, fifty years ago, have gone very far towards delivering the Scotch Church from Erastianism. The decay of the old parish discipline, lamentable as it may have appeared, was in reality a step towards the spiritual freedom of the Church. It was, however, the Disruption that really did the work of enfranchisement.

The postulate underlying Calvin's theory of Church and State—the postulate embodied in his Presbyterianism—is that the New Testament, like the Old, has its prescribed Church economy, and that this economy should hold the same relation to a Christian State as the Mosaic law held to the Jewish commonwealth. The conclusions resulting from this postulate he carried out with intrepid and unyielding logic. His motto, more fitly than Strafford's, might have been " Thorough." Alike in Church theories and in theology, logic ruled, and the conclusions in both spheres were blended and interwoven into one great system. However apparently direct and sound, indeed, might be the logic which led to his Church and State conclusions, it must, as all would nowadays admit, have been in reality fallacious. But Calvin, with his wonderful constructive intellect, completed his *Institutes* and never faltered. .

With him as a theological teacher and preacher, no less than as an ecclesiastical legislator, logic was all in all. This fact accounts for the characteristic defects of his doctrine and ministry. In cleaving to and striving to follow the traces of "truth," the laws and powers of the "life" in Christ Jesus were too much neglected. With this general intellectual tendency the character of his special creed— itself the result of an inadequate though powerful logic, rigorously applied to questions which transcend the sphere of mere logical definition and deduction; combined in such a manner that the office of preacher was, almost of necessity, limited to demonstration and exposition. To reason, to instruct, to build up in orthodox doctrine, in morals and duty—unquestionably noble functions—are by no means the whole of the preacher's work. But Calvinism, when strict and real, as it was at first, could scarcely suffer its teachers to exceed these limits; never, indeed, except when spiritual instinct, and the direct force of some special Scripture utterance, proved too mighty for mere logical inference and theological system.

The great work of the minister was to teach and instruct the elect. The work of "conversion" could hardly be a great, or even a real, part of the minister's responsibility, where personal election was always in view as the eternal master-fact that stood in relation with all personal salvation. All "experimental" aspects of religious teaching were placed at a discount where salvation was regarded, not so much as a matter of present personal experience and of conscious renewal in the participation of a transcendent "life in Christ," but rather as a mystery of the Divine counsels to be disclosed in the eternity beyond the grave. "Assurance," in such a connexion of theological doctrine, could only signify a divinely imparted certitude of personal and eternal election and salvation,—salvation to be hereafter revealed rather than now to be tasted and partaken of, and election unconditionally decreed. To persons inbued with such doctrines as these, spiritual self-confidence or a fatalistic indifference would be the too probable alternatives of experience. Mysterious speculations and abstruse theology would be more congenial than loving, humble, practical doctrine; the tendency would be to cultivate the intellect rather than the heart. Orthodoxy would too often be regarded as presumptive evidence of personal election; and the prevailing tone of the pulpit would be that of instruction in the intellectual aspects of Christianity rather than the experimental.

Calvin was a man of extraordinary gifts; in many respects he was a great divine, and he was perhaps almost an abler expositor of Scripture than divine. He rose far above the mere logical level of his theology in his own teaching. Still the aspects of thought and the tendencies of which I have been speaking belonged essentially to his theology; and in the hands of his "orthodox" successors, narrower than himself, could not but more and more, till the inevitable rationalistic reaction should set in, give character and colour to the Calvinistic doctrine, although again and again divinely taught and gifted men, alike on the Continent, in Scotland, in England, and in America, soared clear of the theology of the decrees, and preached and taught the noblest experimental divinity, extracts from the writings of some of whom may be found in Wesley's *Christian Library*. But, after allowing for all such cases and all modifying influences, it remains that Calvinistic preaching, as a whole, has not been "awakening" in its prevalent character, nor experimental in its dealing with the inward life of the Christian or the growing sanctification, not only through "the word," but "through the Spirit," of the child of God. Of late years, indeed, there has been a profound and far-reaching change in these respects; but, of late years also, the theology of the decrees has been left in the distance. Modern Calvinism is altogether a new thing. It was necessary, however, in writing of Presbyterianism, to take knowledge of its original character and tendencies, especially as these prevailed, notwithstanding the exceptions of which I have spoken, during all its great historical period, and indeed are still embodied in the theology of its most famous divines, and in the Westminster Confession, which continues to be the doctrinal standard of Presbyterianism in Britain and in America.

Presbyterians themselves acknowledge the characteristic defect of Presbyterian teaching of which I have spoken. A recent lecturer of the Established Kirk says that "the tendency of Presbyterianism has all along been too much in the direction of regarding prayer and praise as preliminary or subsidiary to the sermon, and making the service sermon-worship, which in its turn fed with lavish hand the merely intellectual side of the Presbyterian, to the neglect of his emotions. The foible of Presbyterianism is to *know* and to *define*." [1]

Mr. Barclay, the author of *The Inner Life of the Religious*

[1] The Rev. Colin Campbell, in the *St. Giles' Lectures* for 1883-4.

Societies of the Commonwealth, himself a descendant of the famous Quaker apologist, although he was a large-souled critic and is usually generous in his censures, had doubtless in writing a keen feeling as to what Presbyterianism had been to his fathers, and uses searching language in regard to early Presbyterianism.

"The influence of Calvin," he says, " upon the Protestant Churches of Europe was very great. Geneva sent forth into all parts of Europe apostles of a new school. It united the stern principles of the Mosaic economy with a purely intellectual view of the Christian religion. It substituted for a priesthood ministers, lay elders, and deacons, giving to them the semblance of popular approval and the most crushing oligarchical power. The school of Calvin grasped clearly certain important points of Christian teaching; but it cannot be contended that Christian love, without which the Apostle Paul declares that all Christian gifts are nothing worth, was the principle which governed Geneva when Calvin exercised an influence in Church and State more powerful than that of the greatest of the popes. . . . Calvin's system sought to bring every sphere of life under the rigid rule of a Church which claimed exclusive possession of the truth, and was prepared to maintain its position in the field of argument."

I fear this severe summing up is just, but it has only a partial application to modern Presbyterianism, which, take it for all in all, and through all its fields of labour, is undoubtedly one of the noblest and most fruitful forms of Christian organisation. Nevertheless, no system which maintains its original formularies and its original organisation and discipline can altogether escape from its early characteristics and tendencies, unless, indeed, it be by the way of utter degeneracy and apostasy. In the case of Presbyterianism, its modern transformation among English-speaking peoples is mainly due to a baptism of new life, of which the sources were in no small measure from without, and to larger discoveries of truth which have been brought in to interpret and modify the old forms of phrase and thought without impairing the fundamental truth contained, but sometimes disguised, under the Calvinistic language of the original formularies. That, at least, is how many Presbyterians of to-day would desire to regard some modern changes of relation between words and meaning in the use of their doctrinal standards, and how catholic-minded men who are not Presbyterians would endeavour to regard the matter.

There is, however, one foible of Presbyterian theorising which recent Presbyterian authorities do not yet seem to have outgrown. They still, in a mild way, claim Divine right for their Church organisation; and they still, for the most part, cling to the "ruling eldership" as an integral part of primitive Church organisation, as a necessary plank in their ecclesiastical platform. With very much of the Presbyterian theory of Church government, apart from the two points to which I have above adverted, namely, the spiritual rights of the laity and the spiritual claims and power of the Church, Wesleyans generally agree; and, in common with universal Protestantism, we owe Calvin and Presbyterianism a deep debt of gratitude for breaking down the hierarchical theories of the Church of Rome. But this eccentric point of the ruling eldership is one as to which some words must here be said.

In what I have written in the earlier chapters of this volume as to the organisation of the primitive Church, I have intimated the views as to this point which I am about to state. That *bishops* and *presbyters* in the primitive Church were convertible official designations, may be taken for granted; that one of the necessary qualifications for the office of bishop or presbyter was, according to St. Paul's standard, "ability to teach others also," "aptness to teach," is another point beyond dispute; that even private persons with any gift of doctrine or of practical exhortation were free to speak in the primitive Church assemblies, is a third point which is scarcely to be disputed; that any bishop or presbyter in the primitive Church would be precluded, or would habitually keep silence, from all public instruction in the Church, even from spiritual counsel or exhortation, seems incredible, inconceivable. At the same time, that some of the elders may have been less gifted for the work of public instruction than others, and may accordingly have been accustomed to speak less often and at less length than their more intellectually gifted and more largely informed colleagues, seems very probable, especially considering the humble rank of the great majority of the believers; and it appears correspondently probable that the more generally instructed and more highly gifted among the presbyter-bishops might, in a special sense, "labour in the word and in teaching." It is also every way likely that among the presbyters some might be more gifted for expository or argumentative speech who were less gifted with pastoral wisdom, authority, and tact. But on such grounds as these, to institute a necessary distinction among the bishops or elders, according to which, whilst a few were appointed to expound and publicly instruct, the rest were precluded from so doing, and limited of necessity to matters of administration and discipline, would seem to be gratuitous and unwarrantable.

The essential error of the theory appears to be that it erects into a permanent and universal institute that which may probably for a time, and in the infancy of Christianity, have had place in certain localities. It takes the exception for the rule. In virtue of a solitary indication and of a single passage,[1] it takes leave to force a violent interpretation on almost every other passage of Scripture bearing on the subjects of bishops or elders. It claims to stereotype and perpetuate for all Churches through all time that which was the mark of an inchoate and undeveloped condition—a condition which, as there is ample evidence from other parts of Scripture and from the records of antiquity to show, the Churches in general speedily overpassed, and to which they never returned. The effect of such a course could not but have been to bring about a wide practical distinction between the separated and paid teaching elders or ministers and the ruling elders, such a distinction as is incompatible with the style in which St. Paul is accustomed to speak of all elders, without the intimation of any difference of rank or of functions, as if they were alike responsible pastors and bishops, and of all bishops similarly, as if they were each and all equally and alike elders.

The distinction in Presbyterian Churches between the minister and the ruling elders is altogether different from that between a Wesleyan superintendent and his colleagues; is really no less specific and important, if it be not more so, than that between an Anglican bishop and

[1] 1 Tim. v. 17.

his clergy. The ordination of the "minister" is different from that of the ruling elder; his work is different and distinctive, not only in respect of the teaching and preaching function, but also of the part he bears in sacramental administration; and whereas in the primitive Church even the elders who did not "labour in the word and doctrine" were, if they "ruled well," to be "counted worthy" of ample maintenance ("double honour"), the Presbyterian "ruling elder" receives nothing in the way of maintenance.[1] In fact, the threefold model of Ignatius is not merely closely approached, but is even surpassed in the Presbyterian arrangement. Call "the minister" the "bishop," as he surely might properly be called, and Ignatius's three orders—bishop, presbyters, and deacons—are reproduced for each Church; the Presbyterian bishop among his ruling elders, and if there should happen to be any, his deacons, being a much more eminent functionary than the "bishop of the first century," whose office is magnified by Ignatius.[2] For the relative degradation of the "presbyters," as seen in Presbyterianism, no support can be adduced from Ignatius. It is no wonder that "deacons," although recognised in Presby-

---

[1] Knox, however, would have allowed the "ruling elder" some provision for maintenance if and so far as he stood in need of such provision.

[2] "The polity of the Church of Scotland," says Dr. John Cunningham in his *Croall Lectures*, "is a perfect facsimile of this Ignatian episcopacy. Let the minister be called bishop (as he properly may), let the elders remain as they are, but let them be assisted by a body of deacons, as in some cases they are, and you have the episcopacy of the Ignatian Church" (*Croall Lectures*, p. 66). When I wrote the text, I was not aware that my words were so nearly identical with those of a high Scottish ecclesiastical authority. I had not seen Dr. Cunningham's book.

terian theory, have been in Presbyterian practice almost always "conspicuous by their absence"; the elders, in fact, take their place. The primitive Churches referred to in the *Teaching of the Apostles*, which exemplify the true "presbyterian" counterpart in apostolic Christianity to the episcopacy of the Ignatian Churches, show an organisation of presbyters and deacons, under the description of bishops and deacons, in which the primitive distinction and perspective is preserved as between the two offices — that of the presbyter - bishop and of the deacon. They afford no countenance whatever to the Calvinistico-Presbyterian distinction. Calvin was not only a masterly divine, but also an able and adroit statesman; and one is almost constrained to conclude that the convenience of the office for certain ecclesiastico - political purposes suggested the textual interpretation on which it was founded. Dr. Henry explains to us how Calvin was resolved that his Church organisation, whilst it should, as far as possible, be of a popular character, should, at the same time, be essentially aristocratic. By inventing an office, on one side, lay in its aspect, and the holders of which should be ordinary citizens and business men, and yet, on its other side, sacred and dignified in its character, an office not annually elective, but for life, and the nomination for election to which rested with the minister and his colleagues of the consistory or the Church council, he succeeded well in his purpose. The Church was governed by the minister, as a bishop; and so far the government was monarchical. The elders, of far inferior position and office, were, for ordinary Church purposes, the council of the minister—of the bishop. This was a compact and powerful government, and served to keep the chief power well within the hands of the minister. At the same time, the name of bishop was avoided, and the elders had no appearance of a hierarchy, being in all practical seeming mere business laymen. By this arrangement the want of a true Church laity, a real spiritual brotherhood and fellowship, was concealed from view. An imperfect and in part unreal antithesis to Rome was substituted for the true one.

It is no wonder that the question as to whether these ruling elders are true presbyters or mere laymen has been perpetual. The common practical mind, at the hazard of a contradiction in terms, settles the question by calling them "lay elders." According to the theory of Presbyterianism, it would be equally proper to speak of them as lay bishops; for on the absolute identity of the episcopal and the presbyterial office—the bishop and the elder—Presbyterianism is essentially founded. A long consensus of high authorities, including, besides Calvin, no less names than Beza, in his *Reply to Saravia,* Knox, in the *Second Book of Discipline,* Dr. Goodwin, in his *Catechism on Church Order,* Dr. Cheever, in his *Account of the Plymouth Church* (representing the views of the fathers of American Independency), Miller, Guthrie, King, Bannerman, Dr. John Cunningham, Professor Witherow, Dr. Killen, among modern Presbyterian authorities on the subject, and Mr. Macpherson, in his *Handbook on Presbyterianism,* all maintain the eldership to be a real episcopal office, and do not employ the term *lay elder*.[1] On the

---

[1] I observe that Mr. Macpherson gives up the distinction between the teaching and the ruling eldership in any other sense than as an expedient of more or less value and convenience. He gives up the principle.

other hand, the French Reformed, forsaking Beza as well as Calvin in this matter, seem, at least in later times, to have regarded the office as merely a lay office; and I believe that in the modern French Reformed Churches it is not understood to be an office for life. Principal Campbell, of Aberdeen, also, in his *Theory of the Ruling Eldership* (1866), insists that the ruling elder is a lay counsellor, and not a presbyter in the New Testament sense. But if so, then Presbyterianism ceases to be what for centuries it was understood to be; and a great part of all the famous books and standards on the controversy both with Congregationalism on the one hand, and with Episcopacy, even in its most modest parochial form, on the other, is rendered valueless. Given John Knox's "superintendents," and Presbyterianism would then be changed into diocesan Episcopacy. It is no wonder, as I have intimated, that with presbyters holding so ambiguous a position, and discharging, in fact, very nearly the duties which ecclesiastical historians have been accustomed to assign to *deacons*, the office of *deacon* has been almost universally in abeyance among Presbyterians. The Free Church, it is said, has been making special efforts to revive the diaconate. But this can hardly be done generally or successfully without a corresponding enhancement and exaltation of the position and functions of the ruling elder.

In respect to the question of ruling eldership, as in regard to so much besides, the case of primitive Christianity may be illustrated from that of Methodism at the present day. An approximation at least to such a state of things as might have suggested St. Paul's counsel on this matter may have been recognised among Methodists, especially in earlier days, in certain ministerial appointments, in which some ministers of decidedly inferior preaching ability have yet as pastors and counsellors proved to be most valuable. These ministers, on the Wesleyan system of pastoral itinerancy, were of course compelled to take their turn in pulpit services equally with their colleagues, and were equally separated from all secular engagements or ordinary means of support; accordingly, they could not but receive, in the double sense of the word, equal "honour." On foreign mission stations, again, instances may easily be imagined, still more strictly and fully in point, in which native ministers fulfilling the "ruling"—that is, the *administrative*—functions of the ministry, and occasionally preaching or exhorting also, might perhaps be advantageously associated with the foreign missionary as pastors of the flock, though entitled to inferior "honour."

If, from the question of the ruling eldership, we pass to that which it inevitably raises, the question of the spiritual lay element in Presbyterianism, we find,—as respects the main line of Presbyterianism, which may be traced from Geneva through Knox, Andrew Melville, and the Westminster Confession, for Scotland, and through the Westminster Confession also, though with less complete development, for England and America,—that so far as official recognition and organised provision for spiritual service and co-operation were concerned, the claims and laws of lay fellowship were as completely ignored in Presbyterianism as in Anglican Episcopacy. The monopoly of the ordained pastors of the Church was no less complete in the one organisation than in the other. The ruling elders, as we have seen, could by no means be regarded as truly representative of the laity; they were presbyter-bishops, ordained as such for life.[1]

Of free spiritual life expressed in public meetings of the Church there was none; nor was there provision of minor Church meetings for free fellowship; nor was there liberty of lay preaching or exhortation, although Knox, in the *First Book of Discipline*, had recognised such liberty as allowable. That this was so was the just complaint of the "Separatists" and the early Independents in England. In Scotland, where there was no such middle class as in England, and where the helpless and immemorially oppressed commonalty with glad docility welcomed the "ministers" as their masters, and faithfully stood by them in their quarrels with the nobility, submitting with at least passive obedience to the yoke, hard though it often was, of Church discipline, because this was for them the

---

[1] The case of the French Reformed Churches has already been referred to as standing apart from Presbyterianism in its strict and normal development. The Huguenot organisation was not more decidedly political, perhaps, than Presbyterianism elsewhere; but the distinctively ecclesiastical factor in its complex whole, the combined elements of doctrine, devotion, and discipline, did not, as in Geneva at first, and as in Scotland and New England for a longer period, dominate the whole politico-ecclesiastical movement. From the day that the brilliant Condé, mainly, if not wholly, for his own family and dynastic reasons, placed himself at the head of the Huguenots, the political character of the party was determined, for its apparent benefit at first, for its permanent weakening and injury. Presbyterian discipline in a moral sense could hardly be thoroughly or impartially carried out in a community which followed as its great chiefs such men as Condé and the princes of Navarre. The constitution of the Churches was still more aristocratic than in Geneva; the position of the elders was inferior; and, except at certain centres, as, for example, in Nîmes and round about, the Church organisation and discipline were ineffective. Lay preaching was at least as little approved or practised in France as elsewhere.

condition of deliverance from the incomparably worse yoke of the brutal nobles—in Scotland little seems to have been heard of the complaints against Presbyterianism which broke forth on all sides in England, especially from among the middle classes.

The early Separatists of England taught that, whilst every Church ought to have its regular Church officers, the existence of these was not to debar other members of the Church from the exercise of prophecy according to their gifts and abilities. "Every stone," it was said, "hath his beauty, his burden, and his order; *all* are bound to edify one another, exhort, reprove, and comfort one another." Between Barrow and Greenwood, the Separatist martyrs, and the Presbyterians of England, there was as complete an antagonism as between the same confessors and the Anglicans. They complained that the "Puritans would still have the whole land to be the Church," that their reformation was not to be effected by "the Word preached," but "they would have all redressed in one day," by a political change of the outward form of the Church (so called), instead of through "the power of the Word and Spirit, working in men's hearts true repentance and conversion." Barrow reproves Calvin's "rash and disorderly" course in Geneva in "receiving the whole State, and consequently all the profane, ignorant people, into the bosom of the Church, and administering the Sacrament to them." "As for these new officers, these elders"—he insists that their being set up was an injurious device for keeping *the people* from the knowledge and performance of their Christian duties—"they will be the wealthiest, honest, simple men in the parish, that shall sit for ciphers by their pastor and meddle with nothing"; and the people will get nothing but "the smoky, windy title of electing their ministers" (as distinguished from the "elders"), "and not even a pretence of any further power or prerogative."

It is not to be denied that these complaints against the principles of early Presbyterianism were well founded. Nevertheless Presbyterianism, as I intimated in a former chapter, did not a little for the diffusion, through the congregations, of evangelical light and life, and especially for the promotion of spiritual religion in family life. Innumerable journals and other writings of Puritan or Presbyterian saints conbine to attest this great fact. Formal the Church order might be, and unprimitive and unapostolic, in some important particulars, might be the Church organisation; but the great barrier to gospel light and progress had been broken down, and a stream of influence had been set free which could not but deepen and spread from age to age. The superstitions on which all classes had relied for salvation, the Popish sacraments, saint and relic worship, mechanical penances, pilgrimages, all performed as if they operated magically,—these "refuges of lies" Presbyterianism exploded and swept away; priestly juggling and the confessional it denounced and disallowed; it gave the Holy Scriptures to all the people as their light and law; instead of mere collects and forms of prayer,— these and nothing else,—its ministers taught, by their own practice and example, what was the meaning of living prayer, adapted to personal conditions and present needs —taught what it was "by prayer and supplication with thanksgiving" to make known their "requests unto God." The elders also were accustomed on certain occasions— some of them, at least—to offer prayer on behalf of the congregation; and so the example of special and intercessory prayer was brought closer home to the members of the congregation generally, with whom, as citizens in secular life, the ruling elders were so closely allied and united. Family prayer was inculcated on the heads of families; and with the Bible placed in their hands and the examples of public prayer given them by the minister and elders of the Church, the godly naturally learned how to lead their households in their daily collective worship, and to make their homes centres of religious influence.

After the dreary ages of Popish darkness, of worship in a dead language, and of mere superstition, after the reign of priestcraft, with all that was involved in the confessional, such a change as this was like clear sunshine after a noisome night, or a bright green spring after a dreary winter. The first breaking with Popery, the first march from Rome under the lead of one commander, could hardly be expected to carry the reformed and reforming legionaries farther than they had thus been carried in Scotland and England under the guidance and inspiration of Calvin. The first Reformers could only deal with such forces and such materials as those with which they found themselves in contact. Kings, statesmen, and undisciplined crowds, who must be led in mass or not at all, who had no conception of individual religion, and at first had not the Scriptures in their hand—it was with these that Calvin and Knox, as well as our English reforming bishops and statesmen, had to do.

Under such circumstances, it is hard to conceive how they could have organised, to begin with, anything like a Methodist Society or the primitive Christian fellowship. Indeed, having to deal, not individually, but by public manifesto and by national schemes, with potentates and with populations, all of whom supposed themselves to be in the fullest sense Christians, they had difficulties to cope with in the way of spiritual organisation far more unmanageable in various respects than those with which the primitive preachers of Christianity had to contend.

CHAPTER II.

THE CHARACTER AND INFLUENCE OF PRESBYTERIANISM AS
MODIFIED IN LATER TIMES.

FROM the causes explained in the last chapter, it was not in accordance with the original organisation or principles of Presbyterianism to afford facilities for free and general exercise of spiritual gifts, or for the fellowship of spontaneous mutual speech on matters of spiritual experience, among the members of the Church. How, indeed, could such liberty be allowed to the members of the Church generally, when every citizen, as such, was compelled by law to be a member and a communicant, unless he was excommunicated or under discipline, and his position in suspense? State formalism and citizen membership on the one hand necessarily imply, as their correlative, ministerial monopoly of spiritual functions on the other. Birthright membership, whether a State Church right, as among the Presbyterians, or merely a spiritual heirloom, as among the Quakers, has always been, and could not but be, incompatible with the very idea and primary conditions of spiritual fellowship after the primitive type. Accordingly, only by degrees did the truths to which it has been a leading object of this volume to direct attention, as belonging to the very life of genuine Christian organisation, force their way into light and recognition in the Presbyterian Churches—only by degrees, and indirectly and through irregular channels. There was, indeed, with not a little fanaticism, much of the free, primitive force and instinct of the Christian life in the early secessions from the Scotch Establishment. And when these secessions were once set free from political influence and the intermixture of civil authority and prescription, the spirit of true religious liberty and of voluntary zeal and fervour began to assert itself in evangelistic forms. Doubtless the United Presbyterians have inherited a share of that free instinct and energy. The Free Church also, with its striking history of revivals, has often extemporised for itself services and organisations, of more or less permanence, in which laymen have had an opportunity of exercising their spiritual gifts in co-operation with ministers, and of promoting in this way mission work among the needier classes and revival fellowship services in connexion with the Church and congregation.

In truth, as I have already intimated, the spirit of Methodism, alike in respect to its theology and its lay spiritual fellowship and enterprise, has during the last century happily infected the Presbyterianism of Scotland in all its branches. Whitefield, indeed, bore his share in the great Scottish revivals of 1742 and following years, and continued, from time to time, for twenty years, to produce powerful effects in the chief centres of religious influence in Scotland. In later years, the labours of Wesley and his preachers in Edinburgh, Glasgow, Aberdeen, and a few other places in Scotland, produced a deep and critical impression, not striking indeed or violent, but powerful and permanent, which extended far beyond the limits of his Society, and which was the beginning of potent though peaceful influences that have continued to spread and increase. The dictatorial anti-Anglican bigotry, and the stubborn ultra-Presbyterian pedantry and exclusiveness of the Erskines and the "Associate Presbytery," turned Whitefield's influence chiefly into the channels of the Established Kirk, which needed his preaching most, and afforded him by far the widest sphere. Wesley's success in Scotland was doubtless greatly limited by the bitter prejudice against Arminian doctrine. But within the last seventy years a wave of evangelistic life has visited Scotland which has altogether changed the character of what may be called popular Presbyterianism, especially in the large towns. Old Presbyterian springs, the evangelical life and doctrine of Rutherford and not a few more such men, have burst forth again in times more congenial and receptive than those in which they first appeared. The seed sown by Whitefield, Wesley, and many a strong preacher besides, has sprung up abundantly; in Glasgow and elsewhere the influence of English evangelistic work in different forms— in Aberdeen, notably, through the medium of godly fishermen visiting the port—has of late years become increasingly powerful. At certain points, although the points have been few, Methodist preaching, maintained for more than a century past, has told sensibly on some spirits that afterwards became centres of evangelical zeal; and on the minds of not a few thinkers and preachers Methodist writings have produced a critical effect. Above all, the entire change which, during this period, has come over the theological tone and colouring and the preaching form and spirit of English Nonconformity, has produced a powerful effect in Scotland. These things, taken together, have diffused over Scotland and its Presbyterianism a new atmosphere of religious thought and feeling. Presbyterian orthodoxy has felt the strain. Calvinistic doctrine has been left out of sight, but evangelistic life has filled the land. Scotland now sets an example in many respects to England of effective organisation for home mission work and of powerful gospel preaching. Methodism in these respects may learn from modern Presbyterianism.

In America, too, Presbyterianism has modified the tone of its prevalent doctrine, and has long been a great evangelising mission power. There the preaching of Whitefield in the last century was doubtless the greatest among the forces that gave origin and impetus to the movement in virtue of which American Presbyterianism to-day is the living power we know it to be.

Regarded in general, and in all its dimensions, as a Church organisation, Presbyterianism is a masterpiece. In general contour and in generic character there are strong points of analogy between it and Methodism. Methodism, in fact, is now generally recognised as a sort of Presbyterian Church. But Methodism grew up into its present form by the forces of its inherent life and natural tendencies, whereas Presbyterianism was in its original scheme the product of the statesmanlike mind of Calvin. It was his aim to oppose to the hierarchical unity of Rome a union of reformed Christian Churches organised on the New Testament model, and embodying principles antithetically contrary to the superstitions on which Romanism is founded. Although it might be true in certain respects, as Milton said, and as the Quakers and early Independents found by sharp experience, that "new presbyter was but old priest writ large," yet the soul-enthralling superstitions and the parti-coloured "trumpery" and fripperies of Popery were abolished by Presbyterianism, and a fatal wound inflicted on the papal tyranny, with its claims to worldwide primacy and absolute imperialism. The world owes for this a debt to Presbyterianism which can never be paid. It is under the covert of the wings of Presbyterian Churches —taking the word *Presbyterian* in its generic sense—that the evangelical life and liberty of the isolated Churches have found their refuge. It is by the power and array of evangelical Presbyterian Churches that the spread of the hierarchical and so-called Catholic Churches has been limited and held in check. Presbyterianism proper has no peer but Methodism in the spread and growing power of its Churches. The Presbyterianism of Scotland, with its three great Churches, so singularly divided and yet so wonderfully agreed, is a glorious and impressive spectacle. There is in the world no moral ascendency of any force or forces over national character and life equal to that of Presbyterianism in Scotland. The discipline its Churches furnish for the nation is unequalled in its power and thoroughness. Its clergy are the best equipped for their work and the most able in the world. In America, Methodism counts many more adherents than Presbyterianism, and of late years may perhaps have summed up more political weight and influence. But, on the whole, for a combination of culture, wealth, public character, Christian intelligence, and organised Christian influence, scarcely any denomination in America can rival Presbyterianism. Its political influence has always been very great, and it has furnished not a few statesmen of high character to the public service. Presbyterianism may be said to hold in its hands the balance of public influence, alike intellectual and religious, for the United States. The present-day Presbyterianism of England is a modern development. The early English Presbyterianism went out in Arianism and Unitarianism. Apart from synods and all Church sisterhood, destitute of a spiritual fellowship, retaining from the past little more than the intellectual character of the ministry and the good traditions of moral discipline and family virtue, reduced to the position of congregational units under an oligarchical government of trustees and ministers or elders, these Churches chilled down first into cold philosophic orthodoxy, then into Arian heterodoxy, and finally into Unitarian rationalism. The English Presbyterianism of to-day is altogether another thing. Orthodox, fully organised, in fraternal communion with the mother-Churches of Scotland, intelligent, earnest, and liberal, it is a rising power in England of benignant character and influence. Occupying a position of not unfriendly neutrality towards the Established Church, and of fully reciprocated friendliness towards the Evangelical Nonconformist Churches of the country, its presence in England is a great gain. It is one more ally, and one of hereditary virtue and force, in the conflict with Anglican neo-Popery.

Taking into account Great Britain, America, and the colonies, Presbyterianism, as a world-power, is among evangelical forces only inferior to Methodism. Within the same territorial range, Anglo-Episcopacy is probably superior in learning to either Methodism or Presbyterianism, and may be equal in wealth to both combined; but in popular influence the wide world through, it is perhaps not superior to either, and is, of course, immensely inferior to the combined forces of the two. Unhappily, it must be added, its influence, on the whole, cannot be said to be purely or distinctly evangelical. Congregationalism, high as its merits are, in respect especially of learning and ability, is inferior in spiritual power to either of the two denominations—*both* in a just sense Presbyterian—of which I am speaking. The Baptists are numerous in America, being inferior in number only to the Methodists, but their scattered and heterogeneous congregations have no common bond; and the denomination as such, being thus destitute of unity, and, on the whole, inferior in cultivation and intelligence to the other great denominations, has comparatively little public influence. Out of America the Baptists are relatively few, although the wonderful gifts and singleness of purpose of the famous preacher of the Newington Tabernacle, who was also a very able leader and organizer, have during the last thirty years greatly strengthened their denomination in England.

In Geneva, Erastianised Presbyterianism, never rooted in spiritual power or fellowship, has become completely rationalised. The Swiss Reformed Churches generally are blighted under similar influences. In France the cause of the Reformed religion was ruined as much by its own long-standing worldliness and defect of spiritual life, as by the dragonnades of Louis XIV. or the repeal of the Edict of Nantes. During the last fifty years the influence of Wesleyan mission work in France, as is confessed by many of the "Reformed" pastors themselves, has been a chief means in reviving spiritual life among the French Churches. It may be doubted, however, whether the form in which the Presbyterianism of France presents itself to that sprightly and artistic nation is not one of the least fit in which a Christian Church could appear for the purpose of commending its doctrine to the French people. Strange, at any rate, it seems that in a country where at one time nearly one-half of the nation were, more or less loosely, of the Protestant faith, now not more than one-fortieth—less than one million out of nearly forty millions—should call themselves Protestants. In France, as in Ireland, Calvinistic Presbyterianism, with the sombre formalism of its services, with the total absence of any popular element or attraction whatever, with dirge-like music and no relief of artistic form or of pleasant colouring, with intellectual argumentative discourses as the central staple of its worship, has never been likely to impress, but much rather to repel, a gay, mercurial, impressible, and social race. In the fighting days of the sixteenth and seventeenth centuries, and with a keen revolt from priestly iniquity and Popish enormities fresh within their souls, the Reformed worship may have suited the fierce and passionate Southerner of France better than it could suit the French people of to-day. The services, too, may have had in them more fervour, and been quickened by the sense of battling for a great cause,—the cause of liberty as well as of a grand, fresh revelation of religion; but, at any rate, Presbyterianism does not suit the nation now. Something more like Cornish Methodism would perhaps suit the country people better. As for the Protestants of Paris and the towns, the experiment of the late M. Bersier in Paris, his adoption of a more ornate and attractive service, conducted in a more graceful and attractive sanctuary, has been noted with keen and friendly interest. Switzerland, France, and Ireland would seem to have been the only countries in which Presbyterianism has proved a spiritual failure. Of course in the north of Ireland, among the Scotch-Irish, it has been far from a failure. My remarks have no application to that stratum of the Irish population. Taking the world over, Presbyterianism in the future must be looked to as one of the greatest and most beneficent forces for the Christian conversion and evangelisation of the generations of mankind on every continent if not in every land.

In Scotland modern culture and taste have produced some external changes in the aspect of Presbyterianism. Nothing was more characteristic of primitive Presbyterianism, at least in Great Britain, than its intense prejudice against "steeplehouses" and Gothic architecture. Presbyterianism produced an ecclesiastical architecture of its own, of which rude and, to the eye of artistic taste, repulsive utilitarianism was the ruling characteristic. Wesley, who, though he adopted Presbyterian views as to some important points of ecclesiastical principle, never ceased to be an English Churchman as to questions of art and of taste, complained in 1788 of the Methodist chapel at Glasgow, that it had "exactly the look of a Presbyterian meeting-house," adding, "It is the very sister of our house at Brentford, perhaps an omen of what will be when I am gone."[1] The wealth, culture, taste, and ambition of modern Presbyterianism have, however, effected a complete revolution in that respect. Superb Gothic churches occupy the leading sites in Edinburgh and Glasgow, the churches these, for the most part, of the champion sects of old-style Scottish Presbyterianism. Other cities vie, according to their wealth and their more or less advanced development of taste, with the two great centres. As the Free Church has had to build all its churches since the Disruption, and was animated by a natural ambition to eclipse all rivalry, its churches, on the whole, present the most complete contrast to the anti-Gothic baldness of earlier times. The United Presbyterians, however, have, during the last generation, built many splendid churches, some perhaps scarcely

[1] Tyerman's *Wesley*, vol. iii., p. 533.

to be surpassed, if they can be equalled, in Scotch Presbyterianism. The "Auld Kirk," the Established Church of Scotland, having inherited the old parish churches, which, so long as they are reasonably convenient, may well be maintained because of their historic character and their venerable traditions, has far fewer of such splendid specimens of modern church architecture to show than her younger rivals.

This point is really instructive, as showing how far prejudice, especially in the uncultured or undeveloped mind, may be mistaken for principle. Popular Scottish prejudice, such as is represented in a truly characteristic, although exaggerated form in Scott's Andrew Fairservice, would have objected to Gothic steeplehouses no less than to organs ("kists o' whistles"). Modern Presbyterianism has learnt to admire the ancient style in architecture, and is fast learning—in England has fully learnt—to welcome the organ; just as Milton's poetry and musical culture combined led him, levelling Puritan and Independent though he was, to

> love the high-embowëd roof,
> With antique pillars massy proof,
> And storied windows richly dight,
> Casting a dim religious light,

and also to say,

> There let the pealing organ blow,
> To the full-voiced quire below,
> In service high and anthems clear,
> As may with sweetness, through mine ear,
> Dissolve me into ecstasies,
> And bring all heaven before mine eyes.

If a Scotch Presbyterian of the last century could revisit Scotland to-day, with no knowledge of the intervening change that has passed upon the æsthetic tone and temper of his countrymen, he would be far more surprised than the writer of this volume was when he paid his first visit to Scotland, five-and-thirty years ago, at the show of rich Gothic architecture in Presbyterian churches where the savour of the doctrine is strongly evangelical. He would be still more astonished to-day to find that the sounds of organ-music have more than begun to thrill through the aisles of parish churches of the Presbyterian Establishment.

I cannot write this without being reminded of a certain phase in the history of English Methodism. The Methodism of Yorkshire inherited not a little of the character and feeling of the old Presbyterianism of England, which had taken as strong a hold of some parts of Yorkshire as it had of the neighbouring county of Lancaster. Hardly in Scotland itself was the feeling stronger seventy years ago against "steeplehouses" and organs than in Yorkshire Methodism, especially the Methodism of the West Riding. The prejudice against organs was indeed so strong, and the feeling so bitter, that the introduction of an organ into a new chapel in Leeds led to a rent in the Societies of that town, and to the formation of a Methodist Secession Church. That prejudice, however, has long passed away; and there are few chapels now of any size in Yorkshire without an organ. The feeling against "steeplehouses," against spires and Gothic architecture, still, however, holds its ground, although it is not so general as it once was.[1]

---

[1] There can be no doubt that it is much more difficult to adapt the Gothic style of architecture to the requirements of large Methodist Societies in the North of England than of Presbyterian Churches in Scotland. Where there is a congregation of more than a thousand, a Sunday school of more than five hundred children, with all the class-rooms to be provided that are necessary for Society fellowship, and also all the class-rooms required for the fit and full accommodation of a large Sunday school, it is not easy, in harmony with the

In America modern Presbyterianism has during the last twenty years followed the example of Scotland in regard to the sumptuous architecture of its leading churches. This is the case not only in the States, but in the Dominion of Canada, and also, I believe, in Australia. In the States, Baltimore, Philadelphia, and, above all, New York, may be named as affording very fine specimens of modern Presbyterian church architecture. In New York the Dutch Reformed Presbyterian churches, and the Presbyterian church of which Dr. John Hall is the pastor, excel anything I have seen outside British Episcopalianism in respect of complete, costly, and splendid provision of buildings for Protestant worship and fellowship. In the Fifth Avenue the churches to which I refer are only outdone as ecclesiastical structures by the magnificent Roman Catholic cathedral.

How little, in reality, the style and splendour of church architecture have to do with any such thing as Church doctrine may be seen by passing from Scotch Presbyterianism to Irish Romanism. For rude and primitive simplicity of architecture, no early Methodist chapel or ancient and upland Presbyterian meetinghouse can outdo the ordinary type of Roman Catholic chapel in Ireland. It is, as I have said, wealth, culture, modern ideas of taste, and ambition that have revolutionised the outward aspect of Presbyterianism in Great Britain. It is poverty, rudeness

requirements of Gothic architecture, to make all the provision that is demanded. In the case of Presbyterianism the Sunday schools are seldom, if ever, as large as in the case of Methodist Societies in manufacturing districts; nor is there any need of Society class-rooms for fellowship purposes, because Presbyterian Churches are not organised on the basis of mutual spiritual fellowship among the Church members distributed into classes.

of taste, want of culture, that account for the style of the "chapel" in Ireland. If Roman Catholicism in Ireland became wealthy and cultivated, there would very soon be splendid "Catholic churches" throughout Ireland. Indeed, there are already not a few here and there of comparatively recent erection, and particularly in Belfast.

I may have seemed to wander from my line in these last observations, yet not far, I hope. Modern Presbyterianism, the Presbyterianism of the future as well as of the present and the recent past, is included in the scope of this chapter. What I have been saying will serve to indicate that, while maintaining its connexion with a great historic past, its essential features of Church organisation, and the grand evangelical doctrines of Christianity, the Presbyterianism of the future will be found adapted to modern ideas in respect of the style of its public services and the aspect of its churches. It has already greatly modified its presentation of the theology of "the decrees." We are allowed to hope that in respect of what has been especially wanting in the past — in respect of free and mutual spiritual fellowship for its Church members — the enfranchised Presbyterianism of the future will conform to primitive principles. I seem to see signs encouraging this hope. The difficulties in the way are not such as the Church of England has to contend with. When this great point is met, how magnificent a league of Christian forces will be presented by the Presbyterianism of the world!

IV.
CONGREGATIONALISM.

CHAPTER I.

AN HISTORICAL STUDY OF THE PRINCIPLES AND WORKING OF INDEPENDENCY TILL RECENT YEARS.

THE Church of England is a clergy-Church. Its laity are merely receptive. By its constitution it makes no provision for any exercise by them of spiritual gifts, or of active mutual Christian fellowship. Whatever of such privileges may be enjoyed by them is by the personal consideration and concession of the clergy. Regular Presbyterianism, also, is little other than a clergy-Church. There is some show of election, by the communicants, of the ministers, on their appointment to the charge of a church; but of ordinary authority or faculty, whether legislative or administrative, the communicants have nothing. The government of the Church, in every department, according to the original principles and specific character of Presbyterianism, is vested in the ministers and ruling elders—the term "lay elder" being, as we have seen, a misnomer, if we should not say a contradictory expression. The Church members, or communicants, also, according to the original idea of Presbyterianism, are communicants and Church members as citizens, as members of the commonwealth. I am speaking now of the original and historic idea of Presbyterianism. In the "Free" Presbyterian Churches this condition of things has, of necessity, been modified, and members are introduced into the Church on the nomination of the minister, and not without the concurrence of the meeting of elders, or kirk-session. But nowhere has the root-idea of mutual living fellowship found a place in Presbyterianism, as furnishing the true and only legitimate basis of Church membership, as defining the very tissue and growth of the Church's vital organisation, according to the teaching of St. Paul.[1] For the ordinary and constitutional exercise of spiritual gifts, and of active mutual Christian fellowship, on the part of its Church members, Presbyterianism, like the Church of England, makes no provision.

As to this point, Congregational Independency differs fundamentally from Episcopalianism and Presbyterianism. It goes, indeed, in certain respects, to the opposite extreme. It recognises no clergy-nucleus as the central element of force and extension in the Church. It admits of no such thing as an organised clerical brotherhood. A Congregationalist minister is the chosen servant and chief officer of his own particular and independent Church. The office and ministerial relations of each minister are strictly limited to the one Church to which he has been called, and in which he continues to be a "pastor and teacher." The Church members are not so in virtue of citizenship, or hereditary connexion and relation, or of baptism, but only on the ground of individual conviction and profession of faith, and because they have been accepted by the Church into its fellowship. Nevertheless even in Independent Churches the basis of Church recognition is not found in a mutual and actively maintained spiritual fellowship, manifested after the pattern of the primitive and apostolic

[1] Eph. iv. 13-16.

Church, but rather in a more or less general confession of faith, coupled with outward morality and propriety of life. A living, active, mutual fellowship is not the basis of Church organisation. The experimental element is scarcely recognised after the acceptance of a member into the Church, and is hardly a leading element in his acceptance. It was not so in the earliest times of Independent confessorship. Barrow, the Independent martyr (1593), taught that "the members of the Church being divers, and having received divers gifts, are (according to the grace given to every one) to serve the Church." "It belongeth," he says, "to the whole Church, and none of them ought to be shut out."[1] John Robinson, pastor of the Church of the exiles at Leyden, one of the most able and distinguished among the early Independent leaders and confessors, taught that all the members of the Church who "have a gift, must prophesy according to their proportion." He wrote a treatise in 1618, called *The People's Plea for the Exercise of Prophecy against Mr. John Yates, his Monopoly*—Yates being a pastor at Norwich, who wrote to prove "ordinary prophecy" (*i.e.* preaching or exhortation) "*out of office* unlawful." Robinson, in his reply, says that, so far from its being, as Yates declared, a "disgrace" to the officers of the Church for an unofficial member to prophesy *after* them, such an idea was only "the effect of evil customs infecting the minds of godly men." It was only, he said, since those who ought to be "the servants of the Church" have "become her masters," that "one alone in the Church must be heard all his life long, others better able than he sitting at his feet continually." The practice which Yates condemned, Robinson advocates as conducing to "familiarity

[1] Barclay's *Inner Life of Religious Societies*, etc.

and good-will" between ministers and people. It fitted men for the ministry. It tended to the conversion of others.[1]

At the time when Robinson thus wrote, all the Independent Churches, whether Pædo-Baptist or Baptist, appear to have held the same principle and maintained the same practice which he so strongly defends. Nor was it, I think, till the fusion of Presbyterians and Independents took place in England toward the latter part of the seventeenth century, producing a more or less Presbyterianised Independency, that this original and congenial tenet of Independency was abandoned. It is certain that among the Independents of the Commonwealth it was strongly maintained. There was no point of Independency that was more repugnant to the Presbyterians. For nearly fifty years it was a continual bone of contention between the two denominations. Prelatists were not more bitterly opposed to Independents on this point than were Presbyterians. Doubtless some of the "prophets" were empty and presumptuous talkers. It was a great defect in the Churches that there was no sort of discipline or preparation for the advantage of these "prophets." They were not under any kind of regulation. There ought to have been "schools of the prophets"—or something equivalent, though the prophets might continue simple laymen; and besides the public meeting, the "great congregation," there should have been provision of minor and more private meetings for simple and homely fellowship, where the "gifts" of the "prophets" might in the first place be exercised, and, in being exercised, might be tested. In short, the spiritual gifts and rights of the Church members should have been

[1] Barclay's *Inner Life*, etc., pp. 102-104.

at once distinctly recognised, and duly controlled and limited; place should have been found for them, and they should have been guarded from excess or abuse, in the Church organisation and discipline.

If the Independency of the first half of the seventeenth century was free and full of variety, if in its spontaneous energy and unfettered liberty it was liable to outbreaks of eccentricity, and sometimes to wild disorders, the Independency or Congregationalism of the eighteenth century was, for the most part, as tame and sterile as the deadest and most formal Presbyterianism. No one can read Dr. Waddington's *Congregational History*—and a friendlier or better informed authority could not be cited—without being impressed with the fact that not only English Presbyterianism, from which "Rational Dissent," in its most rationalistic form, was directly derived, but, with rare exceptions, the Congregational Churches of England generally, during the middle and the latter part of the eighteenth century, were tainted with doctrinal heterodoxy and blighted by spiritual paralysis. Not until the influence of the Methodist movement reached them did they show any sign of revival. The influence of Whitefield touched them most directly; but there were not wanting links more than a few, of sympathy and unison, even after the death of Doddridge, between the best of the Dissenting ministers and Churches and the Countess of Huntingdon's Connexion. Besides which,—and this was one of the more important factors in the case,—a number of John Wesley's preachers, of whom John Bennet was perhaps the most able and the best known, became Independents, and a larger number of Methodist Societies became Independent Churches.

From these causes, as Congregationalist historians

enable us to see, Congregational Independency began to share in the evangelical revival of which Methodism was the centre. Old seats of Independency, such as Newport Pagnell and Basingstoke, were once again fired with spiritual life. New Churches were founded, evangelical "seminaries" or "academies" for the training of young men for the ministry took the place of the "academies" of an earlier date, which had, for the most part, first become tainted with Arian or Unitarian doctrine, and then died out. From the early part of the present century the steady growth of an evangelical revival may be traced throughout the Independent or Congregational Churches, alike in the counties south of the Trent, where Dissent was oldest and most thickly planted, and in West Yorkshire, where, entering upon the labours of Ingham and of the Methodists, Congregational Independency began to make great progress. The growth of manufacturing populations, and the multiplication of large towns,—towns much larger than the English provinces had ever known before,—afforded a congenial opportunity for the spread of "democratic ecclesiasticism," which, especially in its more modern form of organisation, seems to be best adapted to dense masses of population. In country regions it often assumed of necessity a form and modes of operation more properly to be called Presbyterian than Congregational or Independent —a form and methods, indeed, which sometimes closely resembled Methodism.

For not a few years after the period of the French Revolution, the Dissenting Churches generally ceased to be political. In the middle of the eighteenth century the leaders of the "liberal" advance in political agitation had been found chiefly among the Presbyterian, *i.e.* the

Unitarian, clergy, of whom Dr. Price and Dr. Priestley were the foremost. But a strong reaction had set in among evangelical Christians against principles and tendencies of which such heterodox corrupters of the faith had been the champions, and of which, as it seemed, when pushed to their logical issues, the French Revolution had been the result. Without ourselves asserting that the principles represented by Dr. Price necessarily led to such issues, we may easily understand how the matter came to be almost universally regarded in such a light by peaceful and loyal evangelical Christians. Liberty itself, indeed, was discredited by the revolutionary orgies of France. Hence at the end of the eighteenth century Dissenters were little disposed for controversy or contention. There was a kindly truce between Churchmen and Dissenters. In 1811, however, in consequence of Lord Sidmouth's famous, though abortive, Bill for limiting the right and liberty of public preaching, there was some revival of political activity among Dissenters, a society being formed entitled the *Protestant Society for the Protection of Religious Liberty*. For a few years this society was active and successful, chiefly in obtaining the removal of special disabilities affecting Unitarians. But after 1814 there was a return to peaceful and non-political evangelical progress and development on the part of the Churches. Nor was it till the agitation for parliamentary Reform set in, that Congregational Independency entered upon that course of politico-ecclesiastical agitation which, for fifty years past, has been continually maintained. The "old school"—including such men as the Claytons, Jay, and James—never came heartily into this movement. Some of them, indeed, opposed it. Even Dr. Robert Vaughan, the founder of the *British Quarterly Review*, though a very resolute Congregationalist and Dissenter, disagreed with the spirit and methods of the new movement, as it was organised under the lead of Mr. Miall, and established his valuable journal as an organ of firm but moderate Dissent.

In all this long and eventful history the Independent Churches never reverted to the primary principles and instincts of free evangelical life. Political and religious liberty, first, then politico-ecclesiastical principles of independence and democratic Church government—these were the distinctive points of theory on which they founded their Churches. After the spiritual degeneracy and decay of their Churches in the eighteenth century had been checked, and new life had been infused into them through the influences of which I have spoken, the Church meeting, indeed, became to some extent a fellowship meeting; prayer-meetings were sometimes enlivened by exhortations not only from the pastor, but from the deacons; members, on being received into the Church, were expected to make a statement respecting not only their theological views, but their religious experience; the public services were redolent of the doctrines of grace; family religion was strictly cultivated; the pastor, aided by his deacons, visited his flock somewhat after the pattern of the devout Nonconformists of king William's time; and, after a while, the Sunday school became a growing power among the young, especially in manufacturing districts. Such a Church as that of Mr. Roby, at Manchester, was a mighty spiritual centre of influence and instruction. But yet there was, as a rule, no such thing as lay preaching, nor was a lively and active mutual fellowship maintained. Hence, in comparison with the Methodists, there was a deficiency of aggressive force and of versatile activity in winning converts, a deficiency, too, of means for training and maintaining their spiritual activity and vitality. Nevertheless, with whatever drawbacks, the first forty years of this century were years of great consolidation and of remarkable usefulness among the Congregational Churches. The nineteenth century was proving itself to be the "age of great cities." For great cities, as I have said, Congregationalism has special adaptations. The Congregational Churches inherited the traditions of a trained and well-instructed ministry. In this respect their services often gave more satisfaction to minds of a certain class than those of the Methodists. The evangelical clergy were far too few to meet the demand, especially in the towns, for gospel preaching. Indeed, the number of such clergy was lamentably small during the first quarter of the century. As yet the Church of England, speaking generally, had not begun to revive. Congregationalism, accordingly, was a great evangelical power among the serious classes of our large towns of modern growth. It took hold especially of the middle-class tradespeople. A host of famous names call to mind the greatness of that age of Congregational Independency. I have named Roby of Manchester. But worthy of association with his name, and in some instances perhaps yet more illustrious, are such names as those of James Scott of Heckmondwike, Thomas Toller, J. Pye Smith, George Burder, John Leifchild, W. B. Collyer, Thomas Raffles, Thorp, R. W. Hamilton, John Ely, James Parsons, and many more, in addition to such men among the Baptists as Andrew Fuller, Robert Hall, and Mursell, and some Congregationalist names to which I have before referred—the Claytons, Jay, and John Angell James.

During this period, Congregational Independency was pre-eminently a religious power. It was fitting the middle classes of England, by a training which was profoundly religious, but at the same time distinctly intellectual, for the sober and conscientious use of the political power which was brought to them by the constitutional revolution of 1832. Now the influence of Congregational Independency is not so distinctively and dominantly religious. It is a politico-ecclesiastical power, a power which seems to become every year more and more directly and intensely political. A leading gentleman among the Congregationalists expressed himself some years ago to a friend of mine as wearily impatient of the prolonged Disestablishment agitation, because, if that were only at an end, and the Church of England disestablished, there would no longer be any reason for maintaining the attitude of Dissent and of separation from the Church. Fifty years ago the devout Congregationalist was probably a Whig or Radical in politics: he was opposed to religious disabilities of every kind; but he was a member of his Church for his soul's good, and for the sake of his children's souls as well as his own.

The leading principles of Congregational Independency are three, of which, however, the first is not always taken account of, even by Congregational writers, although Dr. Dale, in his *Manual on Congregational Principles*, gives it its true position and importance. They are: (1) That every member of a Church must profess, and must be assumed, to be a spiritual believer in Christ Jesus, a believer "renewed in the spirit of his mind," and accepted as such by the fellowship of the Church. (2) That the members of every Christian Church form one distinct and collective assembly, self-governing, and independent of every other Church. (3) That the Church meeting as a spiritual republic is the fountain of all authority and official position in the Church; and that in regard to questions of Church government and discipline coming before the Church, each several Church member possesses equal rights with every other member.

The first of these principles, though so seldom adverted to in connexion with the claims and theories of Congregational Independency, should be the most fundamental principle of all. It is certain that, historically regarded, it is the original and primitive tenet of Independency; and that the denomination was, in fact, at first—in England and on the Continent—differentiated from others by this specific principle. Indeed, it would not, I think, be difficult to show that, from this principle, narrowly construed and more or less misconceived, the other two principles were derived. It was conceived that, from the common spiritual life and relationship to Christ of the members of the Church, equal rights for each and all in the government of the Church must be an inevitable consequence; spiritual privileges and claims being thus confounded with provisions of Church government. It was further seen to be impossible to maintain such a theory of equality, in respect of all Church relations, both spiritual and disciplinary, on the part of all the members of the Church, on any other basis than that of the complete autonomy of every Church assembly, the independence of each several congregation of the faithful.

In the early days of New England, these ideas led to the assumption that, as each accepted communicant was, in virtue of his spiritual standing and life, a member of the

Church republic, with full equality of rights as compared with any other, so the Church assemblies in each town or township which owned allegiance to one and the same Congregational communion, were entitled, either in their collective or in their representative capacity, to supreme authority in the guidance of all town or township affairs and in the definition and prescription of principles of action. In these New England Congregational communities, during the seventeenth and part also of the eighteenth century, and in some far on into the present century, Church and State were identified in the towns or parishes, not on the Episcopalian or Presbyterian principle, which made every citizen of necessity a communicant (or else a civil as well as an ecclesiastical defaulter), but on the converse principle, that the "saints" were entitled to govern the commonwealth, and the Church of spiritual believers, as such, to lay down laws for the whole community in its civil aspect. It was long, as is well known, before even the Independents generally learnt the principles of religious liberty. It was a lesson scarcely to be learnt except through the teachings of sectarian conflict and controversy, and of persecution. If the Baptists learnt and taught it thoroughly earlier than any other sect, the reason probably was that, till the Quakers arose, they were of all sects the one most generally—indeed, all but universally—spoken against, and for which none seemed to have any sympathy. If the "Society of Friends" from the very first, thoroughly and with an absolute universality, apprehended, taught, and practised the principles of religious liberty, one chief reason of this doubtless was that, from the first George Fox and his followers were the common butt of scorn and insult, of persecution, always ignominious, and almost always cruel, from men of every class, from professing Christians of every denomination, whilst they themselves could have no hope of becoming an established or dominant sect.

The Independents, at any rate, by confounding in the sphere of the Church spiritual faculties and rights with administrative functions and disciplinary authority, when they found a wide field in America, lost sight of the true spiritual principles which should govern in the organisation of the Church. They made very imperfect provision for the exercise of spiritual gifts, for the "increase of the body"—the Church—in faith and "in love," by "that which every joint" was competent to "supply." Politico-ecclesiastical theories took the place of those primary principles of free spiritual fellowship and activity which the fundamental idea, the first law, of their communion, if it had been received into hearts less addicted to political and religious controversy, should have led them to recognise and provide for in their Church arrangements. And what happened in America in one form has, in a less extreme development, been repeated on this side of the Atlantic. Here, also, politico-ecclesiastical ideas of equality have been substituted for the provision of mutual edification and spontaneous fellowship which represents the first and fundamental right of Christian believers and communicants in every Church.[1]

[1] The pure principles of the best school of spiritual Independency, represented by John Robinson of Leyden, and the Churches of the exile, which had imbibed his large and truly evangelical spirit and followed his doctrine, were carried out by the original Church of the Pilgrim Fathers at New Plymouth, which settlement was not absorbed into the colony of Massachusetts till 1692. The principles of politico-ecclesiastical Congregationalism were carried out in Massachusetts,

As we have seen, this was not the case, or only in part, during the earlier years of the present century. At that time political ideas and tendencies did not, among Congregationalist Dissenters, rule in all the arrangements of the Church, did not dominate and inspire its public relations and appearances. The candidate for Church membership opened his heart and unfolded his Christian experience, first to a few of the official or senior members of the Church, including usually the minister, and then, though not always with equal fulness, to the Church meeting, the general company of believers. The Church meetings were more or less fellowship meetings. The prayer-meetings were also not seldom fellowship meetings, though in a more restricted sense. It is true that, to the view and feeling of a Methodist, not a little was wanting in these arrangements. The general Church meeting was too large to encourage the spiritual confidences of sympathetic and earnest but timid souls, and the meetings were too infrequent to satisfy the wants of

after that colony, under Endicott as governor, was compelled to adopt Calvinistic Congregationalism as its public faith and profession. From 1629 to 1689 this form of established Congregationalism held absolute sway in Massachusetts. It allowed no elective franchise to any Episcopalian, Presbyterian, Baptist, Quaker, or Papist. In 1631 the General Court enacted, " to the end the body of the commons may be preserved of honest and good men, that no man shall be admitted to the freedom of this body politic but such as are members of some of the Churches within the limits of the same"—all except Congregational Churches being disallowed. " The elective franchise," says Bancroft, " was thus confined to a small proportion of the whole population. The polity was a sort of theocracy ; the servant or the bondman, if he were a freeman of the Church, might be a freeman of the Company," *i.e.* of the Massachusetts commonwealth. " It was the reign of the Church ; it was a commonwealth of the chosen people in covenant with God." As to the whole of this subject, I may refer to vol. i. of the late Dr. Egerton Ryerson's valuable work on *The Loyalists of America and their Times.*

those who, surrounded with cares, distractions, and temptations, needed frequent refreshment for their spirits. The weekly prayer-meetings were too public to meet such needs and cravings. Young converts, shrinking but yearning spirits, who would gladly have relieved their hearts by vocal prayer and by simple utterance of some of the feelings that pressed upon their souls, could find no liberty of expression under such circumstances. Besides the minister, in fact, none but the deacons or a few of the senior, more considerable, and bolder among the members of the Church, could venture to take any part in the meetings, private or more public, so far as these were spiritual meetings of fellowship or prayer. In these respects the meetings of the Congregationalist Churches were far below the standard of liberty and fellowship in spiritual life and utterance which was the characteristic of the primitive Church. There was danger lest "cold obstruction's apathy" should chill and deaden the spiritual affections and aspirations of the convert, and induce a chronic state of formalism, which would become the too prevalent tone of the Church generally. Nevertheless, in the hands of the best and most fervent "pastors and teachers," always aware of this danger, and always endeavouring by their pulpit ministry, in their Church meetings, and by systematic pastoral visitation, to counteract it, the Churches were guarded against these evils, more or less effectually, and a fine tone of intelligent piety was maintained. Granting this, however, with all heartiness, and remembering that during the period to which I am referring the Churches of Congregational Independency were strongholds of intelligent evangelical teaching and influence, it is necessary at the same time to note, as one of the great lessons of our historic study, that for want of moulding its spiritual organisation and arrangements in conformity with the requirements of its original principle of spiritual liberty and free Christian fellowship for spiritual ends, Congregational Independency was only partially successful in its spiritual aims. Those Churches, nominally Congregational, best escape from this tendency which, by means of a surrounding network of minor religious meetings, including sometimes what are really dependent (not "independent") Congregational Churches—that is, by means of a quasi-connexional organisation and agency—imitate and emulate, if they do not sometimes surpass, the methods and agencies of Methodism. Of this sort are several powerful Churches in the southern counties of England.

The observations last made, however, do not by any means express the whole truth, or adequately describe that which is the pressing danger of the Congregational Churches of the present day. I do not imagine any person of authority will contradict when I say that the Church organisation of Congregational Independency rests far less on a basis of spiritual character and experience at the present time than it did eighty or even fifty years ago, and that convictions as to not merely Church government, but the relations of Church and State, now occupy a position and fill up a space in the creed and qualifications of a Church member, not merely much more commanding than formerly, but of a different character. The experimental religious qualification has in many congregations diminished, with a steady continuity, until now it has become indefinite, while the politico-ecclesiastical shibboleth, in a form of increasing distinctness, has become, from year to year, a more indispensable qualification. Under these circumstances, what is to become in future of the spiritual qualification of the Church member? Is not all that is expected now, in many Churches, a profession, more or less vague, of orthodox Christian belief (although as to the orthodoxy, where is the standard to be found?)—a reputable position in society, and sympathy with anti-State-Church principles?[1]

[1] See note, p. 201.

CHAPTER II.

AN EXAMINATION OF THE PRINCIPLES OF CONGREGATIONAL INDEPENDENCY.

THE most fundamental and far-reaching error in the theory of Congregational Independency would seem to be the confusion of the laws of spiritual life and activity in the kingdom of Christ with the principles of government in a human commonwealth. But this error is aggravated by the fact that the political theory which Congregationalism assumes as the proper and rightful—if not the divinely ordained—basis of human government is one of which the claims to universal acceptance are far from being proved, and have been, and still are, denied by many of the greatest and most earnest thinkers. There may be at the bottom of this theory a true principle, imperfectly understood; but that principle is at any rate very difficult to define as an abstract truth, and in its practical application it must needs be directed and limited by reference to political and social conditions in each race or nation respectively. The same civil and political rights cannot be claimed for all men everywhere. The principles of political government as understood in England or America cannot be applied as yet in British India, much less in British Kaffraria.

But even though the extreme democratic theory of civil

and political rights and government were better founded, it could not be summarily transferred, as if of Divine right, to the discipline and government of that kingdom which is " not of this world." The governmental authority and polity of all religious communities should be founded on the commission and laws of Christ. Furthermore, and this is a point which needs to be emphasized, the primary rights of every Christian believer are not rights of ecclesiastical *government*, but the rights of spiritual nurture and fellowship, and of free spiritual activity. These spiritual necessities, these vital demands of his soul, are his primary claims.

To which it must be added, that the Christian Church is not to be conceived of as, in its organised character, no other and no more than a settled commonwealth, to be governed and maintained by a balance of the forces of human individuality and conviction. In one of its leading aspects it is an army in a hostile world, acting under the orders of its King, marshalled and led by its officers, who obey His commands, continually advancing its borders and annexing territory, living, if it is vigorous and victorious, in a state, more or less, of perpetual aggression. No army could be effectively disciplined and victoriously led, if the principles of democratic republicanism ruled in every regiment, and not only in every regiment, but in every company. Just as little can the principles of democratic republicanism be applied to the government of a Christian Church in all its discipline and its activities.

And yet the fundamental principles of popular government—that is, of wise and stable popular government—must not be lost sight of in Church organisation. It is true, indeed, that authority in the Church is not derived from the popular suffrage. It is true that no mere popular suffrage can of itself convey the commission of a Christian minister. Nevertheless there must be a just blending of obedience to primitive and apostolic rule and precedent, with a due regard for modern conditions and developments, with respect for the faculties, the sympathies, and the judgment of the members of the living Church, in their various gradations. How this is to be accomplished is by no means a simple question. Nor will any particular solution suit more than a class of cases. But from Scripture itself much may be learnt in the way of suggestion, and much may, and has been, learnt from the lessons of sympathetic insight and of experience. What is certain is, that the *simple* political solution of the problem suggested by Congregationalism is wrong. Only in a certain class of cases can it even seem to work effectively; and in these cases its operation is invariably modified and its strict principles are not carried out.

The difficulties and contradictions arising out of the endeavours of Congregationalists to harmonize their democratic politico-ecclesiastical theories with the requirements of Christian order and progress, and with the injunctions and prescriptions of the New Testament, have been shown at length by myself in a separate essay.[1] The late Dr. King, also, to name one able Presbyterian writer among many, in his work on *Presbyterian Church Government*, has effectually dealt with this subject. He abundantly demonstrates his proposition, that "our Independent brethren, to qualify the unworkableness of democracy, impose such restrictions on the people as in effect to crush their freedom and lodge in the pastorate a despotic authority." Dr.

[1] See *Connexional Economy*, pp. 1–137.

Wardlaw asserts, in capital letters, that "ALL ARE NOT RULERS."[1] He holds that pastors are the *sole* rulers. Dr. Davidson, in his Congregational Lectures on *Ecclesiastical Polity*, demands that while the "elders," *i.e.* the ministers, "rule," the flock shall render "obedience." "In meetings of the Church," he says, "no member should speak without permission of the elders" (teaching elders or ministers), "nor continue to do so when they impose silence. In such meetings no member should oppose the judgment of the presiding elder" (*i.e.* the chief pastor). In his *Christian Fellowship*, the late Rev. John Angell James affirms that "real Congregationalism is not democracy"; that "pastors alone are the *rulers* of the Church," the chief and characteristic merit of Congregationalism being that, "more fully" than other Churches, "it explains the nature and extent of this authority." The "extent," however, as explained by Mr. James, is wider than anything known among Presbyterian or Methodist Churches. "AS LITTLE DISCUSSION," he says, "AS IS REALLY POSSIBLE should take place at our Church meetings. . . . Nothing but the most obvious necessity should induce a single individual to utter a syllable." Mr. James gives the minister an absolute veto on the admission of members to the Church. The late Dr. Campbell (of the Moorfields Tabernacle), in his work on *Church Fellowship*, goes even further, and not only gives the minister a veto, but makes the whole matter of admission rest with him. It is no wonder that in Churches where such an interpretation of the mutual rights of ministers and lay members is admitted and acted upon, there is peace and good order. But where are liberty and popular government, and the fundamental rights of Church members?

[1] Wardlaw's *Congregational Independency*, p. 310.

The truth is, that Congregational Independency is exposed to a pressing dilemma. Where the pastor is a man of great eminence and public power, having received the plebiscite of the Church calling him to office, he reigns thenceforth sole and supreme. Where he is a man of inferior gifts and force, he is under the yoke of the Church meeting, and reduced to the position, which Mr. Angell James describes with so much of mingled pathos and indignation, of a " speaking brother," a brother absolutely powerless in the Church of which he is styled the pastor, being hired to speak from the pulpit, but without any authority to rule—the servant of an irresponsible majority. Or if such a " pastor " escapes from this position, it is by accommodating himself to the tastes and wishes of a select company, the *élite* of the Church, which, though a minority in numbers, wields the power of a majority by reason of the social position, the property, or the general influence of its members, and itself governs irresponsibly in the name of the quiescent majority.

In the midst of a large middle-class population, where an intelligent Church has been gathered and built up by the labours, during more than one generation, of a pastor or a succession of pastors of high gifts and commanding Christian character, the pastor of such a Church will—as I have intimated—exercise a paramount influence, and all matters will be well and harmoniously ordered and organised. Under such conditions Congregationalism is at its best, and offers an impressive example of organised Christianity. A considerable number of admirable men have, during the course of the present century, held the pastorate in such Churches. Evangelical Christianity in England, and Nonconformity in particular, owes very much to the character and influence of these men. Yet such cases, it cannot be denied, are not the rule, but the exception. Many Congregational authorities of the highest mark might be cited to prove this, if any were bold enough to deny it. Mr. Angell James, in the earlier editions of his book on *Christian Fellowship*, gave a description of the position of a pastor in such Churches as constitute the inferior class, but a large proportion, of Congregational Churches. He thought it prudent to omit the passage in later editions, but he would not have written it without good reason. Speaking of the pastor in such Churches, he says: " He has no official distinction or authority. His opinion is received with no deference, his person treated with no respect, and in the presence of some of his lay tyrants, if he has anything to say, it must be something similar to the ancient soothsayers; he is only permitted to peep and mutter from the dust."

The *abstract theory* of Congregational Independency is, in fact, radically unsound. The disparity between the theory of mechanical equilibrium and the laws of life and growth is not wider or more complete, than that between the politico-ecclesiastical theory of Congregational Independency and the laws according to which the Head of the Church has willed that the vital growth and the living order of His Church should be maintained and regulated. One of the primary laws of the Church of Christ, as of all living things which have not attained their final perfection, is that of growth ; and another is that of propagation. But the theory of Congregationalism—I speak only of its *theory*—is in its tendency opposed to free expansion and growth, whilst it is absolutely incompatible with that missionary propagandism which was the great work of the primitive Church, and which should be the characteristic passion of every evangelical Church from age to age. A Congregational Church cannot send a missionary far away to act as a Christian pioneer without contradicting its theory. Indeed, it is very difficult for it to do effective home mission work without similarly violating its principles. Congregational ministers, according to this theory, stand in relation only to the Church for which they have been severally ordained pastors. They belong, as *Congregational pastors*, to no common brotherhood of ministers, a main part of whose proper duty it is to take counsel with each other for the spread of the gospel in " regions beyond," at home or abroad. Any evangelist sent forth by a Congregationalist body to do pioneer or missionary work would, if he acted on the Congregational theory, be a mere lay brother on the new ground, and would have to wait till there had grown up around him a Church which he would have no prerogative to organise, and till that Church—an infant Church, perhaps in the midst of heathenism—had first organised itself on a republican basis, and then called and elected him as its pastor.

The primitive Church, besides its apostles, had evangelists and prophets. Congregationalism has no equivalent ministerial agency. By its apostles and evangelists in the first and second ages, aided also by the "prophets," and by its brotherhood of bishops,—first presiding elders, and afterwards, in the second and later ages, diocesan visitors and rulers,—the early Christian Church preserved its unity. But any such thing as organic unity, as unity carrying with it any directive authority or any ministerial community and intercommunity of charge and responsibility, Congregational Independency cannot consistently admit. In all this it seems to Wesleyan Methodists to be unprimitive, unapostolic, and to be doing violence, for the sake of an incompatible theory, to the primary laws of spiritual life and of the Redeemer's kingdom.

"The old physical axiom that 'a thing cannot act where it is not' applies with a singular propriety to Independent Churches. As Churches, they can consistently project to a distance no influence, or only as a faint and evanescent gleam; they can initiate no enterprise abroad. They may spread slowly, Church after Church, from place to place; but that is all. Their deposition is like that of crystals from a chemical solution. Let the electrical conductor be introduced into the solution at a particular point, and crystallisation will there commence, and therefrom and around that first formation as a centre may crystal after crystal be deposited, till the work is complete. So, yet not so surely or perfectly, might a system of Independent Churches extend themselves among mankind."[1] "Each Independent Church is a monad, self-contained and complete. When most closely associated with each other, they are still but an aggregation of crystals, each distinctly entire, shaped and consolidated by its own internal forces, existing independently by the affinities and cohesions of its own constituent atoms."[2]

I am of course aware that the Congregationalist theory is often much modified in practice. As some men are better than their principles, so in its actual working Congregationalism departs from its theory; and the Churches are not in reality so powerless for missionary work as they would be if they strictly adhered to their principles. But, in argument, we have to deal with a *theory*, a theory which, precisely because of its untenable and unpractical principles, is attractive to a class of minds that are saturated with

[1] *Connexional Economy*, p. 48.   [2] *Ibid.*, p. 142.

political ideas and prepossessions, while they are not well instructed in the laws of spiritual life and progress, and lose sight of the high and Divine principles which should rule in the sphere of Christ's spiritual kingdom. It is accordingly needful to show the confusion of ideas, the tangle of fallacies, in which Congregational Church theories are involved, and to which, in fact, is owing the illusive charm they possess for people with whom certain political principles are a sort of national and social gospel, a panacea for most of the ordinary evils of society. It is no answer to such arguments as we are suggesting against the distinctive principles of Congregationalism, that the Churches escape from their consequences by "modifying" them in practice. The "modifications" are, in fact, in contradiction to the theory. That the distinctive principles of Congregationalism require to be to such an extent departed from in order to success in practice, is not any argument in favour of the principles in question, but in favour of the contradictory principles, by yielding to which evident failure in some of the highest functions of a Christian Church is prevented.

But, indeed, however often and to whatever extent failure may be obviated and averted by a modification in the working of Congregationalist principles, there yet remains enough force in them to produce in too many cases very injurious results. That the description of principles and results I have given above is not a draft of imagination, but is based on truth, may be shown from the guarded admissions of Congregationalists themselves. The following is a quotation from the address of the late venerated Thomas Binney as Chairman of the Congregational Union in 1850.

If Independency," he says, "proceeds to the entire

insulation of every distinct and separate interest from all others; if each Society and every individual insists upon the exercise of their own liberties, unaffected by all connexional relationships; if at the same time the voluntary principle is carried to the extent of all Churches and congregations, of all sizes, and in every place, each for itself finding within itself the means of its own support,—men may say what they please about Divine ideas, or primitive models, or anything else, but the fact is that while on such a system you might have perfect liberty, congregational independence, separation from the State, freedom from the 'supremacy,' and so on, you could not have compactness or power as a body, strength from union, defence from scandal, nor the ability to provide for the spiritual wants of small and poor patches of population. Independency may, doubtless, be carried so far as that Independents shall not be, properly speaking, a body; the Churches shall not be members of a body, or, if members, only like so many scattered and separate legs and arms."

From the writings of the late Dr. Payne and of Dr. Davidson I might quote yet stronger and more sweeping language to the same effect.

Holding that each local Church should be absolutely independent of every other, and that a minister or pastor is only such as related to the particular Church which he serves, and as elected to his office by the members of that Church, the Congregationalist must, as we have seen disallow any organic ministerial brotherhood. There can be no such thing as mutual discipline or oversight among ministers, although this also is one of the duties devolved upon the brotherhood of ministers in the writings of the New Testament. To the weakness and scandals arising from this cause, pointed reference is made in the passage quoted from Dr. Binney. I have refrained from quoting a passage much sharper and stronger, in which, in the course of the same address, he referred to this subject.

But I cannot refrain from citing here two striking illustrations of the practical difficulties that beset the theory of Independency, and the inconsistencies involved when the requirements of pastoral discipline come into competition with the supposed rights of the Churches, which I met with in Dr. Lindsay Alexander's *Life* while the first edition of this work was passing through the press, and which were quoted then in a note.

The first case is that of a minister called Cranbrook, the pastor of a Congregational Church in Edinburgh, who was preaching unorthodox doctrine in his Church. "Having no formal creed," writes Mr. Ross, the author of the biography, "and no 'Church courts' to deal with cases of heresy, but holding by the principle that every Church is independent of external control, it was difficult for Presbyterians, and even for some Congregationalists, to see how ministers and Churches of the Congregational denomination could vindicate their reputation for orthodoxy, and at the same time refrain from interfering with the liberty of the Church and its pastor. No case quite similar having ever been known in Scotland, some doubts arose as to the proper course to take. At length, at a conference of ministers in Edinburgh, it was agreed that those ministers who had taken part in the public services of Mr. Cranbrook's 'induction,' or 'recognition,' should ask Mr. Cranbrook 'to meet them in friendly conference.' Dr. Alexander was asked to send a letter to Mr. Cranbrook, inviting him to the proposed meeting. Needless to say, especially in such a case, Dr.

Alexander's was a courteous as well as a clear letter. To this letter Mr. Cranbrook replied in strong terms, refusing to appear before the 'newly constituted consistorial court and endure the inquisition,' and stating that he was quite prepared to endure 'the penalty of losing the recognition' of those in whose names Dr. Alexander had written " (*Life*, pp. 198-200).

The other case, briefly stated, was as follows. In the Glasgow Theological Academy, in 1844, some of the students had adopted "heretical" views. For this they were dismissed from the Academy; but it was then discovered that a number of the pastors in the west and north "shared with the students in their heresy." The Churches in Glasgow were appealed to on behalf of Calvinistic orthodoxy, and in the end the Glasgow Churches withdrew fellowship from those in Hamilton, Ardrossan, Bellshill, Cambuslang, and Bridgeton. Several of the pastors, however, in Edinburgh and elsewhere, refused to sustain the Glasgow movement, Dr. Alexander among the number, at which Dr. Wardlaw felt disappointed and more or less grieved. Dr. Alexander defends his own course in the following sentences: "Cordially at one with Dr. Wardlaw in his doctrinal views, I yet could not see the wisdom or propriety of involving Churches in a controversy when the point at issue was not whether the *Churches* held the views stigmatised, but simply whether the *pastors* of these Churches held them. In all our Churches, up to this time, it was understood that forbearance was to be exercised with those who could not see their way to Calvinistic views. It was only with pastors that it was not a point of forbearance. The proper parties to judge are, I take it, the pastors of the body to whom each candidate for ordination has to make his confession before he is ordained. As it was their sanction which first gave him the status of an orthodox minister of their body, so they are the only parties competent to deprive him of that status if he shall afterwards swerve from his orthodoxy" (pp. 126–128).

Here are singular elucidations of Independency furnished by the very highest authorities. "There are no Church courts," and every separate Church is "independent of all external control." And yet a small handful of ministers who had taken part in the induction of a pastor into a Church could constitute themselves into a tribunal for judging as to points of heresy, and of their own mere motion, their own assumed authority, from which there could be no appeal, could condemn a pastor as guilty of heresy. And, again, though every separate Church is absolutely "independent," a number of these "independent" Churches agree to proclaim their own separation, and to call on other "independent" Churches to separate, from certain "independent" Churches which they regard as infected with false views of doctrine.

CHAPTER III.

EXAMINATION OF THE PRINCIPLES OF CONGREGATIONAL INDEPENDENCY—*continued*.

THE principle is a just one, that a minister or pastor is only such, in any proper or official sense, in relation to the Church which he serves, and into the ministry of which he has been elected. It is only within the Wesleyan Church that a Wesleyan minister is officially a minister. Until adopted by another Church, if he were to leave Methodism, he could not be received as a pastor or minister within that other Church. To maintain either the indelibility or the universality of the character and office of the ordained minister, merely as such, is a Popish principle. But it is the theory of the absolute independency of each separate Church which deprives the Congregational Churches of the manifold benefits that flow from the primitive principle and institute of an organised ministerial brotherhood, just as the same theory, if strictly adhered to, prevents the possibility of any true sisterhood or any organic unity among Independent Churches. In Wesleyan Methodism the Churches which spring up around a mother-Church are themselves part and parcel of the same united family. The tendency of Congregationalism is to make neighbour Churches into rivals in the same field. There is nothing in the theory of Independency necessarily to forbid a plurality of ministers or pastors in the same Church; but one of the serious practical evils of Independency is the extreme difficulty of working the system on any arrangement other than that of a sole minister for each several Church, except in the case of an assistant pastor to an aged minister. The exceptions to this statement are exceedingly rare, nor have these rare exceptions been usually found to work easily. The evils of Independency are thus aggravated. To combine even two Churches, if of anything like equal numbers, into a joint organisation, with two pastors, would be a departure from the principles of Congregational Independency.

Another result of the system is that, amongst Independent congregations, lay preaching, that great force of primitive Christianity—lay preaching, which must always be the main strength of free and easily sustained evangelistic enterprise, is comparatively little known. The very fault of Presbyterianism against which the earliest Independents protested is, in modern Independency, reproduced in an exaggerated form. There is, as a rule, but one speaker in the Church, and he the minister, who has no elders by his side. If in some nominally Congregationalist Churches there are lay preachers, it is because these Churches have established preaching stations. Such cases, however, are comparatively few; and if these preaching stations grew into such dimensions, or were situated at such a distance from the Church centre, that the members could not attend the central Church meeting and receive the sacrament at the centre, such stations would have to be separated from the parent Church. They would become distinct Independent Churches, and would have a sacred right to govern themselves in all matters, whatever aid they might continue to receive from the centre.

The difficulties arising out of such cases extorted the following protest from the late Rev. John Ely, of Leeds. He is evidently referring to home missionary work done by Congregational County Associations. But the principle is the same as in the case I have sketched. "Nor can I omit to remark," he says, "that a false notion of the rights of Independency seems to me often to interfere with missionary operations. A community of Churches, by missionary zeal, plant a village Church; that Church depends on their funds: as long as they yield support, they have right of supervision and interference. It is with them to appoint the agent or the minister, to demand a statement of operations, to exercise authoritative interference. A *veto* is the utmost that the Church can ask; and in the election of a minister, this perhaps ought to be conceded."[1]

This is common-sense; but it is not Congregational Independency. In fact, the administration of Congregational Home Missions contradicts the professed principles of Congregational Independency. It is no wonder that, some years ago, at a meeting of the Congregational Union where the principles and methods of the Congregational Home Mission were discussed, the general sentiments of the promoters being in agreement with the passage quoted from Mr. Ely, Dr. Parker disturbed the harmony of the assembly by protesting that such fashions of working as the meeting and its managing committee favoured might be Presbyterianism or Methodism, but were certainly not Congregational Independency.

The primitive Church maintained watchful discipline over the ministers as well as the members. It also encouraged free exercise of teaching and preaching gifts among the

[1] Ely's *Remains*, pp. 95, 96.

members generally. And its messengers and evangelists, going forth far and wide to sow the seed of the kingdom, carried with them the right to found and organise Churches, and to exercise over them, especially at first, the needful authority and power of government and discipline. In all these respects Congregationalism is wanting.

The true mean as to government and discipline for the Church of Christ is to be found midway between the Episcopalian theory and that of Congregational Independency. Successionist Episcopalianism—Anglo-Catholic Episcopalianism—begins and ends with the clergy so far as office, authority, spiritual function, are concerned. Congregationalism, on the other hand, makes all Church office and authority to be derived from the vote and original authority of the members of the Church. The true mean between these extremes recognises the fact that Church movements, Church organisation, the very existence of a Church, depend, in the first instance, on the action of the ministers of Christ, but nevertheless that, in the spirit of the primitive Church, provision must be made, as early as possible, for the creation of officers and helpers from among the members of the Church, for the association of an effective representation of the converted brethren with the ministers in the government and administration of each Church, and for a due representation of the different Churches in the joint government and administration of the united body or sisterhood of Churches. The assumption involved in the theory of Congregational Independency, that ministerial authority is derived from the suffrages of the assembled Church members, is negatived by all that Scripture teaches on the subject. It will be well to have this point settled definitively and conclusively.

At the beginning at Jerusalem all office and authority vested in the apostles. The apostles at Jerusalem not only "ministered the word of God," but at the beginning "served tables." They could not but have done so at the first, although they embraced the earliest opportunity of escaping from an uncongenial employment and obtaining the appointment of godly men as "servants" (deacons) of the Church, to take off their hands this "serving of tables." So in the first founding of all Churches the preachers of the gospel have, for the most part, been compelled to attend to every branch of labour and service necessary in order to the gathering and holding together of converts. All the offices of the Church reside initially in the first founder, and he can only part with any of them when occasion calls for it, and fit men can be found to take the work off his hands. As it was with the twelve at Jerusalem in this respect, and with St. Paul in laying the foundations of his Churches among the Gentiles, so it was with John Wesley in the last century, and so it has been with pioneer missionaries all the world over and in every age.

At first the apostles were the sole pastors and rulers of the Church at Jerusalem; its local government was absolutely in their hands. Their commission they held direct from Christ, and the Day of Pentecost was the Divine seal to that commission. But their ministry could not be limited to Jerusalem; their office stood in relation to the whole world. It was their express duty to lead the way in the fulfilment of the Saviour's commission, laid upon His disciples, to go into all the world, and "make disciples of all nations." Hence the number of the apostles resident at Jerusalem seems before long to have been reduced to not more than three or four, while at the same time the number of disciples had increased to many thousands. Hence also, following in this respect most naturally the Jewish order and precedent, at least in general, elders were before long appointed to teach and rule in the Christian "synagogues," of which there must have been many in Jerusalem, and which still retained a loyal connexion with the Temple and its services. Incidentally we obtain a glimpse of these "elders" in Acts xi. They stand out in distinct relief and full dignity in regard to questions of discipline in chapter xv., where they are associated with the apostles in the settlement of the concordat with the Gentile Churches. That they were really subordinate to the apostles in that transaction, although taken into partnership with them, it is hard to doubt. Nevertheless, it seems not improbable that James, of whom we read in the record, and who took so leading a part in the transaction, was no apostle, but chief among the body of elders of the different Churches, the Christian synagogues of Jerusalem : that is, in some sort, already " bishop of Jerusalem," as he is represented to have been by very ancient tradition.

The apostolic office, in its highest sense and scope, the office of the twelve, appointed by our Lord to be His personal witnesses and the founders of His Church, and whose names are inscribed on the foundations of the celestial city,[1] was of necessity an office which could not be continued or transmitted. In so far, however, as the work of the apostles related to the organisation and discipline of the Church,—its continuous development and the provision for its conduct and government,—it was necessary that

[1] Rev. xxi.

they should organise a ministerial succession to whom the government of the Church might be committed. This was done by means of the offices in the Church which have been already spoken of. If the diaconate, as to the date of its institution, took precedence of the eldership, the reason was that the apostles themselves at first discharged the duties of the local pastorate. I omit reference here to the prophetic office, as unconnected with the established discipline of the Church, and as not destined, in its primitive form, to permanency in the Church, although doubtless liable to revival from time to time. The offices of evangelist and of presbyter, taking *bishop* and also *pastor and teacher* as expressions equivalent to *presbyter* in the first age, sum up the organising and governing ministry of the primitive Church. With them was the beginning of ministerial authority and prerogative. Upon them mainly depended the order, life, and progress of the Churches. By "evangelist" in this connexion I mean of course such ministers as Timothy and Titus. The elders or presbyters were, as local pastors, to teach and to rule in the several Churches; but the evangelists were the substitutes or deputies of the apostle. Under the direction of the apostle they exercised decisive authority in the organisation of Churches. They appear to have been not only supreme, but absolute, in their official appointments. They not only appointed presbyters, but exercised discipline over them. They are not found after the first century, because the apostles whom they represented were no longer on the earth. The "apostles" of whom we read in the *Teaching* are not to be regarded as their equivalents, as seems evident from the brevity of their meteor-like appearances. Rather we must find the equivalent, or the revival, of this office in the new and aggrandised form of the episcopate, which grew up after apostles and evangelists had passed away, and which, in the first instance, only gave concentration and unity to the joint authority of the presbytery, but which tended more and more, as the second century advanced, to include something like diocesan functions. The attempt, indeed, of our High Churchmen to make Timothy into a diocesan bishop of Ephesus, or Titus into the bishop of Crete or some wider diocese, is altogether futile. Nor can they in any such way piece out their fabulous hypothesis of apostolic and episcopal succession. But their vain attempts need not prevent our admitting that the idea of an episcopacy or a "general superintendency" (to use the Wesleyan phrase), much wider and of much higher authority and responsibility than the office of the Ephesian or Philippian "presbyter-bishop" of apostolic times, or of the "bishop" of the *Teaching*, is to be recognised as implied in the work done by such evangelists as Timothy and Titus in planting and founding Christian Churches in the apostolic age.

Not any of the ministers known in the Churches of apostolic Christianity would seem to have been appointed or chosen to office by the authority and vote of a Church meeting. We have indeed no evidence as to the appointment of the elders at Jerusalem. But considering how early they were appointed, and the position which the company of apostles, especially Peter, held in the Church at Jerusalem, it is repugnant to suppose that the elders,—however they may have been designated beforehand by various evidence of public esteem and confidence and of personal authority and influence,—could have received their office except by the direct and official appointment of the apostles. Even in the case of the Seven, although the office was only secular,—that of "serving tables,"—and although the suffrages of the Church recommended the Seven to the apostles, nevertheless the apostles reserved in their own hands the authority of final and official appointment. It was they who "set them over" the business. Much more in the case of the spiritual office of eldership would the appointment and investiture rest with the apostles, either in their own persons or through those whom they commissioned.

This view seems to be confirmed in the fullest manner by the detailed record of St. Paul's action as given in the Acts, and indicated in his Epistles. It seems impossible to suppose that Paul would assume a power over Churches composed of Jews and Gentiles greater than Peter and his companions—the men on whom the Lord had "breathed," whom He had acknowledged as His beloved and chosen friends, and had solemnly commissioned as His apostles—exercised over the Church at Jerusalem. And we find that everywhere, as he had opportunity, St. Paul used his personal and undivided prerogative in ordaining elders. What is more, the Apostle of the Gentiles delegated to his trusted followers and representatives, men themselves not claiming any such title or dignity as *Apostle*, the function of "ordaining elders in every city." That is to say, the apostle appointed, of his own authority, not only elders or bishops, but evangelists, who wielded a quasi-apostolic power; and thus provision was made that when the elders were not appointed immediately by the apostle, they should be appointed by men who bore from the apostle a commission to appoint them.

That this principle was intended to obtain, without condition or limitation, in regard to all Christian Churches in the whole future, is a position I am not at all disposed to maintain. I should be bound to hold it, however, if the primitive and apostolic Churches, in the details of their organisation and discipline, had been intended to serve as a model for all Churches in after times. The facts of the first stage are, in this respect, as inconsistent with the pretensions to Divine right of Congregationalism as, in other respects, they are contrary to the claims of High Episcopalianism. But the candid student of the earliest records of the Christian Church is not more likely to adopt one of these views than the other.

A few words remain to be said as to the discipline of the apostolic Churches in its relation to the principles of Congregationalism. It may well be believed that there were no set rules of discipline in the primitive Church. The authority of the apostles was, in fact, supreme and absolute as it was unique. How St. Peter dealt with Ananias and Sapphira we all remember. St. Paul also could deliver offenders over to Satan that they might learn not to utter false and malignant words of slander or contradiction.[1] Regular processes of discipline, it is reasonable to conclude, grew up only by degrees. When St. Paul enjoined Timothy not to receive an accusation against an elder, except on the testimony of two or three witnesses, he was contributing to the foundation of such a process. Dr. Dale, indeed, follows his leaders of the Congregational succession in seeking to prove from 2 Corinthians ii. 6, that modern Congregationalist principles were established in the Corinthian Church, that matters of discipline at least were determined in full Church meeting by the vote of a majority. I apprehend, however, that even in Congrega-

[1] 1 Tim. i. 20.

tional Churches it has been and is the general custom to investigate cases of morality, involving an appeal to discipline, otherwise than in a full meeting of a numerous Church, and that the decision also in such cases is virtually determined before a select company of the Church. The truth is, that the matter referred to in the apostle's letters to the Corinthians was settled, in characteristic fashion, by that Church in its full meeting, precisely because the Church was as yet unorganised. And, after all, it was not really determined by the Church, but by the apostle. At first the Church would take no action in the case. They shielded the offender. It was not till after the apostle had remonstrated, rebuked, and insisted, that the Church assembly, in and over which had as yet been appointed no elders or bishops, repented of its former scandalous laxity, and obeyed the apostle's command by excommunicating the gross offender.[1] It was, in reality, Paul who, by his apostolic authority, determined the sentence and insisted on its infliction. The majority obeyed his behest.

Passing from the " pastors and teachers " to the diaconate of the apostolic Churches, there is little to be said. No intimation is given, unless it be in the sixth chapter of the Acts, of the manner in which deacons were chosen or appointed, although rules are laid down to guide Timothy and Titus as to the class and character of men who should be appointed to the office. It would be natural to suppose that, like the elders with whom they are so closely connected as subordinates, they would, in the Gentile Churches, be appointed in the first instance by the apostle or by his commissioned representative. Nevertheless, the example

[1] Cf. 1 Cor. v. 13 ; 2 Cor. ii. 6.

of the sixth chapter of the Acts remains, at least to teach a principle, if not as an actual instance and precedent to rule the method of appointment. It cannot, indeed, be confidently affirmed that the Seven were precisely deacons, or that they held a permanent office. Still less can it be maintained absolutely that this instance and precedent at Jerusalem, created under exceptional circumstances of popular discontent, would govern the rules and usages of the Gentile Churches in regard to the appointment of deacons. But yet we may learn the lesson that, as far as possible, in the administration of Church affairs, the officers of the Church should have the confidence of the members as well as of the ministers, especially those officers who have charge of the temporalities of the Church. This principle, in its application to Church funds and what may be called stewardships or treasurerships, was indeed signally respected by St. Paul in regard to the collections made in the Churches of the Gentiles for the "poor saints" at Jerusalem, and which were committed to the charge of brethren chosen for this purpose by the contributory Churches. The apostle's principle is plainly expressed when he says, "Avoiding this, that any man should blame us in the matter of this bounty which is ministered by us: for we take thought for things honourable, not only in the sight of the Lord, but also in the sight of men."[1]

All, in short, that Scripture teaches as to the main points which have been under consideration may be summed up in a few words. The appointment of ministers was made by the apostles or by their itinerant representatives.[2] It is *probable* also that the already existing ministry, where

[1] 2 Cor. viii. 20, 21.
[2] Acts xiv. 23; 2 Tim. ii. 2; Titus i. 5.

any existed, joined in sanctioning and authenticating the appointment.[1] How far or in what way the Church in general concurred in such appointments is neither declared nor in any way intimated. And in regard to Church discipline, while it is taught with distinct emphasis that the " elders " or " bishops " ought to " rule "—of course with wisdom and equity—and the people loyally to " obey," [2] what limits should be set to ministerial authority, or what rights are to be exercised by the people, are matters as to which Scripture is silent.

On this general subject it may be well here to add the judgment of the sagacious Neander. " As regards the election to these Church offices," he says in the first volume of his Church History, " we are in want of sufficient information to enable us to decide how it was managed in the early apostolic times."

Even, however, if anything like fair evidence from Scripture could have been discovered in favour of the ecclesiastical principles of Congregational Independency, as representing the original usage of the primitive Church, it would not follow that they ought to be accepted as the rightful principles of Church organisation for all after-ages. Let me, against the pretensions of those who borrow the analogies of secular government to support their own principles of Church government, be allowed myself to use an analogy taken from worldly commonwealths. At first the successors of Clovis met all their freeborn warriors yearly on the Champ de Mai, and these national congresses were the only legislative assemblies ; but afterwards of necessity a more restricted and only partially representative assembly came to be convened.

[1] 1 Tim. iv. 14.
[2] 1 Thess. v. 12 ; 1 Tim. v. 17 ; Heb. xiii. 7, 17 ; 1 Peter v. 1–3.

So the early Witenagemot, at which all freemen had a right to be present and vote, became afterwards confined to a small number of constituents, and finally was modified into the form of the English Parliament. For there can be no doubt that the Parliament of Edward I. was a boon conceded to the old English feeling of the nation, as a fair and practical substitute for the Witenagemot of their fathers in the days of Edward the Confessor, and in the times preceding. So the assembly of *all* the city burgesses came of necessity, and for the better dispatch of business, to be ordinarily narrowed to the council of the mayor and aldermen. In short, universal individual rights of government have everywhere given way to representative popular government. And I venture to think that the frank adoption by Congregationalism of the principle of representative popular government in their Church economy might enable them so to modify their system as to escape from many of the difficulties to which I have had occasion to refer. Already, indeed, something has been done in this direction.

Congregational Independency is a powerful factor in the religious life of England. It has a distinguished history, and has been identified with many great and critical stages in the moral and political advancement of England. But it is capable of adapting itself in the future more perfectly to the requirements alike of social and of religious progress and improvement. What is needed is that its Churches should be united into a mutually helpful organised array—let it be called army or sisterhood, as occasion may suggest ; and that its ministers should be united into an organic brotherhood. Congregationalism should be the true English Presbyterianism, with its town and also country presbyteries, its synods, its General Assembly. The union need not be nearly so close and mutual as in the case of Methodism, and the ordinary local administration of the best-ordered Churches need undergo little or no change. But the evils of which Dr. Binney spoke so strongly in his address before the Congregational Union of 1850 might thus be done away; rivalry among neighbouring Churches might be prevented, and splits in Churches be brought to an end. Arrangements also might then be made, without any of the present inconsistencies and difficulties, for the aid of needy and the support of dependent Churches. Joint and truly mutual provision might be made for the training of ministers, and for mutual help and interchange among settled pastors. United Congregationalism might then really have its own joint Home Mission and Foreign Missions. Considering the views of many eminent Independents, both in the earliest and in more recent times, who have inclined towards Presbyterianism, remembering the spirit of such Nonconformists as John Howe, such a modification as I have indicated would surely be no departure from the best traditions and inspiration of the Congregational succession. Let modern Congregationalism take up the joint inheritance of the Presbyterianism as well as the Congregationalism of England; let it accept and harmonize into one grand system and unity the best elements of both the great historic forms of English Puritanism. Surely this would be a worthy aim to keep in view.

There are not wanting indications of a movement in this direction. Its frank accomplishment, with a wise breadth of sympathy and purpose, would be a grand national blessing. At the bottom of such a movement, however, if it is to be truly successful, must be the distinct recognition and steadfast maintenance of that most fundamental principle of original Congregationalism, that none but spiritually awakened and converted persons ought to be members of the Church, and that for all members of the Church there should be privilege and liberty of true spiritual fellowship, including the exercise of spiritual gifts. A large and effective liberty of fellowship, the play of which is felt as a real force of impression, attraction, and suggestion, throughout all the brotherhood of believers, could not but develop gifts and energies, and habits of counsel and care as to the affairs of the Church, whether spiritual or temporal, such as would naturally mark out those best fitted to discharge Church functions, and prepare an unfailing supply of men to become deacons and ministers. The one-man monopoly might be done away. A large and various diaconate, equipped and ready for every office of lay activity and service, whether in administration or in preaching and testifying, might be continually maintained. Under such conditions the historic glories of Congregationalism in the past would, I may be allowed to believe, be far surpassed by its glories in the future.

I have now done with criticism and argument so far as Congregationalism is concerned. I could have wished that the plan and purpose of this volume had allowed an escape from the task of adverse criticism in this particular case, and that for two reasons. One is that, to borrow an expression of Dr. Guinness Rogers in the *Congregationalist*[1] which, though pleasantly used, is yet true in the sense intended, Congregationalism and Methodism are " natural enemies," and it is impossible to present

[1] For September, 1886.

anything like an honest or thorough criticism of the Congregational system, as seen from the position of a Methodist, without taking an opponent's view almost throughout. The other reason is, that, notwithstanding this fact, the leaders of Congregationalism have, for the last twenty years and more, been generous in their behaviour towards Methodism. It is impossible, however, to give a comparative view of Church organisations, including Congregationalism as well as Anglicanism and Presbyterianism, without treating all alike with impartial fairness. My object is to criticise all round on equal terms, and to criticise from a special point of view, as defined in the opening chapter of this volume. It is simply impossible to expound or defend the principles of Methodism without antagonising the principles of Congregational Independency. At the same time, I have tried to do the fullest justice to the high merits of not a few Congregational ministers. I have not said a word to the disparagement of any, I have brought into high relief the best lines of the Congregational traditions, and I have cordially recognised the great successes achieved by many Congregational Churches, especially under congenial conditions.

I should not, however, like to close this chapter without special reference to some of the able leaders of Congregationalism who have laid Methodism under obligation by their Christian sympathy and public recognition, actuated, no doubt, largely by a characteristic liberality of spirit, but also, perhaps, in part by a chivalrous wish to be generous to the utmost towards their "natural enemy." Of these the grand and massive Binney was one, whom I had the privilege of knowing in his later years of ripest wisdom and mellowed nobleness of spirit. Another was, and happily still is, the able, catholic-spirited, and serenely impartial Dr. Stoughton, who, as a Church historian, has won confidence and respect from critics of every colour. Another was the gifted and amiable minister of Union Chapel, Dr. Henry Allon. Still another is the famous City preacher, Dr. Parker. There was also the loving and eloquent Raleigh, a Scotchman, who had the rarest graces of the most refined type of his countrymen, without a particle of Caledonian hardness. All these, however, have owed not a little, as they have delighted on fit occasion to testify, to the quickening spiritual influence of Methodism, without which they would hardly have been all that they have been. Their testimony on behalf of Methodism was therefore the more natural. Perhaps also the majority of them scarcely represented the strictest principles of their denomination. But, besides these, there are two of the stoutest champions of Independency who have borne themselves very generously towards Methodism. One of these is Dr. Guinness Rogers, who, man of war though he is, and in some respects one of the strongest representatives of the "dissidence of Dissent," —I borrow the expression of a great statesman adopted by a well-known Congregationalist journal,—has proved himself, in his treatment of Wesleyan Methodism, to be also a man of remarkable largeness of view and breadth of sympathy. The other is the late able and truly liberal pastor of Carr's Lane, Birmingham, Dr. Dale, for whose address, in particular, delivered at the last Birmingham Conference, universal Methodism owes him lasting thanks, and who, although so unlike his predecessor at Carr's Lane Chapel, Mr. Angell James, in intellectual character and in political and ecclesiastical feeling and policy, was not inferior even to that saintly man in genuine catholicity of spirit.

NOTE.

In the passage to which this note refers (p. 169) as originally published (*Wesleyan Magazine*, September, 1886), I had used the word *require* where I have now substituted the word *expect*. I used it in the sense of *expect*; and I cannot help thinking the word might well have been understood in that sense, for certainly the pages preceding had not been characterised by a harsh judgment of Congregational history and practice. However, in the *Congregationalist* for October, 1886, I was made an offender for the word *require*, interpreted according to the hardest meaning which it could bear, and the imputation it was supposed to convey was indignantly denied. I accordingly published in the November number of the *Wesleyan Magazine* the following explanation:

"Thus far I had written before I read a passage in the *Congregationalist* for October, which gives a decisive negative to the question with which my first paper on Congregationalism closed. (See *Wesleyan Methodist Magazine* for September last.) I frankly admit that on re-reading my words I see that they are too unguarded, and are fairly capable of a construction which I never intended them to bear. I never meant to imply that any *question* with regard to his political creed was put by any Congregational Church to a candidate for Church membership. All I intended was, that whilst the old experimental requirement in order to Church membership had 'in many Churches' been abandoned or relaxed, the 'politico-ecclesiastical' element in modern Congregationalism was made more distinctly prominent. If the last thirty volumes of the unfortunately now extinct *British Quarterly Review* are compared with the first fifty or sixty, or if the *Congregationalist* be compared with the *Christian Witness* of five and twenty years ago, it will surely not be questioned that the 'politico-ecclesiastical' question has, in comparison with the subject of religious life and experience in the pages of the more recent publications, assumed largely developed proportions. I might further have made an appeal to much voluminous and continuous correspondence in the *Nonconformist* and *Nonconformist and Independent* newspapers between the years 1870 and 1880 as seeming strongly to support the impression under which I wrote the few lines to which Mr. Rogers so sharply objects. Moreover, my strongest sentence is not a statement, but an enquiry and an appeal. That enquiry has been answered in the negative by one much better acquainted than I am with the present condition of Congregationalist Churches. That he is able to return a negative so unhesitating and conclusive, I greatly rejoice; and I cannot altogether regret that the last too hastily written sentence of my article was the occasion of calling forth this reassuring denial. This being so, it is plain that a movement which some few years ago was in full force has happily been checked. Of course, my very question implied that I had reason for fearing that the state of the case was not so favourable as it turns out to be. The fact that the 'anti-State-Church principle' is part of the very *basis* of the Congregational Union looks strongly in that direction. And I may assume that the very able and very genial editor of the *Congregationalist* cannot have forgotten the movement of which he himself was one of the most distinguished leaders—the attempt to do away with the enquiry into the religious experience of a candidate for admission to Church membership which had heretofore been one of the most cherished traditions of the Independent Churches. In the 'series of essays' by the most distinguished Congregational ministers, entitled *Ecclesia : Church Problems Considered*, not the least remarkable is that on 'The Congregationalism of the Future,' by the Rev. J. Guinness Rogers, B.A., in which, with an eloquent and argumentative elaborateness, and by the space of full fifteen octavo pages (490-505), he pleads for the discontinuance of that enquiry. The question was vigorously discussed for a long time in the *Nonconformist* and the *Christian Witness* ; and Dr. Eustace Conder, from the chair of the Congregational Union, lifted up a warning voice against the so powerfully advocated change. I am truly thankful if that warning has been heeded.

"If I have been led, unwittingly, to write anything of which our Congregationalist brethren can justly complain, I am truly sorry. They, on their side, have of late years done nothing to provoke unfriendly or unfraternal criticism on the part of Wesleyan Methodists. The tone of Bogue and Bennett, and of the learned and large-minded Dr. Vaughan during our troubles in 1849-1854, when he seemed really to exult in what he regarded as the imminent disintegration of Methodism, has not been heard for three and thirty years. Nothing could be more kindly, more brotherly, than Mr. Rogers' own treatment of Wesleyan Methodism in his Congregational lectures. I should be ashamed of myself if I did not reciprocate his kindliness.

"On the other hand, it is fair, and indeed necessary, to say that the editor of the *Congregationalist* cannot possibly be unaware that the present is a most anxious moment for *Wesleyan* Methodism, a determined attempt being made to involve *Wesleyan* (!) Methodism in the vortex of party politics. With that attempt, indeed, the *Congregationalist* is in avowed and eager sympathy. In its August number, an injurious statement was made on this subject which had no foundation whatever in fact. And even the fine-spirited article on the Conference in September distinctly takes a side with this endeavour to give this ' new character and tone to the Methodism of the day,' that is to say, to make

Wesleyan Methodists 'political Dissenters.' Our Congregationalist brethren have but to reflect on the disastrous results of all former attempts to complicate Wesleyan Methodism with party politics—those of Alexander Kilham in 1795-97, of the Leeds politicians in 1828, of Joseph Rayner Stephens, and of William Griffith—to be able at least to understand the apprehension with which those who are familiar with Methodist history, and old enough to remember the heart-rending divisions of 1828, 1835, and of 1850, cannot but look upon a repetition of the like ill-omened endeavour."

Since the original publication of the passage so severely resented, I have had abundant testimony, in some instances emanating from high Congregational authority, as to the substantial truth of the intimation which I ventured to convey in that obnoxious sentence. I have judged that there is no need for me to do what I had thought of doing —that is, give conclusive extracts from correspondence in Congregational newspapers on this subject.

In publishing a revised edition of this volume, let me take the opportunity of acknowledging, on behalf of universal Methodism, the signal service rendered by my late esteemed friend, Dr. Dale, in his every way admirable, as well as faithful and searching, sermon on the characteristics of original Wesleyan Methodism, preached in City Road Chapel in March, 1891, in connexion with the Centenary Commemoration of the death of John Wesley.

V.
WESLEYAN METHODISM.

CHAPTER I.

THE METHODISM OF THE WESLEYS—THE DOCTRINE AND THE FELLOWSHIP OF WESLEYAN METHODISM — THE SPREAD OF WESLEYAN DOCTRINE—THE MUTUAL RELATIONS OF DOCTRINE AND FELLOWSHIP—THE SPECIAL CHARACTERISTICS OF METHODIST PREACHING.

METHODISM is universally regarded by its friends as a revival of primitive doctrine. It is not so universally recognised that it was, still more characteristically, a revival of primitive Christian fellowship and discipline —of primitive spiritual life in the individual believer and in the Christian community. This second point is not a whit less important than the first. The two points also are implicated with each other. The revival of the primitive doctrine produced, as an immediate result, the fellowship and discipline, which also proved to be a revival, both in spirit and to a large extent also in form, of the primitive fellowship and discipline. Of this the Wesleys themselves were not distinctly conscious at first. But presently they recognised the remarkable reproduction in their own Society of primitive and apostolic fellowship, and admired the more the manner in which they had been led by Providence. It was not their own deep wisdom and foresight, but their single-minded practical purpose to take the plainest and straightest way to satisfy, from day to day, the spiritual needs of themselves and their converts, that led them to form and mould the fellowship of Methodist Societies, which, by a man like Dean Paley, was soon acknowledged to be the truest representation and revival of primitive Christianity that had been seen in the world since the earliest Christian times.

As a revival of primitive Christian *doctrine*, the Methodism of the Wesleys had two forms of error to combat: the principles of Popish and Anglo-Catholic mediævalism, and, in particular, sacramental superstition, on the one hand; and Calvinism on the other. The predestinarian element in Calvinistic divinity was scarcely less directly opposed to the experimental theology of primitive Christianity than the superstitions of "Catholic" mediævalism. The Methodist preachers taught that living Christianity in any man implies a conscious spiritual life, a life of present consciousness and presently realised spiritual power. This spiritual life in the present was in their view salvation. And this salvation for the present and for the eternal future, they held, was available for every man to whom the gospel was preached; whereas the predestinarian regarded salvation as an immunity and privilege for eternity, conferred on the elect by a Divine decree, and to be revealed as such hereafter by the Divine sentence. When Calvinists spoke of a conscious *assurance* of the salvation of the elect believer, they meant, by this gift and blessing of assurance, a peculiar and supernatural conviction given to the elect that his name would be found in the Book of Life at last. They did not always mean a sense of God's living presence in the believer's soul, a consciousness that his whole being is touched and renewed with a vital quickening of faith and spiritual power and inward peace. The Methodist preachers did not often or characteristically speak of "assurance"; but when they did use the word, it was in the sense I have just described, and in that sense only. They preferred to speak of enjoying peace with God, and the "inward witness," the "witness of God's Spirit with their spirit that they were the children of God."

The conflict, at this point, of Methodist doctrine with the dogmas of Calvin would seem now to have almost come to an end. For many years, under the lead of Whitefield and with the concurrence of the Countess of Huntingdon and her "Connexion," the Calvinistic Methodists attempted to combine the doctrine of conscious salvation with the theology of the decrees. In reality the two are incompatible; and as years have passed, this has come to be more and more confessed. The doctrine of a conscious present salvation—a theology at once experimental and evangelical—has prevailed over the theology of the decrees. Experimental theology has cast out predestinarian theology. Hence throughout England and America the old Calvinism is almost extinct. In Scotland also the same process is rapidly making way. Calvinism has been first modified and afterwards ignored. Experimental theology even in Scotland has all but ousted the theology of the decrees.

With sacramental superstition the conflict is more protracted. Anglo-Catholic leaders like Bishop Wilberforce, Dr. Hook, and even Dr. Pusey, have indeed contrived to amalgamate not a little of Arminian experimental theology —quasi-Methodist theology—with their own characteristic teaching as to sacramental efficacy. But, in this case, as in regard to Calvinism, Methodist experimental theology cannot be logically or permanently united into one and the same system with dogmas which at bottom are radically inconsistent with the doctrine of conscious renewal and sanctification through faith in Jesus Christ, our living Saviour. The Methodist teaching is that of St. Paul : " repentance toward God, and faith toward our Lord Jesus Christ." The Methodist doctrine of inward and growing holiness is that of "sanctification," not only "by the Spirit," but "through the truth"— the "word." The high Anglo-Catholic doctrine, the doctrine especially of Pusey and his followers, teaches regeneration not through repentance, but through baptism, and sanctification not through the saving truth, spiritually received and applied by faith and obedience, but through the duly administered and reverently received eucharistic rite. This, according to the Anglo-Catholic, is the essential foundation; all other lessons and growths of sanctification are founded on this, the sacrament being received implicitly as in itself a quickening rite. There is no way of reconciling such contradictions as these. In the end, lingering as the conflict may be, the sublime experimental doctrine of salvation through faith, salvation through the Spirit, and through "the truth as it is in Jesus" received and assimilated by living faith, will assuredly displace the doctrine of quasi-magical transformation through the sacraments.

The philosophical or metaphysical system of fatalism which Calvin interwove with his otherwise admirable system of theology, had the effect of injuriously rationalising Protestant theology in Great Britain and over not a little of the Continent. It hung a weight round the heart of Reformed doctrine which prevented it from rising and expanding to meet the needs of the world. On the other hand, Lutheranism, retaining the roots of sacramental doctrine, while it provoked scepticism and intellectual rationalistic rebellion, also involved its devotional theology in perplexed and intricate mysticism. Methodism gave to Protestantism, to the Reformed theology of England a breadth and vigour and buoyancy, a hopefulness and a missionary faith and energy, which have sent it forth winged and inspired to undertake the conversion of the world. The specific and differentiating doctrines both of Continental Calvinism and of Lutheranism, especially as these forms of doctrine and discipline were Erastianised by artificial and mechanical State Church settlements, tended equally, although in different ways of influence and operation, to engender rationalism, to produce formalism, to fetter the energies and localise the range of Christianity. Experimental evangelism and missionary instincts and expansiveness are not the natural and congenial results of the theology either of Geneva or of Augsburg. It is the Methodist revival which, in the ordering of Providence, has brought back to Christianity the apostolic impetus and the inspiration of primitive evangelistic faith and zeal.

Still it is not mere doctrine by means of which this result has been accomplished. The Pentecostal inspiration can only be retained so long as not only the "apostles' doctrine," but the primitive "fellowship," is sacredly maintained. The "doctrine" and the "fellowship," in truth, as already intimated, cannot long be maintained in vital reality apart from each other. Let the fellowship be dissolved, and the doctrine even of experimental and evangelical theology will gradually become a mere sentimental or metaphysical theory, a sort of Broad Churchmanship, either of the indefinite latitudinarian school, such as in the Church of England may be typified by the teaching of Dean Stanley, or of the philosophic universalist school, such as that of Maurice. In fact, when Arminianism ceases to be experimentally evangelical, it tends, as has been shown especially in the history of the Church of England, to latitudinarianism of the laxest type. Nor can Methodism flatter itself with the dream that examinations and doctrinal standards will avail to preserve its ministers from rationalism. Where a whole communion gradually loses religious vitality, standards and examinations afford no guarantee of continued orthodoxy. The meaning of words and phrases insensibly changes its colour and content, alike for pulpit and pew. It is the heart alone that can keep the standard of doctrine true, as it is the true ear alone that detects and resents the false note in music. It is the true tradition of evangelical experience which affords the only living and transmissible test of genuine experimental orthodoxy in the public teacher. If the spiritual fellowship of Methodism should gradually decline into a dying formalism, if her class-meetings become mere companies on paper, and her love-feasts come to an end, the Arminianism of Wesleyan Methodism will no more retain its evangelical character than the Calvinism of Geneva has done. The evangelical experience not only answers to the saving doctrine—it tests, preserves, and reproduces it.

When the Wesleys, aided by their Moravian teachers, rediscovered the primitive evangelical doctrine; when, finding that doctrine in the Homilies of the Church of England, they preached the doctrine of the Homilies, illustrated and interpreted to them by their own experience and that of the Moravian brethren, apart equally from the Calvinism and the High Church mixtures with which, in the Homilies themselves, it is variously combined—the apostolic doctrine flashed a sudden illumination on the dark background of the national ignorance and insensibility as to spiritual realities and the life eternal. The preachers reasoned, and the Holy Spirit "convinced" the hearers "of sin, and of righteousness, and of judgment"; of repentance, faith, and holiness; of the forgiveness of sins, and the renewal of the heart; in a word, of the new life in Christ Jesus: and the like result followed as in Jerusalem. There came the new life; and the new life immediately found expression in the new fellowship. The new converts gathered instinctively into bands; they poured out their fresh experience as it welled up from within; they met almost day by day, or night after night; their fellowship was vivid, free, and mutual, and most commonly "from house to house." In the spirit also of the Jerusalem fellowship, their bounty flowed freely and largely forth towards such as were in need.

Like the early Christians also, they were exemplary attendants at the public "prayers" of their Church. After their conversion, they went to church with zealous assiduity and with a regular frequency before unknown. They delighted also, after the primitive pattern, in the Holy Communion, and took every opportunity of being present at "the breaking of bread."

Like the first Christians, moreover, they were full of joy with the light of their Saviour's countenance. *Gladness and singleness of heart* are terms strikingly descriptive of their experience. And even though persecuted, they still, like their prototypes, "rejoiced that they were counted worthy to suffer shame" for the name of Christ.

In still another respect the Methodists were like the early Christians at Jerusalem. They began as a Society within a Church, and only by degrees did they acquire a special and independent organisation. As the apostles appointed deacons, so Wesley appointed stewards and leaders, just as need arose, and according to the indications of Providence. The whole Methodist economy unfolded in this way, as did the organisation of the early Church.

Thus the spiritual economy of Methodism is a vital product, an organism which has grown by virtue of the life within, and is accordingly a true index and a fit vehicle of all the spiritual activities which are necessary to its integrity and its efficiency. But however it may be fitted to develop, it can never create that inner life. On the contrary, if that life decay and fail, this highly developed and organised economy will prove a cumbrous burden, and will rather hasten than hinder decline.

Thus the doctrine, the spiritual life and fellowship, and the special organisation which has grown up for the satisfaction of that life and in response to the instincts of that fellowship, are all in necessary relation to each other, and must stand or fall together. Unless all are maintained, none can permanently endure. It is with a spiritual community as it is with a nation. The vigour and vitality of a nation, the virtue of its institutions, and the character of its men and women, can only be maintained by the actual working out of the national life at once collectively and in the history of the living men and women individually. The character of a noble ancestry can only be reproduced in their descendants if each generation lives after the spirit of its fathers, if the successive generations are vigorous, healthy, and vivid in their lives, and if their children are bred and trained according to the best habits and traditions of the race. Literature and sentiment alone will not keep alive a nation's greatness. The mere name, the idea, the history, of a great race, the mere letter and memory of great institutions, will not avail to preserve the nation from decline, or the institutions from fatal decay. So Methodism cannot live upon its past achievements, nor can its mere organisation save it. It is the vivid, faithful, self-denying life and service of the present which can alone reproduce and transmit as an inheritance for the future the great truths, the precious experience, the vital forces, of original Methodism.

At the same time, it is a point to be noted, that the easiest way for Methodism to decline is the neglect of the means of spiritual fellowship. It is not always seen, although nothing is more certain, that without the maintenance of these the pulpit ministry will presently lose its vital savour and its spiritual power; and it is easy to forget that mere periodic manifestoes of doctrine can never compensate for the loss of those less formal and more frequent helps of both doctrine and fellowship which are provided by Wesleyan Methodism, such as exercise a continuous influence, such as bring home to our social conditions, and apply to daily experience in all the privacies and by-paths of life, the vital and saving truths of religion. So students are apt to forget that exercise and fresh air are as needful to health, and not seldom even to life, as regular meals. It is certain that nothing could compensate Methodism for the loss of its simple, primitive means of fellowship and occasions of spiritual activity.

But, further, there is not only the life-quickening which the fellowship of Methodism ministers: there is the specific training of gifts and faculties which it affords. The opportunity and the easy liberty, in a simple and congenial circle, for the earnest and overflowing soul to voice forth in homely, heartfelt, unstudied words of prayer the feelings which press for utterance, calls out and informally trains the gift and faculty of prayer. The habit of free, though reverent, mutual conversation as to religious subjects and matters of spiritual experience, coupled with the exercise of social prayer in private fellowship meetings, such as the class-meetings of Methodism, calls out, again, and informally trains, the gift and faculty of religious exhortation, plain, unpretending, extemporaneous in its actual form and utterance, although the result of reflection as well as of experience; and thus the exhorter, the extempore speaker, the earnest and telling lay preacher, makes proof to others and becomes more or less conscious to himself, of his gifts for the service of the Church. In this way, in and by the class-meeting, the lovefeast, the stirring prayer-meeting, Methodism obtains knowledge and use of its prayer-leaders, its class-leaders, its local preachers. The class-meeting is the germ-cell out of which the whole vital economy develops. First the gifts are ascertained and more or less developed; thus the fitness for office comes to be recognised by both ministers and people, usually by the people in the first instance. In this way the necessary elements of life and influence disclose themselves. The fitting characters and personalities are brought to light which, gathered and ordered according to their faculties, as class-leaders in leaders' meetings and as local preachers in local preachers' meetings, form the material and basis of official organisation and government for the Societies of Methodism.[1] The Societies being severally organised, the circuit, which is an aggregate of the Societies for a particular neighbourhood, naturally finds its common council in the collective assemblies of the officers diffused throughout it. Thus the liberal Presbyterianism of Methodism, with its large, active, and capable assemblies for purposes of administration and discipline, is dependent for its definition and development on the maintenance of the elementary spiritual fellowship of the Societies. From that primitive life-tissue the whole growth of the system has been evolved. Let that wither, and all must decay; let that die, and Methodism, as such, with all its special qualities, must come to an end. What sort of a *caput mortuum* might in such a case remain, it is hardly worth while to speculate.

I come back to the position which I have been endeavouring to make good: that the spiritual fellowship of Methodism is necessary in order to the life of its evangelical doctrine. Its characteristic doctrine is not only evangelical, but yet more strikingly and specifically is it experimental. Experience—vivid and inspiring experience —is essential to the character and life of Methodism. This experience can no more permanently subsist without such an appropriate and accordant organisation as is the fit vehicle and expression of its emotions and its activities, than the organisation can be maintained in life and vigour without the experience.

The fundamental characteristics of Wesleyan Methodism .

---

[1] As to authority and office being, by the law of natural suggestion and sequence, based on work and service and gifts, see 1 Cor. xii. 4-11 and 28-31 ; xvi. 15, 16.

being such as I have endeavoured to define and exhibit, the style and method as well as the staple material of its pulpit ministrations have been marked by corresponding characteristics. Methodist preaching, not long ago, was easily recognisable by its special features. No Methodist could mistake its identity; and those, not being Methodists, who had once been introduced to it, could not fail afterwards to identify it. If to-day this is no longer so generally the case, the chief reason is that the Methodist doctrine and manner of preaching have spread into other than Methodist communions. Many who have been impressed under Methodist preaching have become preachers in English Congregationalist Churches. Not a few clergymen of the Established Church were brought up under Methodist influences; sometimes, as in the conspicuous instance of the Aitken family, a Methodist tincture of doctrine and experience has descended from father to son. There are many Anglican preachers, especially among the "missioners" of their Church, whose preaching is eminently awakening and experimental. Of these preachers, as might be expected, a considerable proportion are extemporaneous in their utterances. Where the appeal is from heart to heart, from conscience to conscience, where all the forces of mutual sympathy between preacher and audience should be brought into play, where all that is said, as to matter, manner, phrase, and timeliness, is to be adapted with full and exact fitness to the character, the condition, the circumstances of those addressed, the only method for the preacher is that of extempore address, free, unconstrained, sympathetic, at times altogether impromptu. It is no more possible to conceive of the original Methodist preachers, than of the apostles, as delivering their pleadings and exhortations from a manuscript. It ought to be as impossible for read sermons to become the custom with experimental preachers, with Methodist preachers, as for barristers in a criminal court to read their addresses to the jury. It is impossible, as a rule of ordinary practice, for sermons which are the instruments of awakening and persuasive appeal to the conscience to be read sermons. This is a truth which is coming to be recognised in the Established Church. It is, I venture to say, a discouraging symptom that some of the younger preachers of the Methodist ministry are taking to the habit of reading their sermons. Canon Liddon's sermons were written and read; but they were of a special class, as he was a man that stood alone. They were usually condensed and eloquent arguments, dealing with fundamental points of Christian faith and controversy. Such sermons can never be the ordinary staple of any ministry. Not one man in a thousand is called habitually to attempt any such work as a preacher; in Methodism especially, men whose faculty assorts with the practice of reading sermons, and is at the same time a high and valuable faculty, must always be very rare, while the congregations to whom such preachers can fitly and profitably minister must be yet rarer. In the biography of that eloquent Methodist preacher, W. O. Simpson, a man whose life-work signally illustrated the meaning and value of extempore power, we find him quoting a saying of Dr. Osborn's, at the Conference of 1871, to the effect that "extempore preaching is vital to Methodism; he who has it not is not a preacher." I also venture to endorse that saying. The power of the Methodist ministry must decline in proportion to the growth among us of the habit of reading sermons. It may not be improper to read a commemorative historical discourse at a special crisis, or an official and argumentative manifesto of faith and doctrine, or an Ordination Charge ; but habitually to read the sermons delivered in the ordinary course of the ministry is an ominous departure from Methodist practice and traditions.

CHAPTER II.

OUTLINE OF THE ECCLESIASTICAL ORGANISATION OF WESLEYAN METHODISM.

I MUST now pass from the primary considerations on which I have thus far been dwelling, to some other points of scarcely inferior importance connected with the organisation of Wesleyan Methodism.

It has been shown that, besides being, first of all and essentially, a spiritual fellowship wherever it was found, and whether its Societies were large or small, the primitive and apostolic Church was distinguished by its unity of principle, of spirit and sympathy, and, as far as this was practicable, of government. The congregations within the same town and even within the same province were one community, as in the case of Palestine, of Syria and Cilicia, of Achaia, of Ephesus and Proconsular Asia; the unity of the general government of all the Churches founded by St. Paul was maintained by his own authority and by his visits, and by the delegated authority of his representatives, such as Timothy, Titus, and Erastus; the essential unity of the Churches, and their acknowledgment of a common paramount authority, on the widest scale, was strikingly illustrated by the "decrees" of the Council of Jerusalem, which were by Paul and Silas delivered to the Churches in Syria and Asia Minor to be by them obediently observed. The individual Churches, indeed, were too few at that time, and too far apart, communications also were too rare and too difficult, to allow of a close organic connexion between them; but the spirit and tendency were altogether opposed to isolation, and in favour of the closest possible connexion of the Churches and union of counsel and authority in their government. The very troubles of the apostle in Galatia and Achaia arose, to a large extent, from the recognition by the Gentile Churches of a sort of natural primacy as belonging to the Church of Jerusalem and its rulers. It is true that St. Paul found it necessary to restrain this tendency and to assert his own co-ordinate apostolic authority. But he nowhere asserts or implies the independency of the several Churches. Rather he shows, in his Epistles alike to the Galatians and to the Corinthians, that there ought to be no discordance or disunion among them; that St. Peter and himself were associated in council and agreed in the same conclusions; that both were one in and under Christ; that there was and could be no disagreement in any essential or important point between Jerusalem and his own Gentile Churches.

The connexional union of Methodism is closer and more complete than could be the union of the Churches of distant regions in the apostolic ages. But such union is in strictest harmony with the spirit of primitive Christianity. So also the responsibility and power, with which Methodism invests its ministers, to take the lead in all evangelistic enterprise, to initiate Christian missionary effort wherever it is possible to make advances from the ground already occupied, is a point of organisation and discipline in which Methodism is in the strictest harmony with apostolic Christianity. The close mutual brotherhood, again, of the ministers, and their common responsibility for the appointment of their colleagues and successors, and for the exercise of moral and spiritual discipline over their fellows—these are points in which Methodism, more completely than any other form of Presbyterianism, carries out the original principles of apostolic Christianity.

In respect of the manner in which the laity are associated with the ministers of Methodism in administrative and in disciplinary functions, it is sufficient to claim that the spirit of the apostolic precedents is well observed in Methodism. The precise mode in which this point is kept in view and carried out has been determined by the growth and history of the Methodist Connexion. The manner of the growth and the facts of the history determined the law of the organisation. As in the primitive Church, so in Methodism, need and aptitude were the two factors which, from time to time, governed the steps of development and adaptation in the organic growth of the united community. The distinction between clergy and laity is one which had no application, no meaning, in relation to Methodism in the earliest stages of its history. Methodism was at first merely a Society, a sort of extended spiritual guild. As such, it was most effectively managed and governed. There were classes and class-leaders for spiritual fellowship; each local Society had its stewards, who took charge of the moneys contributed in the classes and congregations, and who saw to their proper distribution. When in the course of time the preachers, who had at first been merely lay helpers of the Wesleys, grew into the character of pastors, and when the aggregate Society or union of Societies developed into a Church, the leaders and stewards became the local Church council of each Society. The whole guild-system was, in fact, gradually transmuted into a Church organisation. The leaders and stewards were invested with disciplinary functions; they became a sort of diaconate, the stewards being godly men whose attention was mainly devoted to the secular business and responsibilities of the Church, the leaders being the class of deacons who, as assistants of the ministers, the "pastors and teachers," the "elders," were placed in charge chiefly, but not exclusively,[1] of the spiritual character and condition of the members. Official authority and position were thus founded on appropriate gifts and on service rendered to the Church; gifts and service were the qualification for official status and rights of government (1 Cor. xvi. 15–18).

Another sort of office in our Methodist Church—which some have regarded as a branch of the diaconal service, and others as the modern equivalent to the office of prophet in the early Churches—is that of lay or local preacher. There is in Wesleyan Methodism a distinct local preachers' Quarterly Meeting, over which the superintendent minister of each "circuit" presides. There are also for the "circuit" generally officers called originally "general stewards,"—now called "circuit stewards,"—who receive the moneys from the stewards of the various Societies. There are trustees of the chapels, and trustees' meetings; trustees, who are members of the Society, being also members of the Circuit Quarterly Meeting. All the Society and circuit officers are, according to the practice of the early Church, approved and appointed to office by the ministers, but approved and chosen also by the members of the meeting

---

[1] *I.e.* not to the exclusion of other than merely spiritual functions, Church finance and spiritual fellowship having always gone together from primitive and apostolic times onwards.

into which they are to be introduced; the ministers, on the one hand, and lay members of the meeting, on the other hand, possessing thus a separate power of veto, as well as the right of joint approval, in regard to every appointment. The administration of the spiritual affairs of each Society, or local Church, is vested in the leaders' meeting, and that of the general business of the circuit in the Quarterly Meeting, or collective assembly of the lay officers of the circuit. A circuit of a thousand members may be estimated, on an average, to have a Quarterly Meeting of not less than a hundred and twenty members. These powerful bodies invite the ministers, determine and raise their "allowances" (*i.e.* money payments), review all the interests of the circuit, and send resolutions to the District Synod or memorials to Conference. They have also the right to appoint a circuit jury of appeal from the findings and verdict of a leaders' meeting in certain cases of discipline. Moreover, in case of the enactment by the Conference of a new law, intended to be binding on the circuits and Societies, each Quarterly Meeting has the right of suspending, if it so determine, the operation of the law for one year, until it shall have been reconsidered by the Conference.[1]

The Conference itself—that is, the Annual Assembly which governs the whole Connexion—has, like the local organisations of the Connexion, grown into its present form and functions according to the suggestions of necessity or pressing convenience. The Conference cannot alter the "Rules of the Society," or the settlement of the chapels, or the provisions of the Deed of Declaration by which, in

[1] See Appendix C, on "Circuit Development in Methodism," for a succinct view of the development and functions of the circuit Quarterly Meeting.

1784, it was legally constituted and defined by John Wesley. Before that date, the Conference was the annual assembly of such of Wesley's preachers as he called together to take counsel with himself. In 1784 he gave it a legal constitution, and certain authority and rights in regard to the chapels of the Connexion and the appointment and disciplinary control of the preachers. These rights, and others with which the Conference has in various ways been invested, have received the fullest and most explicit recognition from the highest legal tribunals of the country. The Conference, at the present time, combines two functions: it is, in part, an assembly of co-pastors, annually meeting to exercise mutual discipline and to take mutual counsel in regard to such questions as are specifically pastoral subjects; and, in part, it is a conjoint assembly of ministers and lay brethren convened to receive reports and to deliberate and determine in regard to the general interests of the Connexion. All the points as to its order and method of procedure, and the classes of questions to be dealt with respectively in the two distinct but correlated sessions, are exactly defined. In the first capacity—as the assembly of co-pastors—it sits for about ten days in the second—as the assembly of representative ministers and representative laymen—for a week; the Conference being, throughout both terms of session, regarded as one continuous assembly. Between 1878 and 1890 (inclusive) the two sessions were consecutive. Now the representative mixed assembly occupies the intermediate week, the co-pastoral session meeting in the first and third week. The legal body which gives unity, and, in a sense, identity, to the Conference in both its sessions, is what is called the "Legal Conference," a body of one hundred ministers, constituted and perpetuated in virtue of the provisions of the "Deed of Declaration" already referred to, and which, as a matter of necessary legal form and solemnity, endorses and adopts what has been done in the sessions of the General Conference.

Intermediate between the Conference and the circuits of Methodism are the District Meetings, which are in effect provincial synods. These assemblies, which have been officially described and known as Synods since the Conference of 1893, were originally organised as Committees of the Conference, and, like the Conference, are, during the transaction of certain business,—what has been defined as properly pastoral business,—purely pastoral assemblies; while for all other business, and during its consecutive transaction, they are mixed assemblies; the circuit stewards, and, besides the circuit stewards, the specially elected representatives of the circuit quarterly meetings, the District treasurers of Connexional funds, and the lay members of District committees which have charge respectively of Chapel Affairs, of Sunday and Day School Affairs, of Home Mission Affairs, of Temperance, and of the District organisation of the Foreign Missionary Society, being members of the meeting for the transaction of all such business. At the pastoral sessions of the Synods the ministers exercise mutual discipline, including a strict enquiry into character and administration; they take counsel in regard to their common and also their respective pastoral responsibilities and duties, and the spiritual interests of their work; they conduct theological and pastoral examinations in regard to candidates for the ministry and probationers for the ministry provisionally accepted by the Conference. These are their pastoral responsibilities. In regard to other points of administration, the ministers and laity deliberate and act in common. The general religious interests of the work of the Church, including both the condition, spiritual and financial, of the circuits, and collective action on the part of the District as a whole, so far as that may be practicable, are considered in the full District Synod. These meetings are accustomed to send suggestions or recommendations to the Conference on the points which come under review. The Conference also is accustomed to remit questions for consideration to the Synods, nor can any legislation adopted by the Conference become binding law for the Connexion till it has been ratified by the majority of the Synods. The Synods are also courts of appeal from the circuits. To the pastoral session of the Synod appeals lie on questions of ministerial character or of discipline. The co-pastoral business of the Synod precedes and follows the financial and general business, which occupies in the largest Districts two intermediate days, but in small Districts only one.[1]

It is natural that such an organisation as that of which only the slightest possible sketch has now been given, should be regarded by persons outside the circle of Methodism as not only highly complex, which it is, but as artificial. It is, in fact, the product, not of art, but of experience; it is not a mechanism so much as a growth; it is not the creation of theory, it is no constitution or organisation *à la Sièyes*, first of all speculatively excogitated and committed to paper; it is, from first to last, the outgrowth of living work, and has developed, at every step, in response to actual and well-tested need. It is the result of the co-operative evangelical working of the most practical and

[1] See Appendix B, "The District Synod in Methodism."

successful Christian workers that modern times have seen. Complex, moreover, as it is, no serious difficulty is found in working it thoroughly out. There is less friction now than there was fifty years ago, when its complexity was not so highly developed as it is to-day. Above all, this Conferential system of Methodism, in its general plan and principles, with complexities similar and equivalent, if not the same, is at work all over the world ; and everywhere is working with a success which other communions confess and sometimes almost seem to envy. A great Church, indeed, cannot work thoroughly and effectively under modern conditions without becoming complex. Modern Presbyterianism is far more complex than early Presbyterianism ; in Scotland, especially, it has become a highly complicated system. The stage of simplicity is over also as regards the Church of England, alike in parish, in diocese, and in province. That Church is multiplying rapidly the details and infoldings of its organisation ; and if it is to meet the demands of its most earnest spirits or the requirements of the age, it must speedily develop new and larger and very bold measures of parochial, diocesan, and provincial or national organisation.

Of necessity Wesleyan Methodism is imperfect. Its working, too, is not without its inconveniences ; it has the "defects of its qualities." To only one point, however, of this sort can I refer in this general outline of a vast and manifold organisation. It is one on which, for some time past, there has been here and there a disposition to dwell. I refer to the Itinerancy.

In this case, as in other matters to which reference has been made, a special characteristic of the Wesleyan Methodist Church has grown out of the history of early

Methodism, and has become fixed and settled owing to the exigences of the system as worked in Wesley's time and under his own hands. To keep the system one, to preserve its integrity and its efficiency, it was necessary that Wesley should visit every part of it, and that his "helpers" should be at his disposal to go wherever there might be need of them. After he had established yearly Conferences of his preachers with himself, it became convenient that, in consultation with them, he should at every Conference assign to each of them the station where, unless some emergency arose calling for his removal, he might expect to labour for the following year. Wesley, however, had complete authority over his "helpers," and could at any time remove them from their station. They were, as a rule, men of little education; and at first it was found that twelve months was long enough for a helper to labour on one "round." Freshness and energy were pre-eminently necessary for the work they had to do. If, however, Wesley at first seldom retained them more than a year on the same ground, he sometimes brought them back again to the same ground after an absence of not more than two or three years. After some years had passed, however, more than a few of the preachers had so developed in character, attainments, and influence, that Wesley and his Conference judged it well to reappoint them to the same "round" for a second year. In 1784, when Wesley gave a legal constitution to the Conference, he concluded that it would be wise to give that body the power of appointing preachers to the same chapel or chapels for three years in succession, if the Conference should so determine, but not for more than three years. An exception was made in the case of ordained clergymen. Some clergymen, being beneficed, had been stationed on Wesley's *Minutes of Conference* to "circuits." Such "preachers" as these could not itinerate from circuit to circuit. Some clergymen, again, were fixed in London, that they might "read prayers," bury the dead, and administer the sacraments, at City Road and elsewhere. These also could not itinerate. It was therefore necessary to insert in the Deed of Declaration constituting the Conference, and giving it legal powers, a clause of exemption from the law of the itinerancy in the case of ordained clergymen stationed by the Conference. These cases, however, all died a natural death, in due course, after Wesley's own labours came to an end, and there has been no revival of them. For a century accordingly a rule of strict itinerancy has held good in the case of preachers "called out" and appointed to chapels or circuits by the Conference. Besides the century's usage, there is the legal obligation embodied in the instrument by which the Conference is legally defined and constituted, and in virtue of which it possesses the right of taking into connexion with itself and stationing ministers. This usage and obligation some ministers and laymen desire to break.

But though a considerable majority of the circuits and of the trustees' meetings might be in favour of such a change, so long as even a small proportion of the circuits and of the trust estates held out against it, the legal obstacles would be insurmountable. The opposition of only a few circuits to the change of a legal usage and requirement embodied in the Foundation Deed of the Connexion, and ruling unbroken for more than a century, would, I apprehend, be sufficient to prevent Parliament from giving any power to the Conference to alter the existing law; while it seems to be more than doubtful whether any power whatever, even the authority of Parliament, could be invoked to force upon a single opposing trustees' meeting a rule of administration in direct contradiction to the trust deed when no natural impossibility exists in the way of carrying out the deed. I am no lawyer, but I venture to think that the attempt, by whomsoever made, or on whatever authority, to appoint a minister for a fourth year against the will of the trustees to a chapel duly settled, would simply have the effect of detaching the chapel from the Conference and vesting the appointment of ministers in the trustees.

Fifty years ago, when I began to study this question, I was of opinion that, if practicable, it would be desirable, that a minister of not less than twenty years' standing, being the superintendent of a circuit, if invited from year to year to remain, might be at liberty to continue in a circuit for five or six years. I still think that, abstractly, there is more than a little to say in favour of such a view. But I have learnt in the interval that there is more to say against it than I had imagined; and my doubts as to the legal possibility of such an arrangement have indefinitely deepened and strengthened. There is, in fact, a widespread prejudice against prolonged terms. Change is popular, and is generally believed to be beneficial.

Meantime, the pressure of the inconvenience of frequent removals on Methodist ministers, as compared with the clergy of other Churches, is hardly so great as generally supposed. The average term of residence in the same charge among Congregationalist ministers does not much exceed three years. Among clergy of the Church of England, when beneficed ministers are left out of account, the average must be less; and as to the beneficed clergy, who may preach more or less frequently in their parish churches, according to taste or circumstances, and who have their curates by their side, the case is not parallel. If, instead of being Methodist itinerants, Wesleyan ministers had been Congregational pastors, unless their abilities had been of a very high order, they would have had to bear changes perhaps not quite so frequent, but under circumstances often far less satisfactory and hopeful, than is usually the case when Wesleyan ministers change their circuits. The removal of their books is doubtless a growing inconvenience; but every inconvenience to which the rule of itinerancy exposes them has its bright side.

It would, indeed, be an advantage if in all circuit towns there were ministers resident who had had time, as well as character and faculties, to become well-known and permanent powers in the neighbourhood. There are few who would not sympathise with the longings and aspirations of some of those who are in favour of the extended term. But, meantime, let us remember that there would be danger as well as convenience in any such arrangement. There are already divergences of tendency, even differences of tone and character, between circuits in one part of the country and circuits in another, between districts and districts, between town and country. An extension of the term of residence in circuits would tend directly to aggravate this serious evil, and to impair the unity of the Connexion. Where there is a common pastorate throughout a large Connexion of Churches, all of which are under obligation to observe the same discipline and expect to hear the same doctrine, and where that common pastorate includes hundreds of men, it is impossible to maintain a solid essential unity or the needful identity of organisation without the frequent and systematic interchange of pastors among the Churches; and such interchange can only be organised upon a principle of rotation or itinerancy such as this cardinal feature of our Wesleyan system. Of this system Wesleyan ministers feel the necessary inconveniences, but they do not know the difficulties, the frequent miseries, of the system of a settled ministry. How thankful would many a pastor be, and many a Church, outside of Methodism, if some effective form of itinerant arrangement could be applied in regard to their rule of demand and supply! And what other principle than that of the itinerancy could secure a minister from the danger of being unexpectedly left without a charge or any pecuniary resource?

CHAPTER III.

THE DISTINCTIVE ECCLESIASTICAL PRINCIPLES OF WESLEYAN METHODISM — COMPARISON WITH "REGULAR" PRESBYTERIAN CHURCHES — WESLEYAN METHODISM AND METHODIST SECESSIONS.

WESLEYAN METHODISM, in this respect like the British Constitution, is a highly developed example of the balance of forces; it abounds in mutual checks and compromises. From its earliest legislation after the death of Wesley, in which it recognised and adjusted the mutual rights of ministers and lay officers and members, of circuits or Societies, also, and the Conference, it has worked on this principle. Though, in many respects, it must be regarded as a form of Presbyterianism, yet, strictly speaking, it is neither Episcopal, nor Presbyterian, nor Congregational, but blends some of the characteristics of all the three communions. More popular than the first two, it is less democratic than the third. Yet, though less democratic, it is more pervasively and practically popular than Congregationalism. At the same time, its Superintendents, its Chairmen of Districts, and its Presidents of the Conference give to it some of the spirit and characteristics of Episcopacy.

The Episcopacy of the Anglican Establishment, like that of Popery, has ignored the laity in the ordinary conduct of

Church affairs; Independency is in danger of ignoring the ministers, as such. In the first, the clergy are the Church; in the second, they cease even to be a class. In neither is there any ordinary constitutional check to the abuse of power. In Wesleyan Methodism the scriptural prerogatives of the ministry and the legitimate influence of the people are made to limit and direct each other.

A saying of John Wesley, reported by Samuel Bradburn in his pamphlet entitled " Are the Methodists Dissenters ? " is sometimes quoted. What the founder of Methodism said, according to Bradburn's report, was that after his death Methodism would become a "regular Presbyterian Church." But it is evident that this reported saying cannot be strictly taken. Bradburn himself calls Methodism " mild Presbyterianism." Methodism is Presbyterian as opposed to prelatical Episcopalianism, and again as opposed to Congregational Independency.[1] But there are essential and profound antitheses in Wesleyan Methodism when it is compared with a " regular Presbyterian Church."

In the first place,—and I mention this point first because it is fundamental,—"regular" Presbyterianism, unlike Methodism, is not rooted and grounded in spiritual life and growth. Alike in Geneva and in Scotland, it was founded, as I have already shown, on citizenship. Even in the great Non-Intrusion controversy in Scotland, out of which

[1] "We are not Episcopalians," says Mr. Bradburn; " we cannot be. We are not Independents; we will not be. Therefore we *must* be Presbyterians, whatever we may choose to call ourselves." He also says, "Our Quarterly Meetings answer to those Church meetings in Scotland called the Presbytery; our District Meetings agree exactly with the Synod, and the Conference with the National Assembly." These are vague and general analogies. Much more minute and remarkable correspondences might be pointed out between the discipline and economy of the Friends and the Methodist economy.

the Free Church movement of 1843 took its beginning, the rights of the "heritors" bulked mainly in the contentions of the Free Church champions. Much was said, indeed, about the headship of Christ as against the claims of the temporal power in relation to the Established Church of the nation; but the question of the spiritual relation of the members of a professed Church of Christ to their living Head, of their personal union with Him, was beside the controversy. Nor to this day has the formal basis of the Free Church as to this point been changed. A doctrinal profession of faith, coupled with a reputable character, is the qualification for Church membership; and the community of such members, by a formal election, choose their minister and their lifelong "ruling elders," after receiving advice from the Presbytery or the Kirk Session as to the character and qualifications of the persons proposed for the offices that are to be filled. Not spiritual life, not spiritual fellowship, not spiritual gifts, spontaneously elicited and naturally unfolding into official service and consecration, constitute the basis of organisation and of official work and status, but the acceptance of a creed and catechism, and, as the qualification for office in the Church, a process which savours all too much of electioneering and its ordinary spirit and motives. It is not by imitating this precedent that the organisation of Methodism is to be improved. I would not have written this but that suggestions which have been extensively circulated among Wesleyan Methodists, have compelled me to do so. I am about to quote, as confirmation and illustration of the foregoing remarks, a passage I have lately met with in the biography of Dr. Lindsay Alexander, of Edinburgh, already referred to on a former page. In a conversation with one of the leaders of the Free Church party, on the eve of the Disruption of 1843, according to his own report, he expressed himself as follows: "I pointed out to him," he said, "the fine opportunity he and his friends had for lifting the subject above its merely ecclesiastical and political position, and making a bold effort to form a new Presbyterian Church on spiritual principles, and aiming at having a Church membership based, not on a mere profession of religion, but on personal piety; and I stated my conviction that, though by adopting this principle (which is a distinctive one among us Independents [1]) the seceding body would be numerically weaker than by taking over members of the Established Churches as they were, it would be infinitely stronger for all the high purposes of a Christian body and a branch of Christ's Church. My friend admitted the force of what I urged, for he sympathised with our views on purity of Church fellowship; but he said that that was a matter that could not be pressed at that critical time. They wanted first to get the people over to their side; and when they had them, they would do their best to raise the tone of spiritual life among them." Dr. Alexander added that, though the ministers got the people over from the Establishment, they found that the somewhat "mixed multitude" forming the new body did not in many instances prove so accessible to high spiritual influences and teaching as had been anticipated.[2] It is further stated as Dr. Alexander's view that "mere multitudinism" had, in too many cases, been inherited by the Free Church from the Establishment, and that "the move-

[1] *I.e.* in 1843.
[2] *Life and Work of Dr. Lindsay Alexander*, pp. 117, 118.

ment had become more ecclesiastical than spiritual." Such was, and continued to be, in the judgment of Dr. Lindsay Alexander, the defect of the Free Church of Scotland. Whatever reasons may be assignable to prove that, in the circumstances in which the Free Church and its leaders were placed, it was impossible to carry out Dr. Alexander's suggestions, or substantially to change the basis of organisation for the new Church, a point as to which I can venture no opinion, it is evident—and this is the one point now in question—that no analogy can be fairly drawn from the constitution of a comparatively formal and quasi-national Church, like the Free Church of Scotland, to direct us as to the basis of organisation in the case of a spiritual growth and organism such as Wesleyan Methodism.

The foregoing paragraph has not been written by way of censuring the Free Church, or for the sake of criticising Presbyterianism. Unfortunately an ill-considered cry has been raised that Wesleyan Methodism should be reformed into a regular Presbyterian Church. It is therefore necessary to show how entirely distinct and different in nature, genius, and tendency, is Wesleyan Methodism, regarded as a living organism, from "regular Presbyterianism." Methodism may be destroyed, but it cannot be transformed in the way suggested. Presbyterianism has its own grandeur, as shown in former chapters. The "Free Church" has carried out an impressive protest, founded on great principles. But the world cannot afford to have Methodism broken up or twisted out of its identity for the sake of a politico-ecclesiastical theory. True Methodism is a distinct species, and must be preserved pure in blood and true in form, or it will cease to be fruitful and multiply.

The community of the pastorate, again, in Wesleyan Methodism, coupled as it is with the strictly observed rotation and "itinerancy" of the ministers, is a radical distinction between it and any Presbyterian Church, a distinction far-reaching in its consequences. It is this principle in Wesleyan Methodism which renders fitting and necessary that mutual oversight of the ministers, that strictness of mutual enquiry, not only into character, but into the performance by each of his pastoral and disciplinary functions, which is a peculiarity of true Methodism. It is a case of strict partnership, and each partner is directly interested in the professional character and conduct of all the other partners, in their fidelity to the common covenant, and in the condition of that part of the common field of labour and responsibility of which each has charge for the time.

In "regular Presbyterianism," with its separate and permanent pastoral charges, there is nothing like this. Yet upon this community of the pastorate as its main basis rests the distinction, which is essential to Wesleyan Methodism, between the pastoral and the mixed or general sessions alike of the Conference and of the District Synods.

Furthermore, the Synods and Assemblies of the "regular Presbyterian" Churches consist, as shown in the chapters on Presbyterianism, exclusively of ordained office-bearers of the Church, of "teaching" ministers or elders, and of "ruling elders." Deacons were unknown in the regular Presbyterian Churches of Wesley's day, and are all but unknown in "regular" Presbyterian organisation to-day. Neither deacons nor lay representatives, *properly so called*, are members of the great Church courts of "regular" Presbyterianism; whereas in the assemblies of Wesleyan Methodism the true laity, in large variety of character and status, are united with the ministers. Being thus composed wholly of "elders,"—that is, of ordained Church pastors,—there was no distinction of of faculty or responsibility called for among the members the Presbyterian Synods and Assemblies. Even cases of theological heresy, it was natural to believe, would not unfitly be referred to the whole multitude of such presbyters of the Church, although many of them might not be teaching ministers, but only ruling elders. The experiment, indeed, has not served to demonstrate the fitness of such courts for trying cases of doctrinal heresy. The clamour, confusion, and violence attending on such trials, in many notorious cases, have afforded scandalous entertainment to scoffers, and have greatly grieved the godly. Nevertheless the theory on which the arrangement is based is intelligible. But it is altogether in contrast with the theory of Wesleyan Methodism, which, denying any radical distinction between teaching and ruling presbyters, reserves (so far, indeed, like Presbyterianism) the determination of questions of doctrine and discipline for the pastors (or presbyters) of the Church, but, to carry out this principle, common to Presbyterianism and itself, is compelled, in its large and mixed governing assemblies, to call the ministers together, apart from the other members of the Conference or the Synod, in order to deal with all such pastoral matters. It would be manifestly unfitting that, while the ministers alone submit to mutual and regular examination as to character in all their stated annual assemblies for purposes of administration and mutual consultation, the laity, themselves free from such examination, should take part in the disciplinary examination of the ministers in such assemblies. The absolute community of the pastoral relation, the relation of a common and coextensive pastorate to a common and coextensive flock, while it renders such mutual discipline necessary between the ministers, equally renders it necessary that they should hold their own distinct and separate pastoral council. In "regular Presbyterianism" none but pastors (*i.e.* presbyters or elders) can be members of any Presbytery, Synod, or General Assembly.

Nor are we even yet at the end of the essential distinctions between a Wesleyan Methodist and a "regular Presbyterian" annual Assembly, or Synod, constituted for purposes of formal ecclesiastical government. The itinerancy of Wesleyan Methodism compels the ministers to be removed from, and to be appointed to, their circuits or stations at the yearly meetings of the Conference. In such a case, for the ministers year by year to be stationed directly, and after discussion of their merits, by a mixed assembly of their brother ministers and of the laymen, who would be contending for some and against other ministers, or objecting against some and contending for other ministers, —*these laymen, too, being in many cases the authorities on whom the quality and scale of the ministers' maintenance would directly depend,*—would surely be an unseemly and injurious arrangement. Such an arrangement could not but lower the character and status of the minister, and place him in a false and intolerable position. It would, in short, be a degrading arrangement, quite incompatible with pastoral independence and self-respect, incompatible therefore with pastoral fidelity or efficiency. In a Presbyterian General Assembly there is no such work as this of "stationing" the ministers to be done. In short, the two cases are not parallel, but in contrast.

According to the view, indeed, held by such politico-ecclesiastical theorists as apply to the affairs of Christ's kingdom the extreme principles of democratic republicanism, the arrangement I have spoken of would be the "correct thing." These theorists hold the view which the good and wise Angell James so emphatically denounced, and which may in part have caused such writers as Dr. Wardlaw and Dr. Campbell to advance for the pastorate, by way of precaution or of protest, claims so much higher than any Wesleyan minister ever made, at least in writing. That view is, that the minister is no more than a "speaking brother," the paid servant of the Church which employs him as a preacher and manager. A principle in accordance with this view has, in fact, been embodied in the polity of some of the Secessions which, from time to time, have separated, after a protracted politico-ecclesiastical agitation, from the parent Wesleyan Methodist Church. But, as might have been expected, a principle which in theory is so inconsistent with all that is known of primitive Christianity, and which in practice could not but be so fatal to ministerial independence, has not proved successful in actual working. Successive agitations, originated always in the midst of political excitement and passion, and prosecuted in undisguised alliance with extreme political principles and movements, have had power to grievously disturb and divide the Methodist Church, have driven away many tens of thousands from her folds, but have not been successful in the organisation of such Secession Churches as have proved fruitful in gathering new converts to Christ. In 1797, in 1835 and the period immediately preceding, in the epoch marked by the year 1849, the Conference and the great majority of the Methodist Societies stood firm by the principles of primitive Christianity and of primitive Methodism as to the point of pastoral responsibility and pastoral duty. These same principles were sealed afresh by the happy settlement of 1876-7. Neither the Conference nor the people of Wesleyan Methodism are likely to depart from them now. It is true, indeed, that once again political influences of a disintegrating and extreme character are abroad; it is unhappily true also that there are some who seem to have set their heart upon transforming Wesleyan Methodism into a political organisation; and it is further true that during thirty years of profound peace the study of the distinctive principles of our connexional economy has fallen into neglect. But the lessons of history still remain; the principles of our own economy and of the earliest Christian Churches only need to be restated and enforced afresh; the essential spirit and aims, the vital sympathies and the governing tendencies, of both ministers and people in the Wesleyan Connexion, are essentially what they have ever been; there is no need to fear the result. Such a biography as that of Joseph Entwisle would just now be a seasonable book for ministers to read; while the *Life of Dr. Bunting* is full of instruction for all Methodists, and especially for those of the junior generation.

Political analogies, when applied to questions of Church government, must always, for reasons explained in the chapters on Congregationalism, be altogether misleading. But they are most of all at fault when applied to purely voluntary Christian Societies. It is one thing to give power and prerogative to clergy who, as respects both their ecclesiastical appointment and their maintenance, are independent of their flock, and quite another thing to concede prerogative to ministers who cannot retain their position except by the consent and goodwill of their flock, and are directly dependent on them for their support. It has often been a ground of hostile criticism on the part of the friends of Church Establishments, that the ministers of voluntary Churches, being pecuniarily dependent on their flocks, and especially on the wealthier official members of their Churches, are unable to exercise an honest and impartially faithful ministry. Where, besides the pecuniary dependence, the position of the minister is in other respects little else than that of a mere *employé* of the Church, this difficulty becomes exceedingly great and serious. It is true, indeed, that the "elders" are enjoined by St. Peter not to exercise their "oversight" or "bishopric" as "lords over God's heritage" (1 Peter v.). But it is equally true that the ministers are repeatedly spoken of as "rulers" in the Churches (1 Tim. iii. 5 ; Heb. xiii.); that the members are exhorted to "obey" them (Heb. xiii.); that they are described as called to "watch over souls as they that must give account" (*ibid.*); that it was not only their duty to "admonish," but might be, and in the case of the deliberately immoral, or in the case, after a first and second ineffectual admonition, of the factious and unruly, would be, their duty to "reject" members of the Church (1 Thess. v. ; Titus iii.). Such passages as those now cited cannot, of course, be held to imply that all discipline was to be carried out personally by the elders or ministers, without any proper process or due order; but it cannot mean less than that the pastor must have a special responsibility in regard to the conduct and discipline of the Church, and special rights of initiating enquiry and securing the due enforcement of discipline. It would scarcely warrant the exalted claims of the Congregationalist authorities quoted in a former chapter, but it is utterly incompatible with the theories which have been deliberately and explicitly adopted as the basis of the "Methodist" organisations referred to.

Richard Watson thoroughly understood this question. He was a man of large views, and of generously liberal tendencies. He left the Wesleyan Church to join the "New Connexion" at one period of his life, but, after a few years, retired from that Connexion, and returned, as a private member, to the "old Connexion." Some time afterwards he was received again into the ministry of the Wesleyan Church. He was not betrayed into any reactionary views as the result of his experience. Breadth, candour, moderation of view, distinguished his writings and all his opinions to the end of his life, especially as to questions of ecclesiastical government. But he wrote with the insight, the discrimination, and the force of one whose experience was exceptionally large and various, whilst his intellect was peculiarly acute and comprehensive. The following passage, on the point as to which I am now writing, appears to be eminently worthy of attention:

"The only view in which the sacred writers of the New Testament appear to have contemplated the Churches was that of Associations founded upon the conviction of the truth of Christianity and the obligatory nature of the commands of Christ. They considered the pastors as dependent for their support upon the free contributions of the people, and the people as bound to sustain, love, and obey them in all things lawful—that is, in all things agreeable to the doctrine they had received in the Scriptures—

and in things indifferent to pay respectful deference to them. ... A perfect religious liberty is always supposed by the apostles to exist among Christians; no compulsion of the civil power is anywhere assumed by them as the basis of their advices or directions, no binding of the members to one Church, without liberty to join another, by any ties but those involved in moral considerations, of sufficient weight, however, to prevent the evils of faction and schism. It was this which created a natural and competent check upon the ministers of the Church; for, being only sustained by the opinion of the Churches, they could not but have respect to it; and it was this which gave to the sound part of a fallen Church the advantage of renouncing, upon sufficient and well-weighed grounds, their communion with it, and of kindling up the light of a pure ministry and a holy discipline, by forming a separate Association, bearing its testimony against errors in doctrine and failures in practice.

"In places where now the communion with particular Churches as to human authority is perfectly voluntary, and liberty of conscience is unfettered, it often happens that questions of Church government are argued on the assumption that the governing power in such Churches is of the same character, and tends to the same results, as where it is connected with civil influence, and is upheld by the power of the State.

"Nothing can be more fallacious, and no instrument has been so powerful as this, in the hands of the restless and factious, to delude the unwary. Those who possess the governing power in such Churches are always under the influence of public opinion to an extent unfelt in establishments. They can enforce nothing felt to be oppressive to the members in general without dissolving the Society itself."

"The true view of the case," says the same writer, "appears to be that the government of the Church is in its pastors, open to various modifications as to form; and that it is to be conducted with such a concurrence of the people as shall constitute a sufficient guard against abuse, and yet not prevent the legitimate and efficient exercise of pastoral duties, as these duties are stated in the Scriptures."[1]

The connexional character of the Wesleyan Methodist Church affords special facilities for dealing with such difficulties in regard to the mutual relations of ministers and flock as some that have been glanced at. The minister is sufficiently dependent on his present flock to make it inconvenient and perilous for him to show anything like arrogance or impropriety in his conduct among them, or to "lord it over the heritage" (1 Peter v. 3); and yet, as one of a wide brotherhood, and as in relation with a wide sisterhood of Churches, he is never so dependent as to make fidelity on his part endanger his livelihood and the prospects of his family. In the case of differences, moreover, between himself and his present flock, both parties have the power of appealing to Connexional arbitration, if necessary, for relief or redress.

The position of the pastorate in Methodism in regard to cases of Church discipline is distinctly defined and happily balanced. It is in perfect accordance with the view given by Mr. Watson, and in particular with the last sentence quoted from that able and judicious writer. The minister is regarded as not merely the pastor of the Church, whose calling it is to feed his people with spiritual knowledge and instruction and to watch over their souls, but also,

[1] Watson's *Institutes*, part iv., chap. i.; *Works*, vol. xii., pp. 187-191.

to quote the *Liverpool Minutes*,[1] as a "Home Missionary," who is to lead in all the wise and fitting ways of Christian enterprise and Church extension. He is to be at once captain and shepherd, evangelist and pastor.

Being in this full sense called to the Christian ministry, he is, as already intimated in the general sketch of Methodist polity and organisation given in the preceding chapter, surrounded and sustained, and at the same time guided and informed, by various bodies of official helpers. Of these the chief, in addition to the Quarterly Meeting, are, as already explained, the local preachers' quarterly meeting, and the leaders' meeting, which should, as far as possible, meet weekly. As to this cardinal part of Wesleyan Methodist organisation, the leaders' meeting, a few more words than I have already said may fitly come in here.

The leaders' meeting is, for the particular Society to which it belongs, the court of discipline and the local council of the general pastorate, that is, of the "ministers of the circuit." The stewards, usually two for the Society fund towards the general expenditure of the circuit for the support of the ministry, and two for the local poor's fund, constitute a true diaconate for the departments which they represent. The leaders are the helpers of the ministers in regard to the personal spiritual instruction and discipline of the Church members, the members of the local Society; they also collect and pay in to the Society stewards the contributions of the members in their several

[1] See Dr. Williams's *Constitution and Polity of Wesleyan Methodism*, Appendix III. The document there printed, which is known as the *Liverpool Minutes*, is an admirable compendium of the pastoral duty and proper work of a Wesleyan minister, which, having been drawn up mainly by Dr. Bunting, was adopted by the Conference of 1821, and has since been regarded as one of the chief standards of the Church.

classes towards the ordinary expenditure of the circuit. Each leader meets weekly, for the purpose of close spiritual fellowship, a class of the "Society," or local Church, each class consisting usually of from ten or twelve to thirty members, ten being an undesirably small number, and more than thirty undesirably large. Some, in support of the spurious analogy between Wesleyan Methodism and regular Presbyterianism, have compared the class-leaders to ruling elders and the leaders' meeting to a Kirk session. The comparison, however, is more than inexact: it is misleading. The differences between the office of class-leader and that of ruling elder are important and indeed essential. The ruling elder stands in formal and explicit relation to the whole Church to which he belongs, and is solemnly ordained to his office. He is one of the presbyters of the whole Church, a co-presbyter with the minister.[1] Whereas the Methodist class-leader has the spiritual undercharge of a fractional part of the Society, which Society is itself only a part of the whole spiritual community of which the ministers of the circuit are the pastors. The class-leader is not ordained as a presbyter or pastor of the Church, and stands in relation to the local Society only in so far as he is a member of the leaders' meeting, that being the ministers' council for the Society. The ministers of the circuit themselves are the co-presbyters both of the circuit and of each local Society included within the circuit, there being two or more ministers in a duly organised circuit. Each minister presiding for the occasion over a leaders' meeting has ministerial colleagues or co-pastors, who usually preside in their turn, while, on the most important occasions, the co-pastors may be present together at the leaders'

[1] See Knox's *Liturgy* (Glasgow University Press, 1886).

meeting. The leaders, accordingly, are not presbyters or co-pastors, but form a spiritual diaconate of the highest value and efficiency. Their classes are visited each quarter by a minister of the circuit, who at that time gives notes of trial for Church membership to those recommended by the leader, and gives or renews " tickets " of Church membership to those fully received into " the Society." [1]

A leaders' meeting is a much more numerous meeting, in proportion to the number of Church members represented in the Society, than a Kirk session is in relation to its Kirk or Church, and, unlike that meeting, is not purely pastoral or presbyterial. Moreover, as the stewards are every year changed or re-elected, it is frequently refreshed by changes in the *personnel* of its members.

This meeting is the council of the circuit ministers in regard to the spiritual condition and all the spiritual affairs and enterprises of the local Society, and is also the disciplinary court of the Society. No member, it need hardly be said, can be put away from the Society by the mere prerogative of the minister. Every member, before he is separated from the Society, or, for any cause, ceases to be recognised as a member, can claim a trial before the leaders' meeting, which is to pronounce, by the verdict of a majority, as to the guilt of the accused member, in respect to both the fact charged as an offence, and the meaning and intent of the law he is charged with having violated. When a verdict of guilty has been given, it is provided and enacted that a week's interval must elapse before sentence is pronounced by the superintendent minister of the circuit, after consultation with his co-pastors. In all cases there lies an appeal against the sentence from

[1] See letter of Wesley's at the end of this chapter.

the superintendent to the District Synod, and in the final resort to the Conference. There is nothing in Wesleyan Methodism that commands more confidence than its disciplinary arrangements and its appellate jurisdiction.

The essential distinctions, as to the pastoral office, between the principles of the Wesleyan Methodists and of Congregationalism, have already been indicated in the chapter on Congregationalism. And the essential *differentia* which distinguishes between the constitutional principles of Wesleyan Methodism and those of the Methodist Secessions already referred to, and of which I shall speak more particularly in another chapter, is, that these Secessions have adopted, at least in part, the fundamental principles of Congregationalism, and have endeavoured to amalgamate them with a connexional organisation. The resulting amalgam is of necessity full of theoretical inconsistencies and practical incongruities and dilemmas.

The position of the minister in the leaders' meeting, including pastoral prerogative in cases of discipline, was one of the points on which Alexander Kilham and his followers in 1797 separated from the Conference. They adhered in principle to Kilham's radical republicanism as applied to Church organisation and administration. The minister was to be the servant in all points of the majority of Church members. They made the principle of decision by majorities of Church members, of whatever age or stage, a fundamental law and force in their organisation. In the leaders' meeting the minister was merely the chairman, with no pastoral prerogative whatever. From time to time their original contention in 1797 in regard to the minister in the leaders' meeting was revived by the successive agitations, all founded on similar political principles and analogies, which disturbed the parent Connexion. The last argument on this subject of which I have knowledge was closed in 1852 by a pamphlet of admirable masterliness from the pen of the Rev. W. Arthur. From that pamphlet I quote a few sentences. " That, after a member of the Church was convicted of offences, the minister was to administer or to omit ecclesiastical discipline at the dictation of the majority, is a principle which the Methodist Conference has never adopted; but, on the contrary, the Conference of 1797, on which that principle was urged " [by the founders of the " New Connexion "], " perspicuously guards, in every one of its documents, the freedom of the minister in dealing with proved trangressors; and the discontented of that year felt that this freedom was held inviolate. But in maintaining this, that Conference did give to the people a just and powerful check against its abuse, by providing that no minister should have power to exclude a member until the leaders, on a hearing of the evidence, had solemnly pronounced his crime proved. The leaders are judges of the fact and of the guilt, the minister is responsible for the sentence:—this was the constitutional balance established in 1797; and this is the constitutional balance maintained at this day. . . .

"As to whether Christian ministers ought or ought not to place themselves under the direction of the majority, and to administer their Master's law on *proved transgressors* according to the command of the majority, that is quite another question. You honestly believe they ought; I honestly believe they ought not."[1]

[1] *Has the Conference Broken Covenant?* By William Arthur, A.M. 1852. As to the leaders' meeting, and its relation to the discipline of the Church, see Appendix A at the end of this volume.

Such is Wesleyan Methodism, and such are the main principles on which it is founded. They are, as I believe, in harmony with the essential principles of primitive Christianity, although they are in contrast with the ecclesiastical principles of Congregationalism, and are only in partial agreement with the economy and discipline of "regular" Presbyterianism. They are, moreover, in harmony with the whole spirit and history of the Methodist revival from its beginning hitherto. The Congregational postulate, that all power in the Church of Christ is derived from the Church members, and that all authority and movement must rightly emanate from their majority decisions, is opposed to all the experience of Christ's work as carried on by John Wesley and his followers. It is as contrary to the history of Wesley as it is to that of St. Paul, or to the records of the primitive Church. And if we leave the personal history and acts of Wesley, and regard the history of the Wesleyan Conference, it is no less in contradiction to its whole course. The case of Wesleyan Methodism is, in fact, as respects both history and theory, the precise reverse of that of Congregationalism. In Independency the Church exists before the minister; the minister holds his pastoral office directly from the people. Whereas in the Wesleyan Connexion it is quite otherwise. There the Connexion of circuits depends, and has ever depended, on the prior union of ministers, and the existence and maintenance of individual circuits on the prior existence of the Connexion of circuits; the Societies, again, being the mutually associated parts of the circuit, on which, as a whole, they are severally dependent for government and direction. The united Conference, from the first, has been to Methodism the central directive body, possessing a collective authority and oversight over the whole.

It is, of course, always a question of delicacy and difficulty to decide what checks and limits should be placed upon the pastoral authority in any Church, how difficult may be conceived from a remarkable saying of Dr. Dale's saintly predecessor at Birmingham, in the first edition of his book on *Christian Fellowship.* " The tyranny of a minister," he goes so far as to say, "has some shadow of excuse in the circumstance of his being invested with an office the duties of which are not defined with accuracy; but the tyranny of a Church over their pastor is without apology, as they have no office, and therefore no power." This is a very strong utterance, and if it had come from the pen of a Methodist minister, it would have been quoted by some people as evidence of the arrogance belonging to such a system as Wesleyan Methodism. I may fairly quote it, however, although Mr. James omitted it from the later editions of his excellent little book, as an illustration of the difficulty of defining the just limits of ministerial prerogative. Even from among the ministers of the New Connexion, a voice is occasionally heard which shows how hard it is for any earnest preacher and pastor to accept a position of mere subservience, to consent to such an obliteration of all specific official prerogative as the theory of the New Connexion involves. The Rev. S. Hulme, writing, apparently by authority from the New Connexion Conference, an address to the members of that Connexion, dated September, 1846, after half a century of New Connexion history, uses such words as these: " The same spirit has betrayed itself in withholding from ministers the respect to which their character and office scripturally entitled them. The *authority of the pastor, as the ruler of the Church,* has been reduced to *a mere name*; he has often been left to struggle alone, or, thwarted and dispirited, he has sunk into indifference."

The general principle, however, may be safely laid down —a vague principle, it is true, but not on that account worthless—that, as far as possible, in the spirit of apostolic Christianity, the people shall, in all matters of Church regulation and discipline, be taken along with the ministry. The voice of brotherly love persuades to this; Christian equity requires it; sound and provident policy prescribes it.

But then it must also be borne in mind that the extent to which it is possible for the people thus to be united in administrative functions with the ministers must vary according to varying circumstances.

"For example" (if I may be allowed to quote here what I have written elsewhere), "it will be admitted by all that it would be simply absurd to give to a newly gathered Church of South African troglodytes, or Ceylonese treelodgers, or Australian savages, the same powers and functions which have been exercised by the Church of a Jay or a James in England. It would be an unchristian farce to do this. Such untutored children of the wild must be informed and trained before they can be prepared to take any part whatever in Church discipline, or possess any share of ecclesiastical authority. Now these extreme cases prove the principle. And scarcely less sunk in brutal ignorance than the African negro, or less savage than New Zealanders, were some of the converts gathered into Church association by John Wesley a hundred years ago.

"But, in proportion as the laity of a Church advance in intelligence and the discipline of Christian culture, it is fit and right that they should be taken into closer and more frequent association with the ministry in Church counsels and decisions. Many men in many Churches are eminently fitted to tender advice, and to add authority, in questions and decisions connected with ecclesiastical regulation and administration. And it is the duty of the Church to use, and to find scope for, every faculty possessed by its members."

It is on this principle that the development of the Wesleyan Methodist organisation has proceeded since the death of Wesley. In 1795 the pastoral rights of the minister were settled, in response to the urgent representations and solicitations of the Methodist people. In 1797 the fundamental rights of the laity in relation to the ministers and of the Circuits in relation to the Conference were determined. For nearly half a century afterwards, as is shown in Dr. Smith's *History of Methodism*, and still more fully in the *Life of Dr. Bunting*, there was a steady development of lay power and influence, in connexion especially with the District Committees, the Connexional Committees of Management, and the annual Committees of Review, this development having been chiefly guided and worked out under the master-hand of Dr. Bunting, who, until the feebleness of age began to touch him, and many cares and trials had abated his energy, was the great and the truly liberal and progressive leader in Connexional organisation. In 1852, after the agitation of 1849–1850, Dr. Beecham and the Rev. John Scott led the way in further adaptation and development, bringing the laity into larger, closer, and more influential association with the ministers in the counsels and administration of the Church. This process was continued without break, in accordance with the growth in all respects of the Connexion, until the happy and all but unanimous settlement of the definitive concordat and constitution of 1877, practically inaugurated at the Bradford Conference of 1878, of which I had the honour to be the President, and which determined in detail the respective functions of the ministry and laity in the Conference and in the Committees of the Connexion, and the relation of the Conference to the District Synods and to the Circuits. Since that epoch the same process has steadily continued, the new development having been built upon the foundation laid in 1877.[1]

At present, accordingly, the laity have a most influential position in Wesleyan Methodism. At the hazard of some slight repetition, let me here sum up the case.

In regard to all matters except such as the Connexion at large, under the lead of its most distinguished laymen, and throughout all its Circuits, has agreed and resolved with unanimous accord to recognise as bound up with the proper and common pastoral responsibilities of the united pastorate of the body, the laity are joined in equal numbers and on equal terms with the ministry in the supreme representative body of the Connexion, that is, in the Conference during its representative session. The laity are also and analogously united on equal terms, and in more

---

[1] I have referred above to Dr. Smith's *History of Methodism*. That invaluable work, however, only brings the history of our Connexional development down to 1860. For a view of what has been done since, I must refer to Dr. Williams' *Constitution and Polity of Wesleyan Methodism*, to my own volume on *The Connexional Economy of Wesleyan Methodism*, and to the successive yearly volumes of the *Minutes of the Conference*, all of which publications may be obtained at our Connexional Book Room. The present order of Conference procedure, in its two sessions, the Pastoral and the Representative respectively, is printed yearly in the *Minutes of Conference*. See also Appendix B on "The District Synod in Methodism, an Historical Sketch," and Appendix C on "Circuit Development in Methodism."

than equal numbers, with the ministers in the District Synods of the Church. No new law can be enacted formally by the Conference which has not received the sanction of a majority of the Synods. The circuits, besides, have the right, severally, of suspending for a year the operation of a new Connexional law.

All the Society and Circuit officers who act with the ministers as a diaconate—*i.e.* all the leaders and all the stewards, whether local or general—are nominated by the ministers, with whom they have continually to act, and whose confidence they ought to possess, but must be elected by a majority of the meetings to which they respectively belong. In regard to the appointment of laymen to other offices, the ministers as such have no special right of nomination.

In the administration of ecclesiastical discipline the minister is, as we have seen, bound to act upon the verdict of the leaders' meeting; and although the power of censure, suspension, or excision finally rests with him, it is surrounded by such checks and guards, that he is in little danger of acting harshly or rashly in any instance. The danger now is undoubtedly in the other direction—lest he should find himself too feeble and dependent to exercise necessary discipline in the Church. It is, no doubt, possible that he may, in some instances, fall into the opposite fault of haste or extreme severity. But this is much less likely than that an irresponsible majority of lay officers should do so. And if the minister does wrong, he is not only personally and alone responsible to public opinion, and dependent upon that opinion, to a considerable extent, for his comfort and respectability, but he is directly responsible to the superior Connexional courts, the impartiality and resolute justice of which have been repeatedly evinced.

There are two points, however, the alteration of which would be the destruction of Methodism. The constitution of the Legal Conference is fixed by law, and could only be altered by statute. The system of Methodism, furthermore, is so adjusted in all its departments to this leading fact, that it could not be altered, even if the law would permit, without bringing confusion, discord, and imbecility into the whole working of the system. And the ministerial prerogative in the government of the Societies has been reduced to the minimum compatible with ministerial responsibility either in enterprise or in discipline, and especially, in respect of discipline, with fidelity to Christ and His law. The supremacy of the Conference is, of course, a primary postulate in a Connexional system such as that of Wesleyan Methodism.

NOTE *to page* 251.

WESLEY himself, in his ripest experience and while his judgment was as clear as ever, settled in his own way this question as to Methodism being or being destined to become neither more nor less than a regular Presbyterian Church. Mr. Pawson, one of his elder preachers, an excellent man, but not on the whole a strong man, had allowed Glasgow Methodism to be adapted in some measure to the ideas of the national Presbyterianism. His successor at Glasgow was Jonathan Crowther, the elder minister of that name, to whom, in reply to a letter asking for advice, Wesley addressed the following characteristic letter:

CORK, *May* 10, 1789.

MY DEAR BROTHER,—"Sessions"! "elders"! We Methodists have no such custom, neither any of the Churches of God that are under our care. I require *you*, Jonathan Crowther, immediately to dissolve that session (so called) at Glasgow. Discharge them from meeting any more. And if they will leave the Society, let them leave it. We acknowledge only preachers, stewards, and leaders among us, over which the assistant in each circuit presides. You ought to have kept to the Methodist plan from the beginning. Who had my authority to vary from it? If the people of Glasgow, or any other place, are weary of us, we will leave them to themselves. But we are willing to be still their servants, for Christ's sake, according to our own discipline, but no other.

JOHN WESLEY.

It is a point to be noted in this letter, that Wesley speaks of the Methodist Societies and circuits as " Churches," " the Churches of God that are under our care."

CHAPTER IV.

AMERICAN EPISCOPAL METHODISM.

IRISH emigrants, as might perhaps be conjectured, were the means of introducing Methodism into the American Continent. This was about 1766. Three years later, two of Wesley's preachers, Richard Boardman and Joseph Pilmoor, volunteered, in response to an appeal made by Wesley himself at the Conference then in session in Leeds, to go out as missionaries to America. They went out, not knowing how they were to be supported, or what was to be their sphere of work. Wesley and his preachers made a collection at the Conference to pay their passage-money; the collection amounted to £70, of which £50 went to pay the personal debts and outfit of the missionaries, and £20 for their passage-money and expenses. In 1773 there were 1,160 "members of Society" and seven preachers. Two years later the War of Independence broke out. When the war was over, and America had become an independent republic, the crisis came which determined the character and form of American Methodism. Wesley sent out Dr. Coke as superintendent,—as bishop, in fact,—having first, by a special ordination, himself appointed him to that office, in order that he, in turn, might ordain Francis Asbury elder and bishop, and that Coke and Asbury might be to American Methodism what Wesley, assisted of late years by Coke, had been to English Methodism. Wesley put into their hands, for the use of the newly created independent Methodist Church in the United States, a Methodist Service Book, including a form of liturgical service for congregational worship, and liturgical offices for all Church ordinances and functions,— ordination, among the rest, both to the office of elder and of bishop,—and containing also an abridged and reduced collection of Articles of Religion, twenty-five in number, founded on the Thirty-nine Articles of the Church of England. Thus Wesley may be said to have constituted and organised the Methodist Episcopal Church of America. At that time, it is estimated, the number of Church members was 18,000, with 104 itinerant preachers, besides local preachers and exhorters.

That Church was thus created (*sit venia verbo*) just in time to fill up a great void in the Church conditions of America, and by so doing to secure for itself a vantage-ground, of which its genius as a Church and its organisation enabled it to make the best and most. The Church of England quitted the rebel States, and abdicated its great position in the central seaboard States; Methodism succeeded to its primacy in that region. Methodism, which, from the first, had found a congenial soil in Maryland, now took deep and strong hold of Baltimore and all the territory to which that city was a key. Baltimore, from that time till now, has been the greatest stronghold of Methodism in the States. In the neighbouring State of Pennsylvania it presently obtained a firm footing. From Maryland it easily made good a powerful position in Virginia. Its itinerant system —so precisely adapted to a boundless and sparsely settled territory—and its free and easy methods enabled it to follow the settlers everywhere, to speed westward with the swiftness of an arrow-flight, to surmount the Alleghanies themselves, keeping abreast of the most daring emigrants, and to take possession of Kentucky and the Indian border of those days. Thus Methodism became the religion of pushing, pioneering American settlers, and has retained to this day not a little of its original pushing and pioneering character. Chiefly, no doubt, its adherents have belonged to the English and the Protestant Irish sections of the population. Among Scotch settlers Presbyterianism has often and naturally blocked it out. Converts among Irish Catholics were not wanting, they were much more numerous in proportion a hundred years ago than now; but the great majority of the Catholic Irish have clung to their own religion. During the last forty years, Methodism has taken a wide and powerful hold among Protestant Germans. In New York city Methodism had found its earliest lodging-place; but the Dutch and German Reformed Churches have from of old been very strong there, and the Irish Catholic element has long been perniciously powerful, so that, in that city, Methodism has never been relatively influential.

In the great State of New York it is much more powerful. In Congregationalist New England, with its old Puritan civilisation and culture, it won its way slowly, and even now has not, by any means, a foremost position. But it is the great middle-class Church of the United States— far larger, more animated, more energetic than any other.

In its Church organisation and government it stands apart from all other Churches. Whilst it retains the stamp impressed upon it by Wesley, it nevertheless offers strong contrasts to the Wesleyan Methodism of England. In the spirit and character of its government and administration it is far less popular, far more clerical. It is, said Dr. Ninde at the first Œcumenical Conference, " not undemocratic, but it is thoroughly militant." In fact, it has always been too aggressively and restlessly militant to be democratic. It has more alliance with the administrative genius of the Church of England than has English Methodism.

It started with a Conference as in England, which was to have been to American Methodism what the Annual Conference was to Methodism in England. But the necessities of space and time made it impossible for the Conference to meet annually. Accordingly, after comparatively few years, it became the rule for the Supreme Conference to meet once in four years ; minor or sectional Conferences meeting at first occasionally and irregularly, but afterwards annually. Thus for four years the bishops were always left in supreme administrative power without any paramount Conference to interfere with them, by way of limitation, regulation, or revisal of their acts. The bishops, moreover, —Coke and Asbury,—for seven years ran a course parallel in America to that of Wesley in England, and too far from him to be really under his authority. They, in fact, administered Methodism in America as he had administered it in England—that is to say, on their own authority, consulting with the ministers they stationed and ruled, but exercising strong authority over them, while, as to government or organisation, the laymen had no place. Laymen, indeed, led classes or preached as they were appointed ; but they did not crystallize into conciliar organisations or Church courts. The English leaders' meeting was not—it could not be—established in America, with its sparse population and vast interspaces. As a consequence, quarterly meetings, in the English sense, were never consolidated, though Quarterly Conferences, or, as we might say, " Conventions," were held by the itinerants in their circuits. The English division of the whole Church and its territory into Districts, under itinerant and annually elected Chairmen, with District Committees of the Annual Conference,—an arrangement which may be said in a certain sense to have Presbyterianised English Methodism on a basis of universal ministerial equality,—was not created in England till 1792, when American Methodism was already well started on its special and distinctive course of development. From the necessary conditions of the work, the English District system could not have been adapted to American Methodism. In America the English "superintendent" of a circuit developed into a "presiding elder" with his "district"; his subordinate colleagues being appointed to work under his direction in circuits and stations. These subordinate itinerants held the "Quarterly Conference" of their circuits or stations when the presiding elder was not able to be present. Once a year the presiding elder met his subordinates in the "Annual Conference" of his "district," a purely ministerial or pastoral assembly. It was the rule for a bishop to preside at these Annual Conferences, which embraced two or more districts, thus meeting, to guide and to govern them, the presiding elders and their subordinate colleagues. The bishop, taking counsel with the presiding elders, fixed the stations of the ministers from year to year, of the presiding elders with the rest.

The first General Conference was held at Baltimore at the Christmas of 1784, on the arrival of Dr. Coke from England with Wesley's commission. Coke presided at the Conference, he ordained Asbury; and Coke and Asbury were recognised as bishops, though styled for a short period superintendents (ἐπίσκοποι). There was not another Conference held till 1792, and of that gathering no minutes are extant. After 1792 these General Conferences were regularly held every four years. In 1812 the General Conference became a "Delegated Conference,"—it was henceforth an electively representative assembly,—and met under constitutional restrictions, which gave it the character of a new organisation. It still remained a purely pastoral assembly. Its constitution was not essentially altered till 1872, when laymen were, for the first time, admitted into the General Conference, the Annual Conferences, which had become very numerous, and covered the whole territory of the States, being still unmixedly pastoral assemblies, and remaining such till now. The bishops, in rotation, have from the first presided over the General Conferences.

The foregoing is a slight outline of a grand and wonderful development, to which belongs a history full of heroic episodes, of singular and often of thrilling and romantic interest. Dr. Stevens' *History of American Methodism* will well repay the attention of every student of the world's progress, and, in particular, of the making and progress of the great American Republic. This outline will also serve as an introduction to the more particular account of the distinctive features, as compared with English Methodism, and the recent modifications, in its more modern development, of American Methodist organisation.

It will be understood, from the preceding sketch of the earliest development of Methodism in America, that when, in 1784, Wesley launched American Methodism on its independent course, he took the only effective plan for such a country as America then was—an aggregate of vast territories with an exceedingly scanty population dispersed over them, separated by a wide and formidable ocean from the mother-country, and quite independent of it. He appointed bishops or (as he for modesty would have had them called) *superintendents*, who were to rule and organise the Societies, and whose functions as rulers and organisers closely resembled those which he had himself exercised over the Methodist Societies in England. Such a superintendent or bishop was Dr. Coke in his relations to American Methodism. Such, emphatically, was Bishop Asbury, who, in many respects, may be regarded as the Wesley of American Methodism, who was almost as autocratic a ruler as Wesley, and not less apostolical and devoted in his character and labours. Asbury's successors were men largely of the same spirit, and continued to rule the Societies with a sway almost as absolute. The stationing of the ministers, the settlement of circuit boundaries, and all administrative or disciplinary questions of any difficulty, were in their hands. In a new country, made up of immense mission-fields, fields often separated by vast trackless interspaces, and where only a spirit of heroic courage and enterprise could grapple with the hardships and difficulties of the work, only such men could have led the way to victory, and such men could not but be rulers of almost absolute and unquestioned authority. The bishops, and under them the ministers (or *elders*, as Wesley taught the Americans to call them, with a happy adaptation to the conditions and ideas characteristic of the American States), inherited, in fact, all the ruling and disciplinary functions which in England had belonged to Wesley, and, under him, to his "assistants"; and how absolute these were we know well. They inherited them, and used them in regions where there were very few towns of any size, and where democratic ideas of Church government, such as prevailed in some parts of England, had no existence. The character and development of Methodism were formed and determined among the solitary homesteads, the lonely hamlets, the forest trysting-places, where the adventurous Methodist rider, the itinerant with his saddle-bags, found his way, and where often he was the only visitor from the world of social intercourse and general intelligence that reached spots so sequestered.

The itinerants, accordingly, in America possessed an authority and supremacy, among the members whom they gathered into classes and Societies, even more complete and more unquestioned than ordinarily belonged to the early Methodist preachers in England, high as their prerogative was, and only expressly limited, for the most part, by the power of appeal to John Wesley. The same conditions which made Asbury and his earliest episcopal associates or successors so great and almost apostolic in their authority and sway, made their leading itinerants proportionately powerful. The "assistant," as Mr. Wesley called him, the "superintendent," as in England the chief minister of a circuit was called after Wesley's death, became in America a magnified and exalted ruler of the Societies scattered over vast regions of wilderness. He was distinguished as the "presiding elder," and he exercised a powerful and peremptory sway over his province. He was within his "District" much what the bishop was in the Annual Conference and in visitation. Imagine a very wide, an immense country circuit in England, worked in sections; imagine a quarterly meeting organised for each section, to provide maintenance for the minister or ministers there stationed; imagine the whole put under the charge of one superintendent, who visits and holds each sectional quarterly meeting, and maintains the harmony and unity of the whole circuit. We have here a small and faint outline of the work done by the presiding elders of early times, and which is still done in the remote Western States and Territories of the Union. The presiding elder's District might embrace a whole State, or even more. The bishops, Asbury and his successors, itinerated through the whole Church, presiding at all the Annual Conferences, and thus preserving its unity. The presiding elder, a sort of diocesan under-bishop, itinerates through the whole of his District. The resident minister in each of the stations which the presiding elder visits is a comparatively insignificant person.

In England it is the collective and representative Quarterly Meeting of the circuit—where all the Societies are represented by their leaders and stewards, and all the chapels and trust property by the trustees, where all the ministers of the circuit are present, and all the local preachers have a place—which forms the bond of union for the whole circuit. In America it is the presiding elder alone who maintains the unity of the District through which he travels and which he rules. There is nowhere any representative assembly answering in its character and relations to the English Quarterly Meeting. Neither has the presiding elder any District Assembly to which he stands in necessary official relation, and which corresponds with an English District Synod. There is, in short, nothing in American Methodism corresponding to the all-important District Synods in English Methodism, held in September and May, through which, under the Annual Conference, the unity of the Connexion is maintained. How completely the authority of the presiding elder absorbs—we should perhaps better say effaces—all such ministerial authority on the part of the ministers stationed within his District as, according to English Methodism, would belong, in connexion with each quarterly meeting and the constituent Societies, to the resident superintendent minister and his colleagues, will be evident from the description which the *Discipline* of the American Methodist Church gives of the functions of the presiding elder.

It is his duty to "travel through his District," and "to take charge," except when a bishop happens to be present in the course of his vast itinerancy, "of all the travelling ministers, local preachers,[1] and exhorters in his District"; to change, receive, or suspend preachers in his District, during the intervals of the (Annual) Conferences, and in the absence of a bishop; "to be present, as far as practicable, at all the Quarterly Meetings"—there being, as I have said, one such meeting for each station included within the District; to hear complaints and to receive appeals; "to oversee the spiritual and temporal business of the Church in his District"; to take care "that every part of our discipline is enforced in his District."

Two items more of the presiding elder's duties ought to be mentioned. He is, by a rule made in 1840, "to decide all questions of law pending in a District or Quarterly Conference, subject to an appeal to the" bishop or presiding elder who shall be "President of the next Annual Conference," and (this rule was made in 1844) he is "to report to the Annual Conference the names of all travelling

---

[1] This term includes "located ministers"—"elders" who no longer itinerate, or who have been ordained as local pastors with a strictly limited authority.

preachers (*i.e.* itinerant ministers) within his District who shall neglect to observe the rules."[1]

This powerful and greatly prerogatived minister—who is in very truth a diocesan bishop, but with more power than any such bishop possesses outside of the ancient "Catholic" Churches—is stationed and changed entirely apart from any authority or concurrence of either any other ministers or any representatives of the circuits or the laity, by the bishop who visits his Annual Conference. The presiding elder cannot, however, hold office in the same District for more than four years at a time. Each Annual Conference usually includes in its jurisdiction two or more presiding elders and their Districts. These purely ministerial councils—these Conferences—are considerably more than a hundred in number.

Although the presiding elders are not the mighty functionaries they were sixty years ago, in the heroic ages of Methodist enterprise and extension in America, they are still a wonderful and a most potential order of ministers. I find in the *New York Christian Advocate* for January 7, 1875, a letter addressed to presiding elders by the late Bishop Peck, whose "ruling" faculty will be remembered by all who attended the sittings of the Œcumenical Methodist Conference at City Road, in 1881 ; a few sentences from that letter will bring vividly before us what it still is to be a presiding elder in American Methodism.

The bishop says : " Your twelve to forty charges must all be supervised. The spirit and power of the preaching, the constancy and spirituality of pastoral visitation, the thoroughness of paternal discipline, the care of the children, due atten-

[1] Compare Sherman's *History of the Discipline*, p. 170.

tion to all the great Connexional causes, the enlargement of the work, the proper support of the ministry, other current Church expenses, and even Church book-keeping, must all come under your careful observation." And again : " You are not presiding elders of the District, so much as of the people in the District. This brings us to the pastoral character of the presiding eldership." Again : " This is the great desideratum in the pastoral superintendency : time enough with the people to thoroughly know the work. Form your plans wisely, and see them executed." He presently proceeds to give them advice founded on his own experience as a presiding elder ; he recommends a " method, which," he says, " I have thoroughly experimented. Place the Quarterly Meetings in groups, which will require about four weeks each, more or less. Bid good-bye to your family for the whole time. As soon as the public meetings are over "—*i.e.* the meetings held in connexion with the Quarterly Conference—" move socially and religiously among the people, using evenings, as far as your strength will allow, for special meetings." After more in the same vein, he goes on to describe how the presiding elders should train the people among whom they move : " You will come to know for yourself about the financial condition of your brethren ; gradually educate them in missionary intelligence and demands ; teach them much concerning our educational interests. . . . In short, you will gradually lift them out of local ideas into a great general Churchship; and hence nothing which you or the stationed minister shall present to their support will be new to them."

The whole view derived from the passages quoted justifies the description already given of the presiding eldership as a vastly magnified superintendency, of the sort known in

England a hundred years ago, but wider and larger still, modified in its organisation to meet the requirements of stations scattered so far apart, and extending collectively over so immense an area; an office endowed with prerogatives far more searching, sweeping, extensive, and peremptory than at any time have belonged either to Wesley's assistants or to the superintendents of Methodism since the times of Wesley.[1]

It must be noted, at the same time, that, however insignificant is the authority and responsibility of the "preacher in charge," when compared with that of the presiding elder, yet, on his own station, within a limited sphere, and in the absence of the presiding elder, he has considerable and unshared power. By his nomination he appoints the leaders and stewards. The leaders' meeting has no prerogatives whatever: it is not, as in England, the council of the pastorate, nor is it a Church court. In the two *Histories of the Discipline* which I possess, both of them of high authority, I find in the very full index the word "class-leaders," and the heading, "appointed by the preacher," but the phrase "leaders' meeting," or any equivalent to it, is not to be found in Bishop Emory's *History*, and only occurs once in Sherman's *History*. There are leaders, every member's name stands on some leader's list, although there is no visitation of the classes by the minister in charge. The minister in charge is instructed, " wherever practicable," to hold a meeting of the leaders and stewards.

---

[1] In the columns of the *New York Christian Advocate* for April 9 and May 14, 1896, Bishop Walden has at great length set forth a view of the office of presiding elder in strict agreement with that given by Bishop Peck. He frankly speaks of the office as that of a "diocesan bishop."

This is described as a Board Meeting; and is supposed to meet quarterly. But there is no official leaders' meeting in the old Wesleyan Methodist sense. In the *Notes on the Discipline*, by Dr. Coke and Bishop Asbury, the date of which is 1796, leaders' meetings are recognised, —such as were known in early Methodism,—and the value of them to the preachers in their pastoral work is noted. But that is the last heard of them till 1868, when an attempt was made to revive them in the way just described, as pastoral aids to the minister in charge. No attempt is made to give the meeting any disciplinary authority, or any necessary organic or constitutional character. The meeting may recommend probationers to be admitted into full membership in the Church, and persons to be licensed as exhorters or preachers within the limits of the station. All else done is the furnishing of useful information to the pastor.

It is abundantly evident that American Methodism has been, much more absolutely than English Methodism, the creation of the pastorate, of the indefatigable itinerant pastorate, the riding preachers. "Local preachers" have had much less to do with the work than in England. We read of local preachers attending the Quarterly Conferences, but of these a large proportion are locally ordained deacons or elders, or else "located elders,"—*i.e.* elders who have itinerated for some years, have settled down in business, usually to farming, as the only way of making due provision for their families, but have still continued to preach and perform other ministerial functions as they may be able. Of these located elders, some, having secured the competent provision they needed, afterwards resumed itinerancy. When all the classes and varieties of local preachers, however, are taken together, their aggregate number is less than that of the itinerant ministers (elders and deacons). There has been such an immense and continually growing demand for preachers to enter the itinerancy, that the young local preachers or exhorters, if they combined in any fair degree competency with zeal, have been absorbed into the itinerant work as fast as they gave evidence of their gifts. Thus, as I have said, American Methodism has been, in a direct and special sense, a pastoral creation.

If for a considerable period American Methodism had been confined within narrow limits around Baltimore and Philadelphia, and thence had worked its way by comparatively slow degrees wherever fair-sized towns were established, with a fringe of townships or hamlets around them, it might have developed in a way more nearly resembling the development of Methodism in England. The original Rules of Wesley, sustained and expounded by the *Notes on the Discipline* of Coke and Asbury, would have tended in this direction. There would then have been leaders' meetings watching over concentrated Societies; and there would have been Quarterly Meetings of the circuits, in which meetings the leaders of the Societies and the stewards of the leaders' meetings would have formed the chief constituents. But the rate at which "the saddle-bags" followed through the forest, over the mountain, across the prairie, "the rifle and the axe" of the settler, fixed another law of development for the Church. The ubiquitous bishop, whose flight was wonderfully swift, and whose movements, made as he liked, were so mysterious, whose visits were welcomed as those of a celestial guide and teacher, and the daring, devoted, heroic presiding elder, whose work and whose qualities made him an absolute leader and disciplinarian, these carried Methodism over the whole land, and what, under Providence, they had thus created, and were still creating, the people looked to them and to no other, to rule and preserve. Among a simple and primitive people this patriarchal economy was the only one possible. Hence, when, towards the end of the decade which began with 1860, public attention at length woke up widely to the wonderful spectacle of a vast Church in the American Republic entirely and absolutely governed by its clergy, there was, for those who believed in lay rights, plenty of ground for criticism.

Not that there had been no stirrings at an earlier period against the existing condition of things. Between 1820 and 1830 there was agitation on the subject of lay rights, and in 1830 the "Methodist Protestant Church" was founded on a basis of lay representation in government and without bishops. That Church, however, has made slow progress, and remains an insignificant community in point of numbers, although it has counted able men among its clergy. For twenty years after that secession the question rested. Then again began an agitation on the subject. The agitators were fairly and kindly met. But for ten years and more the great body of both ministers and people remained adverse to the movement. In 1860, however, some able ministers placed themselves at the head of an organised movement for bringing about lay representation in the General Conference. Some leading laymen united themselves with these ministers, the movement having its headquarters, as might have been expected, in the older States, and especially in Congregationalised New England and Presbyterianised New York. The result was the adoption in 1872 of the plan of lay delegation which still holds the ground, but which the late Dr. Perrine[1] maintained, and not a few distinguished ministers and laymen have agreed and do agree with him in asserting, was a mistaken way of effecting the lay co-operation that was needed.

After all, however, it was but a veneer of lay conjunction and co-operation which was laid upon the surface of the system in 1872. The spirited and impressive lay development of office and influence which had long been established throughout English Methodism—in the circuit Quarterly Meetings, in the two annual District Synods of the Church, in the Managing Departmental Committees, in the Committees of Review, as these had been organised for many years before the admission of laymen into the English Conference in 1877-8—had no equivalent or parallel in American Methodism. In Dr. Perrine's book a passage is cited from the *New York Independent*, which contains a true description and criticism, though no doubt a tart and unfriendly one,—as was natural considering the quarter from which it came,—of the constitution of American Methodism, *after* lay delegation had been adopted by the General Conference of 1872:

"It is dimly believed by the uninstructed that the adoption of the principle of lay delegation by the Methodists gave to the laymen of that denomination some practical share in the administration of Church affairs. That belief rests, however, upon very slight foundations. To the Annual Conferences, where all the important work of the

---

[1] See *Principles of Church Government*, by the late William H. Perrine, D.D., arranged and edited, with a Review of the Lay Delegation Movement in the Methodist Episcopal Church, by James H. Pott, D.D.

denomination is done, they have not been admitted. When the session of the Annual Conference, which is held previous to the meeting of the General Conference, is assembled, a lay electoral convention, composed of delegates from the several Churches, is called at the same time and place. The laymen meet by themselves, and elect delegates to the General Conference; then, commonly, a place is made for them in the room where the Annual Conference is in session, and they walk in and are addressed by the bishop, to whom one of their number responds, after which they withdraw, and the work of the Conference, which has been interrupted by this interesting episode, proceeds. Their only relation to the working body of the Church consists in their being permitted, while the Conference is in session, to march up the aisle and then march down again. In the General Conference, which meets once in four years, and which is the law-making body of the Church, the laymen will have a voice; in the Annual Conferences they have neither part nor lot."

So far the Independent critic. But then we must bear in mind that, on the principles of Independency, the American continent could never have been covered with Christian Churches. The Methodist Church advanced under the command of its bishops and elders, who sped like apostolic missionaries over all the land, who appointed elders and deacons, and who at once led and ruled. The Independent Churches, each apart, were governed by their stationary ministers and deacons. The results of the two methods were that Independency, established in the oldest and leading States a century and a half before Methodism, having hold of the two ancient and distinguished universities, Harvard and Yale, possessing learning, and training, and social influence, and by far the strongest political position and the highest popular prestige in the Union, has sunk to a fourth-rate place among the Churches, while Methodism has become by far the greatest aggregate of Churches and Church members in the American nation.

There are, nevertheless, some weak points in American Methodism. One is the absolute dependence of the whole Church for the maintenance of its energy and unity on the presiding elders. Let the well-considered words of the experienced Bishop Peck, who knew perfectly what he was writing about,—words, part of which I have already quoted,—be pondered, and they will be found to be almost ominous, to be seriously alarming. The bishop is addressing the presiding elders. He speaks of them as " knowing how indispensable is this bond of union between the Churches, how suddenly and inevitably without this we should drop apart into a confused Congregationalism, how impossible it would be for the larger connexional bond"—he is referring to the episcopal order—" to grasp the charges, excepting as they are grouped and bound indissolubly by this subordinate superintendency"—that is, by the presiding elders, who are superintendents subordinate to the general superintendents, which is the definition of the bishop's office given in the early *Discipline of American Methodism.* Here, then, the bishops and presiding elders are represented as the sole and absolute upholders and guardians of the unity and the whole discipline of the Church. But for them, and especially but for the presiding elders, the Methodism of the Church would at once come to an end, its connexional character would be destroyed, its discipline would be dissolved, it would "suddenly and inevitably drop apart into a confused Congregationalism";—vigorous, definite, decisive words; the words of one who had a complete mastery, in principle and in detail, of all that related to the economy of his Church. The Church of England is not more dependent as its bond of union on the bishops, and is less dependent for its discipline on its archdeacons and its rural deans, than the American Church is for both on its presiding elders, acting under its bishops. In this country Methodism is not similarly dependent on any order of its ministers. The development of lay co-operation in English Methodism, and its general Presbyterian, rather than Episcopal, character, save Wesleyan Methodism in this country from any similar dependence on a paramount executive order of ministers. It is not so dependent on its superintendent ministers. They have ministerial colleagues, who form a brotherly council, by their side, and who in the District Synods are their equals ; these together, and not the superintendent alone, officially represent in the Quarterly Meetings the discipline of the Connexion. And the entire Quarterly Meeting, under the presidency, but by no means under the personal control, of the superintendent, and including a numerous body of lay officers, leaders, local preachers, stewards, trustees, gathered from all the Societies of the circuit, maintains the union of the Societies and the identity and continuity of the collective whole. Each Society, again, is maintained in its integrity, not by any minister, but by its leaders' meeting—its meeting of leaders and stewards— presided over by one of the ministers. The District Synod, again, is not, in English Methodism, a mere assembly and council of the ministers of the District, preserving, by their clerical or ministerial coherence and union, the integrity and unity of the Church within its boundaries, as in America the purely clerical Annual Conference, presided over by one of the bishops of the Church, maintains, and alone maintains, the union and unity of the Church within the boundaries of the Conference. In the Methodist District Synods of England, all the circuits are represented by their chief lay officials, while a large organisation of District Committees, composed equally of ministers and laymen, has charge of all the departmental interests of the Church. The chairmen of Districts, it need scarcely be added, have no such powers or predominance as the presiding elders. They are little more, often nothing more, than moderators of the Synods and general advisers to their brethren when appealed to.

If the presiding eldership were done away, Bishop Peck says that American Methodism would fall asunder "into a confused Congregationalism." There would be left the stations, now almost always solitary stations, and the pastors of these stations, with a number of class-leaders, sometimes merely nominal, and with a register of members, attendance at any time at class being no condition of enrolment or continuance on the class-list, but with no quarterly or systematic visitation of the registered members, with no official spiritual council or assembly of any kind, with not even the possibility of a Church meeting in the strict and spiritual sense of elder evangelical Nonconformity. That is what the bishop meant by a "confused Congregationalism." When Bishop Peck published his *Letters to Presiding Elders* in the "great official" journal of American Methodism, formidable agitation was going on against the institution of presiding eldership, which was defeated not without a severe struggle at the ensuing General Conference (1876). Happily it was defeated, at least for the time.

Nevertheless, the fact of such an agitation could not but direct attention to the peril of having no other defence, except that of the threatened order, against such a calamity as the dissolution of American Methodism "into a confused Congregationalism." Nor is it without significance that the assault on this vital institution, the presiding eldership, proceeded from the same sections of the country in which the movement for lay delegation had originated which brought about the new constitutional settlement of 1872. Confused Congregationalistic ideas had influenced the movement which had its headquarters in Congregationalistic New England between 1860 and 1872. And Congregationalising tendencies originated and sustained the agitation against the presiding eldership which filled bishops and conservative Methodists with just alarm between 1872 and 1876.

The view given in the preceding pages will have shown that a fundamental reform in the direction of bringing the laity of the great Methodism of the States into official recognition and into distinct co-operation as partners with the clergy in respect to the legislation and administration of the Church was unquestionably necessary. Our English ideas and experience would have taught us that such official co-operation, and such frank recognition, should have begun much earlier, and in the first instance much lower down in the organisation—in the leaders' meeting, in the presiding elder's District, in the Annual Conference. As, however, this had not been brought about, it is not surprising that in 1872 it was determined at once to make a place for lay delegates in the General Conference of the United States. This alteration was made seventy years later than the first admission of laymen into the District Meetings of English Methodism, and much more than a generation after the managing departmental Committees of Review, preliminary to the Annual Conference in England, had been organised, in which ministers and laymen bore their part, in equal numbers and with identical official position and functions. What was done was, indeed, as I have already said, very like veneering the official organisation with a lay film on the surface; it still left the underlying arrangements as they have been described; it left the whole body of the Church, for all ordinary and working purposes, absolutely in the hands of the clergy, save for the influence of lay opinion; it left the Church open to such criticism as that which has been quoted from a Congregational critic. But it was nevertheless a great stroke, and it might have been consistently followed by other and more pervasive reforms. The mere abolition of the ruling eldership, which threatened to be its immediate sequel, would not have been reform, but dissolution and destruction.

The whole system of lay co-operation, as developed in English Methodism during the present century in Leaders' Meetings, Quarterly Meetings, District Meetings, and Mixed Committees managing and controlling every Connexional department of activity, a system culminating for many years in the Committees of Review, preparatory to the Conference, and now for eighteen years past in the mixed representative session of the Conference, has had no equivalent in American Methodism. It was under such circumstances that the agitation for lay representation in the quadrennial General Conference, at the centre and supreme place of legislative authority and appellate jurisdiction, took form and gathered force during the decade following the General Conference of 1860, and that lay delegation was introduced into the General Conference in 1872. In other respects, throughout the entire body of the vast Church, and from one General Conference to another, the whole organisation remained in all important respects as before, and has been similarly administered by its pastoral executive of bishops and presiding elders.

The plan of constitutional reform by way of admitting lay delegates to the General Conference was formulated and presented first to the General Conference at Chicago in 1868. As the principle of lay delegation involved a distinct departure from the constitutional platform of principles which had, since 1808, been recognised as the basis of the organisation and polity of the Church, it could not constitutionally be adopted without the consent of three-fourths of the members of the Annual Conferences, which at that time numbered seventy-two, nor, even after such consent, without a majority of at least two-thirds in the General Conference. The principle, accordingly, was submitted to the Annual Conferences for their vote thereupon. It was also directed that meetings should be called in every presiding elder's District of all the Church members within the District, and the principle submitted to these meetings. What was submitted, however, to the Annual Conferences and to the people, was, as Dr. Perrine seems fully to prove, *not the plan* which had been submitted to the General Conference, but only *the principle* involved in it. That principle was, that laymen in certain proportions for each Annual Conference should be elected, at Electoral Conferences of Church members called for that purpose, and should in some way be associated with the ministers as members of the General Conference. But in what precise way that association should take form and effect was, the highest authorities held and declared, left an open question. There was, in fact, a very general agreement among the ministers themselves as to the principle, whilst as to the plan actually submitted there was considerable diversity of opinion.

In regard to one point, however, anticipatory action was taken by the Conference of 1868, which, for want of full explanation, tended to confuse the ideas of both ministers and laity as to the position of the question. In anticipation of an affirmative response from the ministers assembled in the Annual Conferences as to the principle of lay delegation, and to prevent a further delay of four years before the principle could be carried into effect, the Conference directed that lay delegates should actually be elected by the lay Electoral Conferences, so that they might be ready to take their places in the General Conference, as soon as, the principle having first been adopted, the plan also of association and union between the ministers and the lay delegates in the business of the General Conference should have been agreed upon.

Bishop Simpson, with whose views agreed also such authorities as Bishop Ames and Bishop Janes, thus stated the case as it stood in the interval between 1868 and 1872: "It was admitted by all that the last General Conference [1868] had not *enacted* any plan, but only *proposed* it, and that the last General Conference had no power to bind the next." He said further: "If three-fourths of the numbers of the Annual Conferences should vote for the alteration of the rule, it could not be accomplished until two-thirds of the ensuing General Conference should concur; that no part of the plan submitted could go into effect except the election of the two lay delegates (for each Annual Conference) as prescribed, before the next General Conference. That before their admission into General Conference, not only must the rule be altered, but a plan for their introduction and duties must be enacted; then a vote must be had on their formal admission." This was Bishop Simpson's exposition of the law and statement of the situation, when presiding at the New Hampshire Annual Conference. In that Annual Conference the requisite three-fourths proportion was not found agreeing even with the principle of lay delegation. The vote in favour was sixty-eight to twenty-five. In the Michigan Conference, also, it appears that the votes were ninety-four to fifty. On the whole, however, the votes cast throughout the seventy-two Conferences showed a very few more than the requisite three-fourths majority, and thus the principle of lay delegation was affirmed by the suffrages of the ministers. It remained for the Conference of 1872 to settle the plan.

The plan, as submitted in 1868, and as adopted and acted upon in 1872, was as follows:

"The lay delegates shall consist of two laymen for each Annual Conference, except such Conferences as have but one ministerial delegate, which Conferences shall be entitled to one lay delegate each.

"The lay delegates shall be chosen by an Electoral Conference of laymen, which shall assemble for the purpose on the third day of the session of the Annual Conference, at the place of its meeting, at its session immediately preceding the General Conference.

"The Electoral Conference shall be composed of one layman from each circuit or station within the bounds of the Annual Conference, and on assembling the Electoral Conference shall organise by electing a chairman and secretary of their own number; such laymen to be chosen by the last Quarterly Conference preceding the time of its assembling; provided, that no layman shall be chosen a delegate either to the Electoral Conference or to the General Conference who shall be under twenty-five years of age, or who shall not have been a member of the Church in full connexion for the five consecutive years preceding the elections.

"At all times when the General Conference is met, it shall take two-thirds of the whole number of ministerial and lay delegates to form a quorum for transacting business.

"The ministerial and lay delegates shall sit and deliberate together as one body, but they shall vote separately whenever such separate vote shall be demanded by one-third of either order; and in such cases the concurrent vote of both orders shall be necessary to complete an action."

At the General Conference of 1872, the assent of the Church having been given to the principle of lay delegation, the important question to be considered should have been, so Dr. Perrine argues, and so Bishop Ames and other men of distinguished ability thought at the time, in what plan that principle should be embodied. Others, however, held that the vote of the Annual Conferences and of the people had carried the plan as well as the principle; while a larger number, even though they might concede that the question of the plan was before the Conference for its consideration, were nevertheless of opinion that the question was ripe for settlement without any more discussion; that public opinion had, in fact, declared itself in favour of both the principle and the plan, and that the sooner a vote was taken, with however little discussion, the better would it be for the Church. The chief leaders of the movement, who had, four years before, committed themselves to the plan which the General Conference had agreed to submit to the Church " for consideration," naturally urged that the matter should be pressed strongly forward, and settled without delay. Meantime the lay delegates, already elected by the Electoral Conferences of the laity, were present at the doors of the General Conference—were in the galleries of the hall at Brooklyn, where the Conference was meeting—and were awaiting the decision of that body.

It is true that other plans, besides that which it was agreed in 1868 to submit to the consideration of the Church, had been proposed, and among others one formulated by no less an authority than Bishop Ames, which, in its principle, agreed with Dr. Perrine's ideas, and which would have made the General Conference to consist of two assemblies, one ministerial and the other lay, each presided over by a bishop, the lay assembly taking its own part in " all matters except such as relate to ministerial administration and character," concurrence and mutual consent on the part of both assemblies being necessary to the determination of all questions of general legislation. But there was no disposition, on the part of the leaders of the movement, to discuss the merits of any plan. They regarded the one which they had proposed at the previous General Conference as the plan in possession, and they were determined, having a majority, to force a vote upon it without delay

They knew that, with the lay delegates present as spectators and auditors, few, even of those who would have preferred more detailed consideration, would like to vote against the plan, if they were obliged immediately to vote *Ay* or *No*.

Bishop Simpson had announced that of the ministers voting in the Annual Conferences, to the number altogether of 6,512, besides four who did not vote, 4,915 had voted for the admission of lay delegates, whilst 1,597 had voted against it, the number of affirmative votes being thus twenty-eight more—and only twenty-eight—than the necessary three-fourths of the whole number of ministers, *viz.*, 4,887.[1] Thereupon a skilfully drawn minute was submitted, the effect of which was to ratify and adopt the plan, as embodying the principle which had been sanctioned by the votes of the ministers in the Annual Conferences. "We shall not attempt," says Dr. James H. Potts, the editor of Dr. Perrine's writings on this subject as contained in the volume from which I have quoted, " to describe the scene, far less record the resolutions offered and speeches made, which followed this adroitly worded paper. The haste and excitement, the indisposition to hear the remarks of any opponent of the ' plan,' were not creditable to a body of Christian ministers called to deliberate upon the weighty matters of the Church."

Eventually, it was ordered that two votes should be taken, one on the *principle*, the other on the *plan*. The first was carried almost unanimously, the votes being two hundred and eighty-three to six, and three abstaining from voting. The second vote was the one which related to the debatable points. The closure, how-

[1] $\frac{6512}{8616} = \frac{3}{4}$.

ever, or, in American parliamentary phrase, the "previous question," was at once called for and voted by the majority, after which the vote being taken showed two hundred and fifty-two for and thirty-six against the motion. It only remained to move that the roll of laymen should be called, and they be admitted to seats in the General Conference. This was carried by two hundred and eighty-eight to one— Dr. Perrine being the solitary dissentient. All this was done on the first forenoon of the Conference. The scene which followed may be much better imagined than described —the excitement, the tumult, and the inrush, from galleries and upper side aisles or passages and lobbies, of the lay delegates who had gathered from all parts of the Union to the vast Assembly Room at Brooklyn, and had been waiting in intense expectation for this result — for the vote and the admission. The prevalent feeling, however, doubtless, on the part of both ministers and lay delegates, and of the whole Church, was one of profound thankfulness that the Church had been preserved from serious or permanent division, and that a great principle had been carried with general consent, and so as to promise well for the continued unity of the vast Church to which they all belonged. So much as this must be confessed on all hands, and even by those who, like Bishop Ames and Dr. Perrine, could not agree that the conjunction of the laity with the ministers in the Conference had been accomplished in the best and wisest way. Here let me add that the clerical delegates—for the quadrennial General Conference had from the beginning, in 1808, been a Conference of Delegates, *i.e.* of ministers elected by the Annual Conferences — numbered two hundred and ninety-two, whilst the lay delegates were only one hundred and twenty-nine, considerably less than one-half.[1]

Dr. Perrine's argument against the actual plan of lay delegation embraced three chief points, which, however, rather underlie his argumentation than are categorically defined and set forth. Of these the first is that it was unfair to the laity, who were compelled to be always in a decided minority in the Conference, who could never frankly and thoroughly discuss questions as a body of laity, holding distinctive relations, as such, towards the clergy, and who could not call for a separate vote freely, and after fitting discussion among themselves, or without the danger of exciting jealousy or mistrust. The second point is that it was also unjust to the clergy, inasmuch as they, holding a special and distinctive call and commission from the Head of the Church, and underlying peculiar responsibilities to their Divine Master, ought to have the opportunity of mutual conversation and discussion on any question raised which affected their proper duties and responsibilities, ought to meet and take counsel together as the representatives of the common pastorate of the Church; whereas, under the existing constitution, not only are they debarred from exercising this needful right of their ministerial calling, but they are unable even to call for a separate ministerial vote without the danger of exciting more or less of suspicion and ill-feeling. He further contended, and on this branch of his argument he bestowed not a little labour, that for a great community such as the Methodist Church to be governed by a single assembly, was contrary to the recognised principles of high statesmanship and to the constitutional basis of principle on which the govern-

[1] Sherman's *History of the Discipline*, p. 63.

ment of the Union itself is established, and, in the interests of equity, wisdom, and good government, ought not to continue. He would, for these reasons, substitute for the one mixed assembly two assemblies, one ministerial and the other lay, so combined and mutually related, as, with the bishops, to constitute one General Conference.

The second of these points of argument rested on principles which had been recognised and acted upon in American Methodism more fully, more absolutely, and in a more unqualified form than in any other Protestant Church in the world. The whole statesmanship of the Church had been ministerial—clerical. The whole power of legislation and discipline, as of executive and administration, had been vested in purely ministerial assemblies. Nor is it to be supposed that vague and crude writing about the universal priesthood of believers, such as Dr. Perrine severely criticised, had revolutionised the ideas or effaced the instincts and habits derived from Asbury and his coevals, which ninety years of government by bishops and presiding elders, in Annual Conferences and the General Conference, had confirmed and developed. It was no doubt assumed that, with loyal laymen in a comparatively small minority as members of the General Conference, and with the power of separate voting on any critical question, the essential requirements of the case were met in harmony with the traditions of the past. It was a first attempt in the way of introducing lay co-operation in the government of the Church; the problem had not been calmly or thoroughly studied; the plan was drawn up in haste, and never really discussed. The difficulties which experience revealed had not been seen beforehand.

In all that relates to such comparisons and discussions

as have been under consideration, the important and far-reaching differences between English and American Methodism must, no less than their fundamental points of agreement, be kept in view. The English Annual Conference combines in its range of responsibilities all that belongs to the numerous Annual Conferences of America, and also what has been legally devolved upon it as the General Conference of English Methodism by Wesley's Deed of Declaration and by all the history of the past. The American General Conference, on the other hand, is the great legislative council and appellate court which, relieved of the immediate functions and responsibilities of the Annual Conference discipline and enquiries, meets once in four years to pass laws and hear appeals connected with the administration of a Church of more than continental dimensions, and including considerably more than a hundred Annual Conferences—a Church which might almost be called the National Church of the States, counting its ministers by thousands and its members and hearers by more than a few millions.

No wonder that, in view of the range of dominion belonging to such a General Conference, coupled with the fact that it meets but once in four years, thoughtful and far-seeing men like Bishop Ames, Dr. Perrine, and Dr. Buckley should wish for the security of a "second chamber," for the mutual checks and guards of "two houses." The Conference meets during one month in four years, and only meets for legislative purposes during short morning sittings. The afternoons and evenings are occupied with committees and public services or assemblies of some kind. Even the whole of the forenoons cannot by any means be always given to points of legislation or appeal. Business from all the Annual Conferences—more than a hundred—and from all departments of public administration, domestic and foreign, has to come before the General Conference. Rarely, if ever, in recent years, has the whole business properly belonging to the Conference been transacted. Sometimes the Conference session is brought to an end by the diminution of the attendance until it falls below a quorum. Hence the business must needs be done in great haste. Questions of the gravest importance, and touching delicate and difficult principles, are customarily settled in discussions limited throughout by a rule which forbids any speaker to exceed fifteen minutes. Sometimes the limit is reduced to ten or even five minutes. The speakers are eager, numerous, competitive; and the time is painfully inadequate to meet the demands of the subject or the desires of the speakers. Hence hurried debates, debates by no means of a calm or deliberative character. Hence, too, such applications of the closure power, under the dominance of a majority, as those which Dr. Perrine refers to in vivid and biting phrases. Worst of all, what is done hurriedly, if wrong, is incapable of correction or revision, till four years have passed away. Hence the emphatic demand of Dr. Perrine, which has made so deep an impression on the most thoughtful and statesman-like minds of the Conference, for such a process of legislation, by means of two concurrent houses, as should "compel" the needful delay and deliberation in important and critical legislation.[1]

[1] Notice was given of a Resolution on this subject at the General Conference of 1896. But the Conference cannot sit longer than a month, during which period, whatever is left undone, an immense mass of routine and economically necessary business must needs be done. Also three subjects, not indeed of more intrinsic importance, but of more pressing or hasty urgency, were brought before the

The conditions under which the Conference meets and does its work are widely different in England from what they are in America. The English Conference meets not quadrennially, but annually. This makes it less urgent to close a question in any given year; postponement has in the past been usually preferred to hasty or perilous legislation. Every new decision affecting Circuits or Societies, before it is confirmed, must go to the District Synods for their judgments thereupon. Even when it has become law, after this reference, if the new law appears to be unjust or impracticable as applied to any circuit, the Quarterly Meeting of the circuit can suspend its operation till the next Conference. Nor does the Conference adopt important and general legislation in any year, except on the recommendation of committees which have been considering the question during the year, having been appointed for that purpose by the preceding Conference.

These considerations may suffice to show that the reasons for a "second chamber," which are felt to be so powerful in American Methodism, have little force as applied to our English Conference arrangements.

In certain respects, of course, English Methodism has now the advantage of a "second chamber." If the Conference in its Pastoral Session should adopt any resolution, or make any proposal relating to general Connexional administration, it cannot take effect unless adopted in

Conference, of which one related to episcopal duties and administration, another was the election of a larger number than usual of bishops, while the third related to the proposed admission of women to the Conference, as lay delegates; and these so preoccupied the weeks of the session, that the Resolution I have referred to, with other matters of high interest and importance, was not reached, through effluxion of time, and must wait till the Conference of 1900.

the Representative Session. If, on the other hand, any recommendation of the Representative Session should have a bearing upon questions of spiritual discipline or fellowship, or might be regarded as affecting the doctrinal strictness or integrity of the Connexion, such recommendation of the Representative Session could not become law without its having been referred to the Pastoral Session.

The English Methodist Church is not, either absolutely or relatively, so vast, nor is it, either politically or socially, nearly so powerful, as the American Church. But, I venture to think, it has its own points of superiority to that great Church. The grand position secured many years ago by the Methodist Church in America having made it the popular Church, there is a tendency to relax the conditions of membership analogous to that which besets an Established Church. As to this point I may quote the words of Dr. Buckley, the distinguished editor of the *New York Christian Advocate*, the "great official" journal, as spoken at the first Methodist Œcumenical Conference (1881): "The Wesleyan Connexion is much more strict in the class-meeting test than most of the Churches reporting such large figures from the United States. If the same principles which are applied by the Wesleyan Church or Connexion upon the class-meeting were applied to our statistics, but a short period of time would elapse before many of them would shrink in a marvellous manner. As to the wisdom of the course which we pursue, *or which pursues itself* in the United States, that is not a matter which can be discussed at this time."[1]

[1] *Report of the First Œcumenical Conference*, p. 64. The words printed in italics are very significant.

English Methodism has also, no doubt, its points of inferiority to American Methodism. At present, however, it is not only admired, but even reverenced by its magnificently developed sister Church. So long as the Methodism of England adheres to those grand principles which the two Churches in common have derived from their apostolic and saintly fathers and founders, and on which Dr. Perrine in his able work — a valuable legacy to his Church—has so luminously insisted, the Methodism of the States will, it is no presumption to affirm, continue to study with admiration and to regard with reverence its elder sister of the Methodist family.

I have spoken in this chapter of American Methodism collectively. Before the chapter is brought to a close, I must refer to the divisions which have separated the Methodists of the United States into various Churches. To the small non-episcopal Protestant Methodist Church reference has already been made, and no more need be said. The secessions to which I am about to refer still maintain substantially intact and identical, not only the doctrine, but the discipline of the mother Church. They are Methodist Episcopal Churches. By far the most important of them is the Methodist Episcopal Church South, which separated from the Church in the Northern States in 1844 on the slavery question. This is a large and energetic Church. With this Church the Methodism of England has—in consequence, it may perhaps be said, of the Œcumenical Conference — entered into close fraternal relations, by sending a deputation to visit its General Conferences, a practice which has been maintained between English Methodism and the parent Episcopal Church of the States during more than two generations. These two

Churches of the States do not divide the territory of the Union strictly between them. The organisation of the parent Church extends more or less throughout the Southern States; while the Church South has a few outposts, here and there, within the Northern States. Besides these two great Churches, there are five others, of which three are coloured Episcopal Churches, included within the array of the Methodist Episcopal sisterhood of Churches in the United States. Collectively all these Churches count about 35,000 ministers, and between five and six millions of professed communicants. The parent Church claims about one-half of the aggregate. The Church South claims as Church members about half as many as the parent Church, or nearly one-fourth of the whole; but, using lay preachers and leaders much more largely than the parent Church,—being, in these respects, more "primitive" in its character,—its ministers are fewer in number than one-third of those belonging to the mother Church.

In 1776 eleven different denominations were counted in the American Colonies. The Methodists were at the bottom of the list, with eleven churches and twenty ministers. The first four in order were Congregationalists, Baptists, Episcopalians, and Presbyterians. At the present time the Methodists head the list; and the five next following are Baptists, Presbyterians, Roman Catholics, Congregationalists, Episcopalians.

I have now finished the main body of my undertaking, what remains to be said being incidental or supplementary. After giving a summary view of the characteristic features and the church arrangements of truly primitive Christianity,

I have, according to my ability, passed in review, and compared with each other and with primitive Christianity, the chief systems of church government among Protestant and Reformed Christian communities. It will be proper now to restate the great lesson which I have striven to elucidate. The most vital defect in any Church system is to have no equivalent for the fellowship of the primitive Churches. This fellowship may be provided in different ways, though a Methodist may be allowed to prefer the arrangements of his own Church to those of any other. But to have no provision for such fellowship is of all defects the most fundamental and fatal in a Church. If this defect were but effectively remedied in all the Reformed Churches, how mighty would be their united antagonism to the errors of the Church of Rome, fatally strong as that Church is by her perversions of the true principles of Christian communion! How splendid is the history of Presbyterianism! yet in this respect there has been defect. How great have been the great men and the strong Churches of Congregationalism! how special is the strength of the system in certain respects! A little modification, and in this respect, in particular, a true return to first principles, are all that is needed to make Congregationalism powerful, stable, and vital, as it has never yet been, even in its palmiest days. The various Churches have each its special genius, each its adaptation to special tastes and stages of development, intellectual or social. Methodism is, in various respects, weaker, while, in other respects, it is stronger, than the other great Churches. But in this one cardinal point it is stronger, more primitive, more apostolic than other Churches—that its fellowship is wide open to all who desire to come to Christ, and to make their "calling and election sure "; and that this fellowship is distinctively spiritual and evangelical. " Whosoever will may come"; and only persistent and deliberate neglect of the fellowship, or proved misconduct, can separate a member from that closely knit and widely diffused Society which, in various branches, is now fully developed and organised as the Methodist Church. If only all Churches were vital fellowship Churches, how greatly would they be strengthened, and their Christian fruitfulness increased! Their variety of form and colour and character would but multiply the attractions and add to the strength of our common Christianity.

VI.
SUPPLEMENTARY.
METHODIST SECESSIONS AND METHODIST UNION.

METHODIST SECESSIONS AND METHODIST UNION.

THE Methodist secessions referred to in the third chapter of the previous section as having resulted from agitation, and as based on politico-ecclesiastical considerations, are those at this time represented by the Methodist New Connexion and by the United Methodist Free Churches. As to each of these it is necessary, in order to answer questions which have been widely discussed of late among the Methodist Societies, that more exact explanations should be given than could conveniently be inserted in that chapter, and it is necessary also to deal with the question of Methodist union. I shall proceed accordingly in this final section to speak both of Methodist secessions, as matter of history, and of Methodist union, so far as regards the questions of principle and of policy involved in that subject.

In the last edition of the *Encyclopædia Britannica*, the subject of Methodism, including all varieties of organisation embraced under that general title, was entrusted to me by the editor; and I did my best to give a clear and dispassionate summary of all that related to the subject, so far as the limits of space would allow, avoiding, as much as possible, all irritating or fairly disputable matters. As to the New Connexion, my statement, from which I shall quote some passages, is very succinct:

"No sooner was the sacramental controversy [of 1791-5] settled, than the further question as to the position and rights of the laity came to the front in great force. A comparatively small party, led by Alexander Kilham, imported into the discussion ideas of a republican complexion, and demanded that the members in their individual capacity should be recognised as the direct basis of all power; that they should freely elect the leaders and stewards; that all distinction in Conference between ministers and laymen should be done away (elected laymen being sent as delegates from the circuits in equal number with the ministers); that the ministry should possess no official authority or pastoral prerogative, but should merely carry into effect the decisions of majorities in the different meetings. In the course of a very violent controversy, pamphlets and broadsheets, chiefly anonymous, from Kilham's pen, advocating his views, and containing gross imputations on the ministers generally, and in particular on some not named, but distinctly indicated, were disseminated through the Societies. The writer was tried at the Conference of 1796, condemned for the publication of injurious and unjustifiable charges against his brethren, and by a unanimous vote expelled from the Conference. In the following year he founded the 'New Connexion,' the earliest of the organised secessions from Wesleyan Methodism."

In a later passage in the article the following sentences are added: "The" [parent] "Connexion after 1797 had a long, unbroken period of peaceful progress. The effect of the 'Kilhamite' separation, indeed, was after 1797 not greatly felt by the parent body. The number of Methodists in the United Kingdom in 1796, the year of Kilham's expulsion, was 95,226 ; in 1797 it was 99,519 ; in 1798 the New Connexion held its first Conference, and reported 5,037 members, the number of the parent body being 101,682. Nor was it till 1806 that the New Connexion reached 6,000."

In October, 1885, a valuable article appeared in the *London Quarterly Review*, entitled " The Origin of the First Important Methodist Secession." The writer was the Rev. John S. Simon. It is a strictly historical article, authentic throughout, founded on large and undeniable documentary evidence, rigidly temperate in its tone. It gives Mr. Kilham credit for the abilities and organising faculties he undoubtedly possessed. If it is in any sense hard upon him, it is not the epithets or invective of the writer, but the facts brought out clearly from Kilham's own writings, which make it hard. The last paragraph of the article has so close a bearing upon the subject under review that I will quote it almost entire :

" We have given to this article a title which recognises the secession led by Kilham as important. Its importance consisted chiefly in the settlement of principles to which it led. Among many good practical suggestions, of which not a few were either adopted at the time or have been adopted since, Kilham's proposals included three which were fundamental, and which the Conference could not accept. The Conference would not accept the principle that the minister was to be essentially little, if anything, more or other than the hired preacher and officer of the Society, pecuniarily dependent, on the one hand, and, on the other, denuded of all pastoral authority or prerogative whatever. Nor would they be parties to the breaking up of the Conference as the common pastoral council of the Connexion, in which the united brotherhood of ministers consulted with each other as to their special and distinctive duties and responsibilities, and kept watch over each other as well as over their common charge. Nor would they consent to introduce the principle of elective republicanism into every Church meeting, and even into the spiritual fellowship meetings, as, for example, in the choice of leaders for the 'classes.' On these principles the 'New Connexion' was constituted. The result of the respective principles of constitution for the two Connexions, the 'old' and the 'new,' is to be found in the development and in the present position and condition of the two communities. In no spirit but that of friendliness and entire good feeling would we refer to these matters of old history. But, old as they are, they are of cardinal importance, and for Methodists their interest can never be exhausted, nor their lessons become obsolete."

I have given the number of members with which the New Connexion started on its course in 1797 as 5,037. In 1896 it numbered in England and abroad 36,024, and in Ireland 1,078 (including those on trial), the corresponding numbers for the parent Connexion being 466,711 and 27,576.

The slowness of growth in the New Connexion is all the more remarkable, because the proportionate rate of increase in a Church is usually greater when it is small than when it has grown large. It might not be difficult for a Society of six members to double itself in a year, but would scarcely be possible for a Society of a hundred thousand. When any association has once made itself felt throughout a whole community, and attracted to itself from among those not firmly attached to other associations all in that community to whose sympathies it could offer strong attractions, it cannot be expected afterwards to increase as rapidly as during its earlier history. This principle must be borne in mind in forecasting the future of the Salvation Army. It has received ample illustration in the history of the "Primitive Methodist" Connexion.[1]

In regard to the other politico-ecclesiastical secessions from Wesleyan Methodism, I proceed to quote some passages from the article on Methodism already referred to in the *Encyclopædia Britannica*:

"The development of the pastoral position and character of the ministers of the body after 1797 could not but advance on a line parallel to the development of the position and claims of the laity. In 1818 the usage of the Conference was conformed to what had long been the ordinary unofficial custom; and the preachers began to be styled in the *Wesleyan Methodist Magazine*, and in other official publications, 'Reverend,' a fact which may seem trivial, but which in reality was of important significance.

"In 1834, after the idea had been long entertained and the project had been repeatedly discussed, it was determined to establish a theological institution for the

[1] For full and exact information in detail as to Kilham's case and the origin of the New Connexion, I would refer to the second volume of Dr. Smith's excellent and authoritative *History of Methodism* (Longmans & Co.). Dr. Smith was an eminent Wesleyan layman and local preacher, a Cornishman of great ability and learning, no mean author, and in theology and ecclesiastical history a man of remarkable attainments. Also, I should refer to what Dr. Gregory has written on the subject in his valuable Catechism on Methodist "Church Principles," and to a pamphlet by the Rev. John S. Simon, issued since the publication of the first edition of this volume, entitled, *Wesleyan Methodism Vindicated: a Reply to the Rev. Dr. Watts' pamphlet, entitled, " Liberal Methodism Vindicated."*

training of ministerial candidates. . . . In 1836 the practice of ordination by imposition of hands was adopted.

"Such advances, however, as these in the general organisation and development of the Connexion, and especially in the status and professional training of the ministers, could not be made in such a body without offence being given to some whose tendencies were to disallow any official distinction between the ministry and the laity, and who also objected to the use of the organ in public worship. This levelling element was strong in the West Riding of Yorkshire; and in 1828, on the placing of an organ in Brunswick Chapel, Leeds, by the trustees, with the consent of the Conference, a violent agitation broke out. The consequence was a disruption, the first since 1798, and the formation of a new Methodist sect under the title 'Protestant Methodists.' But this was absorbed, some years later, in a more considerable secession.

"In fact, the Connexion was in 1828 entering on a period of agitation. The current of political affairs was approaching the rapids of which the Reform Act marked the centre and the point of maximum movement. A body like Wesleyan Methodism could not but feel in great force the sweep of this movement. . . . Accordingly the elements of disturbance which only partially exploded in the Protestant Methodist secession continued to make themselves felt, in different parts of the Connexion, during the following years of political controversy. The decision of the Conference in 1834 to provide a college for the training of ministerial candidates gave special offence to the malcontents. Such an occasion was all that was wanting for the various discontents of the Connexion to gather to a head. The demands made by the agitators proceeded on a basis of democratic ecclesiasticism such as it is very difficult to apply successfully to a system of associated Churches. The result was a third secession, based on the same general ground of ecclesiastical principles as the two preceding, which was organised in 1836, and with which the 'Protestant Methodists' eventually coalesced. This new secession was known first as the 'Wesleyan Methodist Association'; but for a number of years past it has been merged in a still larger body of seceders, designated 'The Methodist Free Churches.' Its leader at the first was the Rev. Dr. Warren, who left it, however, not many months after it was formed, and took orders in the Church of England.

"The effect of the secession of 1836 on the general progress of the Connexion was not great. The number of members reported in 1835 in Great Britain and Ireland [and on the foreign mission stations] was 371,251 (there being a decrease in England of 951), in 1836, 381,369, in 1837, 384,723. For the next ten years the advance of the Connexion in numbers and in general prosperity was apparently unprecedented. The Centenary Fund of 1839–40 amounted to £221,000. In the midst, however, of all the outward prosperity of Methodism—partly, perhaps, in consequence of it—very perilous elements were at work. The revolutionary ideas of the Chartist period (1840–48) and of Continental politics (1848–49) reacted on Wesleyan Methodism as the political ideas of 1791 and of 1831 had done at those epochs. The embers of old controversies—ecclesiastical, quasi-political, and personal—still smouldered, and at length burst into fresh flame.[1]

---

[1] I have not cared to go into the painful details of this agitation. I may refer those who desire information on the subject to Dr. Smith's *History of Methodism*, vol. iii.

"A disastrous agitation followed. No distinct secession took place until after the Conference of 1850. The union of the 'Methodist Free Churches,' in which was incorporated the 'Wesleyan Association' (of 1836), was formed by the seceders. The 'New Connexion' also received some thousands of the seceders into its ranks.[1] But by far the greatest part of those who left went with neither of these bodies.

"Between 1850 and 1855 the Connexion in Great Britain and Ireland lost 100,000 members, and not till 1856 did it begin to recover. In that year the numbers [for Great Britain and Ireland, *excluding* the Foreign Missions] were returned as 282,787, showing a small increase over the preceding year. Since then peace and unity have prevailed unbroken."

The latest returns, as mentioned previously, amounted to 466,711 members at home and abroad, including those on trial.

More than forty years have passed away since the last terrible secession came to the end of its disastrous history, and forty years since restored peace began to bring back renewed prosperity. In those years the Connexion has increased more than fifty per cent. in numbers; and in many respects, including Sunday-school work and home missionary activities, has increased much more largely. During the same period, or at least the latter part of it, the history of the United Methodist Free Churches has been by no means one of settled unity or of continuous progress. From the article in the *Encyclopædia* I take the following brief summary of the principles of this body of Methodist Churches:

[1] A New Connexion critic objects to this estimate as too large. It would be beyond contradiction to say "hundreds."

UNITED METHODIST FREE CHURCHES.

"This organisation in its original form must be identified with the Wesleyan Methodist Association of 1836. That body first absorbed into itself in great part the 'Protestant Methodists' of 1828. It was afterwards greatly increased, and its organisation in some points modified, when a large number of the seceders from the parent Connexion in 1850-52 joined its ranks. The main body of its Conference does not consist, like that of the New Connexion, of an equal number of circuit ministers and elected circuit lay delegates, but of circuit delegates, whether ministerial or lay, elected without any respect to office, ministerial or other. Its circuits also are independent of the control of the Conference. The Connexional bond, accordingly, in this denomination is weak, and the itinerancy is not universal or uniform in its rules or its operation. The amalgamation between the Wesleyan Methodist Association and the 'Wesleyan Methodist Reformers' of 1850 took place in 1857. At that time the combined Churches numbered 41,000."

The number of members, as we have seen, in 1857, was 41,000, a small remnant gathered from successive secessions. But the fact of the union gave éclat and impetus, and during some years the increase was large. Many of the members whom the agitation had left stranded or scattered came into the new body. Of late years, however, the condition of things has gravely altered. The return of members for 1885 having been 67,081, being an increase over 1875 (i.e. in ten years) of only seven and a half per cent, in a characteristically manly article in the *United Methodist Free Churches' Magazine* for August, 1885, the late Rev. Marmaduke Miller gave his views on this subject.

After referring to the decreases among the Free Churches during the preceding ten years, and to the smallness of the total increase during that period, an increase smaller than that of any other Nonconformist Church, except the Friends, this able and candid writer says :

"In the first place, there is little doubt that the decay of our class-meetings is one chief cause of our decreases. In some circuits they are completely gone, and in many others they are slowly dying. No doubt this is an incalculable loss to the community. A class-meeting, conducted by one who is fitted for the post, is a most helpful means of grace. . . . Where there are no class-meetings, a member of the Church may gradually absent himself from public worship without a single person making any enquiry concerning him. . . . We may take it for granted that, unless some other system of shepherding the flock be adopted, there will be great leakage in Churches and circuits where class-meetings have been given up.

"Next to the decay of our class-meetings, we think the chief cause of our want of progress is the lack of the evangelistic spirit. We lack enthusiasm and enterprise. The population of the country keeps rapidly increasing, but we are putting up few new chapels, and the number of our preaching rooms is decreasing. . . .

"The decrease in the number of our local preachers during the last decade is another sign of the lack of the evangelistic spirit."

That is to say, as the gifts of local preachers are, in their earliest beginnings, stimulated and elicited in the class-meeting, and as the class-meeting (*i e.* the fellowship life of primitive Christianity) is the very spring and seed-plot of all that belongs to the evangelistic spirit and character, the disuse of the class-meeting, in a body originally organised as an evangelistic fellowship, leads directly to spiritual decay and apathy.

According to the latest returns, the "Methodist Free Churches" counted 76,105 members in Home Districts and 13,513 in the Colonies and on Foreign Mission Stations.

Besides the two Methodist bodies to which the preceding pages refer, there are other two, not accurately to be described as organised secessions, to which, for the sake of clearness and completeness, I must refer in this chapter. These are the "Primitive Methodists" and the "Bible Christians." Both of these were irregular outgrowths from Wesleyan Methodism, founded by lay preachers who did not find within the liberties of Wesleyan Methodism, as regulated by the *Minutes of Conference*, free or adequate scope for their own methods or the working out of their own ideas. Both have been developed under very similar impulses and inspiration, although there are material differences in their organisation. Both alike were organised, in all earnestness and simplicity, without any reference to questions of pastoral authority or of the pastoral office in any sense. In both it has been found scarcely possible, as the bodies grew in numbers, to rectify this original defect. If we could imagine the Methodism of John Wesley suddenly deprived of the guidance or presence of the Wesleys, of Fletcher, of any clergyman, of any scholarly men like Benson or Adam Clarke, of any men of general culture and superiority like Henry Moore or Joseph Cownley, with only those among the most fervid of the lay preachers, to act as itinerant evangelists, who were also the least instructed, such a residuary Methodism of Wesley's middle period would not inaptly correspond in character with these fervid and hard-working revivalist communities in the earliest stages of their history. Of the origin of the "Primitive Methodist" Connexion and also of the "Bible Christians," a candid and kindly account has lately been given in the *London Quarterly Review* by the writer of the article to which I have already referred on the origin of the New Connexion.[1]

From the article on Methodism in the *Encyclopædia Britannica* I extract the following brief statements as to the organisation of the two bodies:

PRIMITIVE METHODISM.

"In this earnest and hard-working denomination, the ministers, of whom some are women, are very literally 'the servants of all.' The Conference is composed, in addition to twelve permanent members, of four members appointed by the preceding Conference, and of delegates from District Meetings. The principle of proportion is that there should be two laymen to one minister or 'travelling preacher,' and the 'travelling preachers' have no pastoral prerogative whatever. The Conference is supreme, and the Connexional bond is strong. This body was founded by Hugh Bourne and William Clowes, local preachers who were separated from the Wesleyan Connexion, the former in 1808, the latter in 1810, because of their violation of Conference regulations as to camp-meetings and other questions of order. The Conference had, in 1807, pronounced its judgment against camp-meetings, which had been introduced into the

[1] See the *London Quarterly Review* for July, 1886 and 1887.

country from America, whereas Bourne and Clowes were determined to hold such meetings. Founded thus by zealous and 'irregular' lay preachers, 'Primitive' Methodism, as the resulting new body called itself, bears still in its organisation, its spirit, and its customs, strong traces of its origin. It has been a very successful body, aiming simply at doing evangelistic work, and is now numerous and powerful, numbering among its ministers not only many useful preachers, but some of marked originality and power, and also of superior cultivation. There has for many years past, if not from the beginning, been a very friendly feeling between the old Wesleyan Connexion and the Primitive Methodists."

BIBLE CHRISTIANS.

"The Primitive Methodists sprang up in the Midland counties, the Bible Christians in Cornwall. These closely resemble the 'Primitives' in their character and spirit. Their founder was a Cornish local preacher called O'Bryan. Hence the Connexion is often known as the Bryanites, and Cornish emigrants have propagated this denomination widely in the colonies. The Conference is composed of ten Superintendents of Districts, the President and Secretary of the preceding Conference, lay delegates, one from each District Meeting, and as many of the travelling preachers as are allowed by their respective District Meetings to attend. In general, it may be said that the ministerial and lay members of the Conference are about equal in number."

There has never been any controversy between Wesleyan Methodism and either of the two zealous offshoots now in view. It has been generally recognised among Wesleyans that their co-operation has helped in the most important way the total work of evangelisation for the country and the world. Nevertheless, the differences in organisation and the divergences in tendency have been much too important to admit, among serious and responsible leaders of opinion on either side, the expectation, at least in the near future, of organic union, or the belief that, if such union were attempted, it would conduce to the "unity of the spirit in the bond of peace."

As having a direct and important bearing on this point and on the whole subject dealt with in this and in the preceding chapter, I will here quote the following passages from Mr. Simon's article in the *London Quarterly Review* on the "Origin of the Primitive Methodist Connexion":

"In searching for the origin and tracing the development of the Wesleyan Methodist Church, the investigator is constantly compelled to ask, 'What is the peculiarity of character, organisation, and work which justifies Methodism in assuming and retaining a position which separates it from other English Churches?' The justification of a separate Church lies in the fact that by the retention of its position it answers a purpose, and effects moral and religious work which otherwise would be lost to the world. Methodism possesses qualities which differentiate it from all other ecclesiastical communities, and those qualities fit it for the special sphere which it is designed to fill. It is pre-eminent for its evangelistic enterprise and success. But evangelism does not exhaust its definition. Some of its most treasured and effective doctrines demand the treatment of the cool and lucidly profound expositor. In the hands of the mere mission-preacher they are apt to become sources of mental and spiritual danger. The work of the awakening evangelist in Methodism is initial. It must be taken up and continued by other men. When the 'revivalist' has done his initial work, the converts whom he has won pass into other hands. The class-meeting receives and trains them, and they are instructed from the pulpit by men who are specially fitted to explain to them the deep things of God. They are led through the stages of progressive experience until they leave the first principles of the doctrines of Christ and go on to perfection. Conversion and Christian perfection are the distinguishing doctrines which especially define the objects of the Methodist Church, and both the evangelist and the 'pastor and teacher' are necessary to their full expression. The ideal Methodist preacher is a man in whom these offices are united. He is equally at home in a revival prayer-meeting or when initiating the most mature Christians into the hidden wisdom of God. The mission of Methodism is to rescue men from the world, and to educate them in the highest truths of the Christian religion. The attempt to compel Methodism to consider itself exclusively as an agent for the conversion of the degraded masses, is fatal to her special mission. The doctrine of conversion fascinates ardent young workers, and never loses its force of appeal in the heart of a man who has himself experienced the sorrows and joys of awakening and renewal. But those who look before and after, and who have large discourse of reason, cannot be acquitted of unfaithfulness if they do not keenly watch questionable movements, and emphatically rebuke any spirit which endangers the mission of Methodism. Whilst thus explaining the Methodist position, we wish it to be understood that we have not the slightest desire to cast any reflection upon those Churches in which revivalism is an exclusive characteristic. They, too, have a special work to perform; but the work that they have to do is only part of that which Wesleyan Methodism has to accomplish. . . .

"Another lesson may be learnt; *viz.*, that it is not easy for one and the same strictly organised Church to provide with efficiency and completeness for the evangelisation, and for the spiritual instruction and development, of 'all sorts and conditions of men.' The gospel itself is adapted to all varieties of class, grade, and social or national development; but it cannot be said that each, or perhaps that any, particular Church is so adapted. The 'Primitive Methodist Connexion' has adapted its methods and organisation to the social conditions and special tastes of certain classes of society. Wesleyan Methodism could have met the *needs* of these same classes; but if to their *tastes* and *preferences* everything else had been sacrificed, it would have lost hold of the middle classes, and would not have had a ministry adapted to deal with persons of solid thought and educated mind and character. The Primitive Methodists in their earlier history did a work not altogether unlike that which has lately been done by the 'Salvation Army.' Though they affected no military titles or trappings, their spirit and tone, and even many of their methods, were not dissimilar. Since those earlier times the tone and methods prevailing among the Primitive Methodists have, to some extent, been modified. They have now among them an appreciable proportion of well-educated persons, not a few middle-class people of good social standing, and many able ministers. They are developing culture in all directions, and find it necessary to do this, if they are not to decline. The consequences of this development, necessary as it is, are not all favourable to apparent progress,—to present advance in numbers,—though doubtless they will contribute to consolidation and permanence, and to eventual progress and success. The 'Salvationists,' with whom even the 'Primitives' cannot compete in their special line, are occupying part of their field. Altogether they suffer from a temporary apparent conflict between the needs and demands of the more thoughtful and educated among their people and the tastes and wishes of the less educated. In the end, however, true taste and Christian sobriety will prevail against their opposites. Wesleyan Methodism is now doing more work among the lowest classes than for many years preceding. Education is, in fact, reaching many among the lower classes, and elevating their standard of taste and propriety; while, on the other hand, thoroughly educated ministers and members of the Church, in the spirit of the founder of Methodism, are learning more and more how to preach the gospel to the poor. Still, however, there is, and is likely to be in the future, a need among Christian Churches for 'division of labour.' Episcopacy, Presbyterianism, and Congregationalism, Wesleyan Methodism, Primitive Methodism, and the Bible Christian body (the 'Primitives' of the west of England), and also, we must add, although we wish we could do so with less of inward qualification and misgiving, the 'Salvation Army,' are all contributing to meet specific wants and tendencies in different classes of society, and are helping forward the Saviour's kingdom. They ought to regard themselves as different branches of the great visible Christian Church, and to make it their sacred and cherished purpose to maintain 'the unity of the spirit in the bond of peace, and in righteousness of life.'"

The passages quoted above apply in spirit, and indeed

almost in every word, to the case of the "Bible Christians" as well as to that of the "Primitives." I may add, however, that the organisation of the "Bible Christians," on the whole, resembles that of Wesleyan Methodism more closely than that of any other of the Methodist bodies to which I have referred, and that at present it appears to be the most prosperous. Whether, when it has attained to the dimensions of the "Primitives," it will still retain its present apparent superiority in cohesion and success, is a question which remains to be solved.

The preceding historical discussion has not, however, exhausted the considerations of primary importance relating to the subject of Methodist union, although it will have suggested several which lie at the threshold. It may be doubted, indeed, whether some considerations which are less obvious are not still more critical and important. Let us ask ourselves what is involved in a project of union between two denominations. Many speak and even write as though all that were necessary in order to a union between two denominations were the favourable disposition of a number of the leading persons in the two bodies, backed by the pressure of some outside opinions, or what a sanguine person might describe as public opinion. A few years ago, on this hypothesis, assuredly the Scotch Free Church and the United Presbyterians ought at once to have coalesced. There was an absolute identity of doctrine and an all but absolute—a radical, and largely also a detailed—identity of discipline, while as to practical ecclesiastico-political questions there appeared to be no real difference between the two bodies. Moreover, it seemed for several years as if a majority in both the General

Assemblies were favourable to the fusion and union. And yet the union was found impracticable. Similarly there is identity of doctrine and discipline between the two great American Methodist Episcopal Churches, the parent Church, and the Methodist Church South; there is a general feeling outside these bodies, and there is not a little inside, especially within the larger and more powerful one, favourable to union between the two. Nevertheless, such union seems farther off to-day than twelve years ago.

Even if a majority in each of the Conferences representing two Methodist Churches were predisposed in favour of union, that would not of itself be a conclusive argument in its favour, and might be impotent actually to bring about a real fusion and union of the two. The most vital question is whether the Societies which by a decree of union between the two Churches would have to be fused with each other, and the circuits which would have to admit new Societies and additional preachers and chapels into union with themselves, are prepared to accept and to carry into effect the proposed union. Conferences cannot in Christian equity, nor in wisdom of policy, force Societies together against their will, or compel circuits, without their cordial consent, to admit into organic union with themselves important elements which are likely to completely change the conditions and character of the circuits. The final decision of any question of union must lie with those who are to be directly united, not with majorities not immediately affected. Whatever resolutions might be adopted by Conferential majorities, there are hundreds of Societies which, with their local history and local knowledge, would regard with dismay, and with a sense of grievous and oppressive injustice, any attempt to compel their union in the same close spiritual fellowship and the same ecclesiastical home with other Societies, with whose members, nevertheless, as neighbours of other Christian denominations, they live on terms of cordial friendliness.

But we must look yet more carefully and more fully into the question.

The union of two Methodist Churches or Connexions of Churches with each other is a very different thing from what can be imagined by outsiders, who are supposed to make or to represent "public opinion." It is an operation very different indeed from what any one who has not thought it out closely can realise, far more complex and manifold, far more profound in its stirring and searching of all the life, all the organised faculties and functions, of the Connexions that are united with each other, than can easily be understood. It is altogether different from the mere union of two provinces into one dominion; it has no analogy with the mere bringing together of two collections of electrical or galvanic forces into one dynamic combination, or with the mechanical union of two aggregates of mechanical force. It is infinitely more than the entering into partnership of two closely knit companies. Even a Siamese-twin analogy would completely fail to indicate what such an operation must mean. It means the transfusion into each of the uniting bodies of the life and life-blood of the other; it means the complete interfusion throughout each of the whole circulatory system of the other, the interfusion throughout the two made one of the conjoint circulation of both; it means, at the same time, that the two centres of the two systems should be concentred into one homogeneous common heart. It is the united and itinerating pastorate, and all that is involved in that central fact, which makes the operation such as I have described.

The union of two Methodist Connexions with each other involves, in fact, a number of distinct and difficult operations. Into each Connexion would have to be received a large number of ministers who have not been accepted as candidates or trained for the ministry in that Connexion, whose standard and style of preaching have been formed under conditions more or less foreign and unknown, and who have been accustomed to administer a discipline differing more or less (in the cases in question differing essentially) in its principles. As the effect of the union, also, would be to amalgamate some, perhaps many, Societies and congregations, whilst all the ministers would claim to be provided for in the united Connexion, the number of ministers would thus be increased out of proportion to the number of circuits, of chapels, and Societies, a disproportionate augmentation which might prove, in various ways, a serious inconvenience.

A large number of chapels would have to be taken over, with their chapel debts. This would be for Wesleyan Methodism an exceedingly serious consideration. The Wesleyan Methodist Church, it must be remembered, has spent infinite care and pains during more than half a century, and hundreds of thousands of pounds, in relieving its trust-estates from debt. To begin the work again would be a painful and burdensome operation.

The leaders' meetings of the Wesleyan Church are organised and conducted on essentially different principles from those of the other Methodist bodies. These principles have secured for the Societies of Methodism settled peace and a close spiritual fellowship, such as one may be forgiven for dreading to see disturbed or changed in its nature by the infusion of new and strange elements into the management alike of leaders' meetings and of class-meetings. There is nothing so sacred to Methodism as its class-meeting fellowship and its leaders' meetings. It is pardonable to pause long ere, for the sake of adding, in any suggested case, a small fraction to the number of its members, we infringe on rules and traditions which are coeval with Methodism, and which have contributed to make the spiritual fellowship of English Methodism the envy of other Christian Churches, even of other Methodist Churches, throughout the world.

At present Wesleyan Methodism has maintained, even in these perilous times, its clear utterance and its evangelical orthodoxy in its pulpit ministrations. It may be doubted whether any other Methodist Church in this country can say the same with equal frankness of meaning and fulness of confidence. From the first, Kilham led the way, as a matter of principle, in cutting himself and his followers loose from the doctrinal standards established by John Wesley. Of late years, it is true, the theology of the New Connexion seems to have become settled, and guards and securities for sound doctrine are not wanting in its constitutional settlement. Nevertheless the history and the traditional influences of the New Connexion, in regard to the vital point now touched on, make the question as to the wholesale acceptance by the Wesleyan Methodist Conference of all the ministers, to which must be added all the local preachers, of the New Connexion, the more serious and difficult.

Such are the points, in addition to those vital and

fundamental questions of Church principles, the principles of organisation and administration, referred to in the preceding pages, which necessarily arise when we come to a practical and thorough consideration of all that is involved in the question of Methodist union.

So far as I have gone, I have applied the principles indicated in this chapter especially to the case of union, as some have suggested, with the New Connexion. If the case were that of union with the "Methodist Free Churches," the question arising on the point relating to doctrine would certainly not be less grave. As to other points, the difficulties would be at least as great; as to constitutional principles, they would be even greater. The principle of circuit independency, which is a fundamental point in the "Free Church" polity, and of the working of which some idea may be gained from Mr. Miller's remarks already quoted, is so absolutely contradictory to Connexionalism, that the New Connexion have found this alone fatal to the project of their union with their "free" brethren; with whom, on the whole, and not with the Wesleyan Methodist Conference, it might have been expected that they would look for union, since on all points of any importance save this one there would seem to be no material variance between them, and as to this one the "Free" Methodists have but gone farther in the direction in which the "New" Methodists led the way. That fatal principle, however, is now sensibly and even visibly producing such broad variations and such manifest disintegration in the "Free Churches," that it is intelligible why the New Connexion prefers to remain, with its small numbers, still isolated, rather than join the less settled and more disorganised, although more numerous body.[1] If, however, the small and isolated New Connexion shrinks from union with the "Free Churches" because of the still larger concession to democratic and local majority principles which would be required of it, far as it has itself gone in the same road, how can it be supposed that, for the sake of securing the accession to itself of the very small body of New Connexion adherents, the great and peaceful Wesleyan Connexion, with its organisation but lately revised and now so complete in its compass and its working, would consent to violate the integrity of its organisation, to abandon its most characteristic principles, and to make full surrender and do public obeisance to the New Connexion? All considerations that can influence an historical Church—considerations of policy and principle, considerations of human credit and expediency, and of the highest Church efficiency in relation to both doctrine and discipline—combine to negative the proposal.

The question of union between Wesleyan Methodism and the two revivalistic offshoots of Methodism, the "Primitives" and the "Bible Christians," is one which has not yet been seriously pressed, one indeed which the most practical among the leaders of the Primitives have discountenanced. The account already given is sufficient to suggest the reasons why this is the case. Of the two bodies, the difficulty, on some accounts, would, in respect of discipline and organisation, be less in regard to the "Bible Christians" than the other Church. But the extent to which the pastoral principle is in abeyance in both these bodies would of itself be sufficient to render union imprac-

---

[1] Since the first edition of this volume was published, the two bodies have been negotiating for a union. As yet, however, the negotiations have not been effectual.

ticable. There are also educational standards and conditions, relating to the ministry and all that ought to surround it, which in a question of organic union between Wesleyan Methodism and other Methodist bodies could not be ignored.

The want of pastoral influence and prerogative has indeed been the great defect of the "Primitives," felt more and more as the body has increased in numbers; and it may be anticipated that the same want will be felt increasingly among the "Bible Christians" as that denomination increases in numbers. Forty-five years ago, it fell upon me to defend the principles of Wesleyan Methodism, during our great agitation, from the attacks of writers who represented the then existing Methodist secessions, including one New Connexion divine, with whom, some years afterwards, and till his death, I was on the friendliest terms, and in whose pulpit I have preached. This gentleman referred in a pamphlet to the increase of the Primitive Methodists as neutralising an argument on behalf of Wesleyan Methodism. I shall venture to quote my words in reply, because they are as applicable to-day as they were forty-five years ago, and because they serve to illustrate the point just touched upon. The following, then, were my words in 1851: "The simple reason why I made no reference in my essay to the numerical statistics of the 'Primitive Methodists' was, that I had no controversy with them whatever. They have ever conducted themselves (as a whole) peaceably and kindly towards the old body. It has not been their wont to mingle with hostile intent in the controversies which have agitated our community. We wish them, then, God-speed. We do not attempt to criticise their Church organisation and discipline, since they are content to leave ours unassailed. We would labour together harmoniously in the field of the world; and we wish our own chief care, as that of the Primitive Methodists, ever to be, not to be the apostles of what is called 'ecclesiastical and political progress,' not to dispute about forms of government and unprofitable niceties of religious polity, but to 'seek and to save that which is lost.'

"The Primitive Methodists have largely increased. We thank God for it. But what is the reason of their increase? Not the excellence of their polity, but the zeal and labours of their preachers and members, and the singleness of purpose with which they have so perseveringly laboured. . . .

"Notwithstanding, however, the great real success of the Primitive Methodists, their success is, after all, considerably greater in appearance than in reality. Had their discipline been stricter, and their standard of requirement for membership in all respects higher, their numbers would have been less, but, at the same time, their real influence for good greater and more permanent. With the unquestionable good which they effect, there is ordinarily mixed a considerable alloy of evil. In this opinion Wesleyans proper are not singular. . . . In the Jubilee Volume of the New Connexion occurs the following remark: 'Whether the Primitive Methodist Connexion is adapted for perpetuity is a problem often propounded in conversation by intelligent observers of the constitution and operations of the religious sects in Great Britain. Perhaps time only will solve the problem.'"[1]

Such were my frank words at that time, words which the history of the generation that has passed since they were written has confirmed. I never met with or heard

[1] *Principles of Wesleyan Methodism*, second edition, pp. 122, 123.

of a Primitive Methodist who resented these words. I have received the greatest kindness, the most cordial respect, from some of the leading ministers of the Primitives during the interval. All the real *primitive* Wesleyan Methodists highly value the labours of the secondary "Primitives," who doubtless, in certain respects, have had not a little of the primitive spirit. Nor is there after these forty years any question as to the permanence of the "Primitives." At the first Œcumenical Methodist Conference, held in London in 1881, the masterly ability, the clear-cut thought, the tempered boldness, of several of their ministers, were conspicuous among all the members of that assembly. Few abler men, or men with clearer insight into the needs of the times, were found among the whole assembly. And yet their Church has had to struggle of late, and is struggling still, with the results of ill-regulated zeal and of lax discipline. I, for my part, follow their course with sympathy and admiration. But I do not see that it would be the best or happiest thing for their body to be organically united with the Wesleyan Methodist Connexion; or that any such result is necessary in order to secure true Christian unity, the best possible mutual feeling, and the widest and largest results of Christian fruitfulness. Such results, I believe, can be best promoted by each body pursuing its own course, learning something the while continually from the other.

I can understand, indeed, and, in certain aspects, sympathise with, the desire for an actual union among all the Methodist bodies, if such a union could be really effected, —a thorough union, in the sense already indicated, a union in which Wesleyan Methodism would lose nothing of spiritual power or influence, would maintain and even improve upon its present efficiency of discipline, its Christian culture, its peace and unity, its missionary power. I can see that the Methodist Church would become a very numerous Church, might exercise a large public, and, if so disposed, political influence, would before the world bulk much vaster than it has hitherto done. But I have indicated some of the difficulties of the problem, which seem to me to be insurmountable. Nor can I regard mere numbers or bulk as of the highest importance. A vast Conference is by no means a necessary blessing. To be choice and good, to be spiritually powerful, to set an example to the whole Methodist family not unworthy to be followed, to live in true though unostentatious union of spirit with all that is best in the other Methodist communities, and to cultivate the kindliest relations with them—these ends seem to me more certainly right and good, and better worthy of desire and effort to attain, than a mere organic union under existing circumstances. I can see no real ripeness for such a union, judging according to the criteria which I have endeavoured to indicate.[1]

How long is it since Methodists began to hold the view that organic union was the true unity by means of which

[1] In 1891, when officiating in a large chapel belonging to one of the Methodist Secessions, having been asked to baptize two infants, I found that that Methodist body possessed no Book of Offices nor any Church Form of Baptismal Service. On subsequent enquiry, I learnt that the Primitive Methodists stand alone among the minor Methodist bodies in having their own "Order of the Administration of the Sacraments and other Services." The New Connexion, it appears, has never had a Service-Book, and their Book Room knows of no enquiries after one. The Free Churches' Book Room is seldom asked for one; if any is used, it is that of the Wesleyan mother-Church. The Bible Christians occasionally use a Service Book, which is published by Hodder &

the kingdom of Christ is to be advanced? That has been ever the doctrine of the Roman communion, and of those Churches which arrogate to themselves the title "Catholic," especially the "Anglo-Catholic" section of the Church of England; but it has not hitherto been the doctrine of Protestant Nonconformists. Is there any reason why the view, which has been held so widely outside of the "Catholic" Churches, that Christ's work, within due limits, is best carried on by varieties of agency and by "division of labour," so to speak, among different organisations, should not also hold good as among and between the different Methodist Churches? Given the common link—a precious one, if it be only held good and true—of experimental fellowship among the various bodies of Methodists, are there not great and marked distinctions and divergences in other respects among those who own this common link, such as make separate organisations desirable? Who can doubt that there not only are, but are always likely to be, many persons who are unable to distinguish between the sphere of religious and of political organisation, who must carry their political instincts, sympathies, tendencies, with them into their Church meetings and arrangements of every description? If there are such men, is it better that they should remain conflictingly mixed up in one Church with those who distinguish sharply between ecclesiastical and political organisations and agencies, or that they should be united in communities organised after their own heart? Is it

Stoughton. This condition of things is highly significant. It tells, perhaps, of arrested development, certainly of rooted differences of feeling, training, and tendencies, especially as regards family religious life and observances, among the various bodies claiming the same Methodist parentage.

not the fact, again, that there is another class of Methodists, and a very large class, who cannot endure to breathe a political atmosphere, and to be pursued by political ideas and aims, in connexion with spiritual agencies and worship and enterprises, and of whom many, if they could not find a peaceable habitation in a non-political Methodist Church, would undoubtedly retreat from the sounds of political or quasi-political agitation, or exhortation, or insinuation, or discourse, or allusion, into the shelter of the Church of England ? Is it wise, by insisting on a fusion of all Methodist bodies, to distress these peaceful and simple-hearted (perhaps at the same time able and cultivated) experimental Christians, of the ancient Methodist type, and to drive many of them out of Methodism altogether ?

The existing Methodist denominations make full, and on the whole convenient, provision for such varieties of character, cultivation, taste, and religious tone as have been indicated. They make provision also for those who have dominant revivalistic tendencies, and likewise for such a division of labour as reaches the lowest sections of society and the most out-of-the-way corners of the land, such a provision as could never be accomplished by the agency of one vast, unwieldy, and heterogeneous denomination, the polity of which, as a united denomination, would have to be modified in ways hitherto unexampled, modified, too, in such a way as to give to each individual of the great multitude a greatly diminished opportunity of reaching the centre of affairs, or being brought into direct personal relations with the great governing body.

I may be told, indeed, that there are two cases of

Methodist fusion or union, lately carried into effect, which afford a practical demonstration of the feasibility and advantage of such union.

Let us examine these cases: the case of Ireland and that of Canada. We shall find that in their conditions they are remarkable contrasts to the problems with which in this country we have to deal. They do not disprove, but go to confirm, my arguments; they are of the nature of "exceptions" which "prove the rule."

First, then, as to the case of Ireland. The "Primitive Wesleyans," a very different body from the Primitive Methodists of England, and exceedingly small in numbers, coalesced, in 1878, with the original Connexion, itself numbering not many more than twenty thousand members. This "Primitive" secession was formed in 1816, because the Irish Wesleyans, following after twenty years the English example, had resolved that their own Societies might receive the sacraments at their own chapels and from their own ministers, instead of at the parish church. After the disestablishment of the Anglo-Irish Church in 1870, this small secession body seemed to find its basis dissolved. The reason of their separate existence was discredited by the parliamentary action taken in regard to the Church to which they had clung as a national Church, and as a link with the State and Church of England. The result was a strong desire on the part of most of the preachers and the leading men of the body to be united to the Anglo-Irish Methodist Church. They accepted fully and absolutely the constitution and all the rules and regulations—the whole discipline—of the Wesleyan Methodist Church in Ireland, and were absorbed accordingly. This accomplished, Methodism in Ireland was left one undivided body. The transaction was accomplished with happy unanimity, at least in the contracting Conferences, and by effective majorities throughout the circuits and Societies. In the completely changed circumstances of the "Primitives," an Act of Parliament was obtained without difficulty providing for the transfer of the chapels and the needful change in the trusts. It will be seen how simple a question this was. No principles were at stake. It is true that in the Primitive Conference there had been no distinction between pastor and people; how could there be when the preachers had no pastoral status, and never administered the holy sacraments? The question therefore did not arise, and there was no sacrifice of principle, when the Irish Primitives came over, in accepting the pastoral distinction in the united Conference and District Meetings of Methodism, as maintained in Ireland no less than in England. And it was no mean result to have regained for Ireland the absolute unity of Methodism. Nevertheless, for this most desirable result there was a very heavy price to pay, a price which, as actually paid out from year to year, was found to be heavier than had been anticipated. There was more discontent with the arrangement among the members of both communities than had been anticipated. Of the annexed community not two-thirds of the estimated number of members—out of nearly 7,000 less than 4,000—actually came over to the united Church. But all the ministers, to the number of sixty, came over, an accession which involved complex and difficult financial operations, and which compelled the Conference for some time to refrain from accepting any candidate for the ministry. The chapels had all to be taken over, with all their debts, a serious burden. A large fund had to be raised in order to meet the expense of the whole transaction, without which the operation must have been financially impracticable, and which has not sufficed to prevent serious financial difficulties. It will be evident that such a case affords no parallel and no encouragement for any suggestion of Methodist union which might be raised in this country.

In the case of Canada the conditions were singularly favourable for Methodist union; and the advantages to be gained, if the problem could be well solved, were very great. The Wesleyan Methodist Connexion in the Dominion was not only much the largest Methodist body, but it stood, in its principles and organisation, centrally between somewhat widely separated extremes. In all respects it held the key of the situation. There was at one extremity—at the high pastoral and quasi-episcopal pole, so to speak—an ancient offshoot of the Methodist Episcopal Church of America, itself episcopal, and with the highly developed pastoral prerogative of Methodism as it reigns in the great republic; at the other extremity there were Societies belonging to the New Connexion, the Primitives, and the Bible Christians. The economy of Wesleyan Methodism was the happy medium between the opposite extremes. Then, as to the pastoral position in the Conference, that was not likely to cause trouble in respect of the New Connexion or the other bodies whose Conferences in England ignore or minimise the pastoral distinction, because most of these bodies in Canada, under their own local Conferences, were virtually independent of their parent Conferences in England. To join the proposed union was to gain real rights and privileges; to stand out on grounds of theory because of the constitution maintained in their Conferences in England would have been an unavailing loss to themselves. To which it must be added that on Canadian soil there were no polemical Methodist traditions; that in an entirely middle-class country, without an Established Church, like the Dominion,—as in the United States, but much more so, —political questions are not identified with religious and social distinctions, and do not enfibre themselves with Church institutions, with Church organisation and administration, nor lend a bitter tone and an offensive colour to Church distinctions. The question, in particular, as to the pastoral office and lay rights is not an embittered question, or one mixed up with secular politics. Moreover, the equality and similarity of educational and social conditions strongly favoured ecclesiastical unity and identity; while, at the same time, the sparseness of the population throughout the Dominion, with the exception of the Roman Catholic city of Montreal and two or three considerable towns besides, made the existence of two, three, or four different forms of Methodism in the same place peculiarly inconvenient and disadvantageous. All these reasons together gave special advantages in dealing with the subject, difficult as it was with the difficulty of complexity, and at the same time made it worth every effort safely and wisely to accomplish it. To secure one united and powerful Methodism, a Methodism founded on well-balanced principles, and animated by a peaceful and kindly spirit, in a thinly peopled but grand young empire like that of the Dominion, was worth the united efforts of the best men in all the various Methodist communities. The successful result has been a great achievement. It is true that there has been some friction, but certainly not more than might have been expected. All our sympathies must go along with the united Methodism of the new Dominion.[1]

As respects that great field and the union there accomplished, I may fitly quote some passages from the address of the British Conference of 1886 to the Conference of the Dominion:

"We have heard with much interest of the successful accomplishment of the project for the union of the different Methodist Churches of the Dominion. In a country like yours, free from the extremes of society, and lacking the varieties of social condition which are found in our own land; a country also where the people are scattered over a vast territory, and nowhere aggregated in such multitudes as to allow of the very large and varied development of Church life and activity among separate Churches having a general family likeness in doctrine and discipline; we cannot wonder that the ministers and laymen of the different denominations could no longer recognise, as your Address expresses it, any 'justifiable ground for separation and rivalry.' You have no very large number of persons lifted by their position out of easy fellowship with the masses of the people on the one hand, and no very large degraded classes on the other; but a population, to a great extent,

[1] This great work was accomplished at two stages. Under the skilful guidance of Dr. Punshon, in 1873, the union was consummated between the Wesleyan Methodist Connexion and the small community of New Connexion Methodists. This was accomplished without any concession of principle on the subject of the pastoral prerogative of the minister. Rather that position was made in Canada more secure by the conditions of the union. That first operation in the way of reunion having been successfully accomplished, and a good precedent thereby established, the further union of the other bodies with the Wesleyan Methodist Connexion, so as to constitute one Methodist Church for the Dominion, was consummated in 1883.

homogeneous, and largely on a level. For such a homogeneous population it might well seem desirable that one Methodist Church should make spiritual provision. Moreover, the formerly existing divisions among the Methodist bodies, not being native to the Dominion, but imported, for the most part, from the mother country, seemed to have no proper roots in your soil. Happily, also, the intermediate position of the Wesleyan Methodist Church among the different uniting bodies offered a peculiarly favourable condition for union on the basis of the essential principles of Wesleyan Methodism." [1]

There is one point in the question of union which in the foregoing observations has not been mentioned, namely, the waste of power and sometimes the conflicts of feeling in some villages and a few towns arising from the competing presence of several different forms of Methodism. This is an admitted difficulty, and sometimes an obvious evil. But it is one capable of being mitigated if such a spirit as alone can prepare the way for anything like actual union among the different Methodist Churches rules on all sides. Certainly it is one that should not be aggravated by wanton invasion of each other's spheres in the mere spirit of rivalry. Admitting this evil, but remembering also that the sole presence of one of the Methodist Churches might also be, and sometimes has been or even is, an evil,—for Methodist Churches are not everywhere and always what Methodism ought to be, not always truly primitive in either doctrine or discipline, not always energetic or pure, not always free from a local endemic spirit of acrimony or from practical antinomianism,—it surely cannot be contended that, merely for the sake of removing this difficulty here and there in

[1] *Minutes of Conference*, 1886, pp. 333, 334.

relation to one, or, though very rarely, two of the smaller Methodist bodies, premature action, action not resulting from ripe and spontaneous conviction and feeling, ought to be taken, action which would sacrifice the cherished principles of the most ancient and most highly honoured Methodist Church in the world, a Church larger than all the other Methodist Churches together.

To myself it has not been pleasant to reopen a chapter of controversy in regard to which, for a generation past, I had confidently counted on having borne my final testimony. I have been personally friendly with brethren of all the Methodist Churches. I have preached for all the Churches. I have felt that there ought to be frank good-will both between the Churches and among the ministers. I have been more than content that there should be diversities of tone and tendency among them, and that, being fully persuaded in their own minds, brethren of different politico-ecclesiastical opinions should home together in different Methodist communions. I rejoiced, so far as it was maintained, in the spiritual fellowship within each Church which was the common link of special sympathy between them.

I have enjoyed special opportunities of extending practically the right hand of fellowship to members of other Methodist denominations. In 1871 Wesleyan Methodism completed, at Westminster and Southlands Colleges, its provision for training schoolmasters and schoolmistresses. We found ourselves then in a position to receive pupil-teachers from School Boards and to train teachers for Board schools. It was once agreed that, ours being, by necessary requirement of the Conference, and in accordance with the mind of the Connexion, Methodist colleges for training religious young people to be teachers, all candidates for training who were members of other Methodist Churches should be admitted on equal terms with our own. On that principle we have acted now for twenty-five years. We have had pupil-teachers of all Methodist varieties in our colleges. We have desired to show a liberal and brotherly spirit, to act as the eldest branch of a family, having a distinct but roomy home of its own, might do to guests who are members of other branches settled in their own domains.

And, as time advances, while it is hardly to be expected or even desired that there should be only one form of Methodism for this great and various realm of England, any more than for the wide world, it may be hoped that there will be a confederation of Methodist Churches, combining for many great Christian objects, and recognising each other with frank and cordial fraternity. To me this seems to be the fitter, and for old England even the greater, ideal. If, however, there is to be organic union in any measure or to any extent, it would more naturally be accomplished first between the New Connexion and the Free Churches, and then between the Primitives and the Bible Christians. There would then be three Churches instead of five, embodying respectively real and important distinctions of character and type.[1]

[1] Between the Primitives and the Bible Christians there seems to be reason to expect such a union to take place; between the New Connexion and the Free Churches, the negotiations have not thus far proved successful.

APPENDICES.

APPENDIX A.

THE CLASS-MEETING IN WESLEYAN METHODISM

THE most important disciplinary document issued by the Conference during recent years is "The Report of the Committee on Church Membership, as adopted by the Conference of 1889, having special reference to the Class - meeting." From that document I extract the essential passages, which are as follows:

THE PECULIAR POSITION OF THE CLASS-MEETING IN METHODISM, AND ITS RELATION TO ALL PARTS OF THE METHODIST ECONOMY.

THE Class-meeting is not merely a gateway of entrance into membership; it is not merely a gauge by which fitness for continuing in membership with a living and spiritual Church may be tested. It is all this, but it is more. It is an opportunity systematically provided for the giving of testimony to the power and willingness of Christ to save the soul. It is an organised form of Christian fellowship, and is at least one of the modes of that Christian fellowship which is enjoined by the New Testament upon all believers. It is a form of fellowship also which the history of our Church has proved to be, when duly administered, of the highest efficiency and of manifold and far-reaching influence. It is pre-eminently a method for sheltering, encouraging, and developing the spiritual life. It brings every member under godly oversight, and subjects him to a thorough but congenial discipline. Such a system, moulded for us by the hand of Providence, hallowed and sanctioned during a century and a half by the manifest and abundant blessing of God upon its continual use,—a system after which, or some equivalent for it, other Evangelical Churches are anxiously feeling,— we surely ought not in any way to weaken or discredit, but rather bend every energy to make it more widely and spiritually influential.

The relation of the class-meeting to all the agencies of Methodism must not be overlooked. It is to be feared that in many cases the class-meeting is not now what it once was, and what it might again be made. The class-meeting, when rightly conducted, is a fountain of incalculable blessing. It is in the class-meeting that the young convert first tests his power to speak of the things of God. In the prayers and testimonies of the class-meeting are to be found the first training of prayer-leaders, mission workers, Sunday-school teachers, local preachers, and ministers. But for the practice of simple and fervent utterance in the class-meeting, it is very doubtful whether such a harvest of Christian workers as has been reaped, year by year, could ever have been grown or gathered amongst us. In the class-meeting the finest evangelical instruments have been shaped and tempered.

Nor must the relation of the class-meeting to every part of our Church organisation be overlooked. The leaders' meeting, our first court of discipline, is, as its name indicates, mainly a meeting of "leaders of classes," and its jurisdiction extends as far as the classes themselves extend. But the leaders' meeting represents and embodies in a peculiar way pastoral care, because the leaders may be described as sub-pastors, and are links between the members and the ministers. In a leaders' meeting, if it be rightly and regularly conducted, the minister is made aware of the condition of the Church; the needs of the poor, the sick, the spiritually feeble and tempted, are brought under his attention, and pastoral oversight is thereby made in all cases easier, and, in some cases, possible where it would otherwise have been impossible.

Further, the leaders' meeting, embracing as it does Society and Poor stewards, is also a large constituent of the quarterly meeting; and it is difficult to see how the economy of Methodism could be preserved in any of its characteristic features if the class-meeting unit were broken up or suffered to dissolve into a vague and shadowy existence.

Nor should the relation of the class-meeting to many of our most precious means of grace be forgotten. All will agree that to the solemn Covenant Service admission should not be indiscriminate. Further, some at least of the meetings of the Society ought to be confined to the members, and admission to the regular lovefeasts should also be guarded, and be limited to those who are members of a strict and spiritual Church fellowship; or are, after conversation with the minister or duly appointed leader of the assembly, specially admitted, with the hope of their becoming members. But if a special fitness for these intimate exercises of Christian fellowship is to be demanded, the class-meeting supplies a ready, appropriate, and efficient test.

In a still stronger degree these remarks are applicable to the Lord's Supper. This has often been spoken of as "the test of membership in the Christian Church." For such a view no New Testament authority can be pleaded. The Sacrament of the Supper is a sign and seal of membership in the Christian Church, but cannot, with propriety, be called the test of such membership. No Church theoretically admits communicants to the Lord's table without requiring evidence of their fitness; and it is to be regretted that, contrary to the original rule and usage of Methodism, admission to this sacrament has for many years been allowed without the showing of the "Society" ticket, which is a certificate of fitness on the part of the communicant.

The class-meeting, then, is not a mere appendage to the Methodist system—not a limb which can be removed without endangering the vital organs, but is the very heart of the system, having relations most intimate and essential to all the discipline and fellowship of Methodism. The class-meeting fellowship has been, in fact, the very tissue and substance of living Methodism, from its beginning hitherto. It has indeed been said by some that this vital and essential element of Methodism has lost its former hold upon the attachment of our people. In some parts of the country this is lamentably true. Too many persons attend the class-meeting very irregularly. In other cases, membership is very lightly estimated, so that absence for any reason during a few weeks leads to a quiet abandonment of it. Often through carelessness, sometimes of set purpose, removal to another place becomes the occasion of ceasing to meet. Complaints of this character are by no means new in Methodism. They are indeed as old as the days of Wesley. But the evil has been aggravated by the circumstances of our modern life. Removals from place to place are much more frequent than formerly. The claims of secular business are both more numerous and more urgent than ever. Social life is more restless, and makes greater demands upon the time of our people, especially in the evening. Religious meetings are multiplied; so that the class and week-night services are no longer the only calls on the religious interest and attention of our people when the business of the day is over. Perhaps, too, an increase of self-consciousness, and the growth of a fastidious spirit arising from the influences of modern culture, may, in some cases, have fostered a distaste to speaking freely of the deepest thoughts and feelings. On the other hand, we have gratifying evidence that many of our educated people value not less than others the privilege of class-meeting fellowship; and that, even in many parts of restless and busy London, the classes are exceedingly well attended.

Of the causes which militate against regular attendance at class some cannot be removed. We can only contend against them to the best of our power. Where the condition of the class-meeting is unsatisfactory, it might, we think, be greatly improved if devout and earnest attention were given to the following points:

I. The strengthening and deepening amongst all our ministers of a profound sense of pastoral duty and responsibility. It must be remembered that no system can be more effective than the men who work it. Patient, diligent, minute attention to the meeting of the classes is necessary, if our knowledge of the flocks is to be thorough, our returns of membership trustworthy, and our influence upon the members powerful for good. If a minister speaks lightly of a class-meeting, or treats lightly the quarterly visitation, hurrying through it, unduly crowding the classes together to save time, or (as there is reason to fear has sometimes been done) even sending the tickets to a leader instead of meeting the class himself, both leaders and members will be apt to think of it and treat it as lightly. Time and energy devoted to larger and more popular religious gatherings will by no means compensate for any neglect, even in villages, of conscientious pastoral care in the meeting of the classes. Society meetings should be held more frequently than of recent years. If not on every Sunday evening, as in earlier Methodism, they should be held once a month, or at least twice a quarter, and should be appointed on the plan, that they may not be overlooked.

II. Much difficulty and confusion have arisen from the varying standards in the minds of ministers as to the occasions which would warrant the withholding of a ticket from a member. It should be borne in mind that it is our rule that no member shall, either upon the recommendation of a leader, or otherwise, be left without a ticket, until he has been personally visited by a minister. It must also be understood that there exists no rule which requires a minister to refuse a ticket solely on the ground of irregular attendance at class. It must not be forgotten that to exclude a person from membership is the most serious and painful exercise of ecclesiastical discipline, to be undertaken only when necessity demands it, and under a sense of solemn responsibility. Indeed, in the independent ecclesiastical position into which Methodism has been led by the providence of God since the death of Wesley, exclusion from membership in the class-meeting involves, for the time being, excommunication from the visible Church. It is therefore the duty of the minister to allow the name of no one to be removed from the class-book who has not been carefully visited, patiently borne with, faithfully exhorted, earnestly entreated; or for any other than grave moral or spiritual reasons, or decided and persistent disaffection. And even in such cases, every person so excluded from the fellowship of the Church must have the opportunity, if he claims it, of having his case judicially decided at a leaders' meeting, according to the provisions of our discipline.

III. In many places, persons who would, in the first instance, shrink from joining any other class, would willingly join one of which a minister is the leader. By means of such a class, conducted with tact and judgment, many might be drawn within our closer fellowship, who would otherwise decline to enter it.

As bearing directly upon these matters, the Conference directs that, in our theological colleges, instruction, theoretical and practical, in all the points of our pastoral discipline, especially in those which relate to our class-meetings and leaders' meetings, should be regularly given as a necessary part of the routine of college study.

IV. It is of the greatest importance that the leaders' meeting should be restored to its former place of spiritual influence and power. It should be remembered that the leaders' meeting is not a mere instrument for collecting the contributions of the classes, for administering poor relief, and for making certain administrative arrangements. Its purpose is to enable the ministers, with the help of the leaders, to guard and promote the spiritual well-being of the Societies. The meeting should therefore be held frequently and regularly; if possible, weekly, according to rule. The class-books should be examined by the minister, and note taken of any members who, because of affliction or poverty or spiritual declension, need special attention. The leaders themselves should be conversed with as to how they are prospering in their own souls, and how their classes are prospering. In accordance with a regulation passed many years ago, and productive of great blessing, an entire meeting should at least once a quarter be given up to prayer and testimony, and heart-searching conversation in reference to the leaders' special work. Further, the introduction of a new leader should be made with all solemnity; our rules as to his examination being carefully observed. In a word, the leaders' meeting should be made the spiritual centre of the Society. If this were done, not only would the existing leaders be more efficient and useful, but the succession of competent and spiritually powerful leaders would more easily be maintained.

V. It is highly important that new leaders should be appointed with reasonable frequency. Even though there should be classes, under existing leaders, the attendance at which is few and feeble, it is important to appoint leaders, selected for their promise of vigour and enterprise, as well as for their other gifts, to commence new classes. It is very important that suitable *young* men and women should be appointed to this office. The best leaders have usually entered while young upon the office, and many who in mature life refuse to become leaders would have accepted the office at an earlier age. There seems to be no reason why leaders, if otherwise suitable, should not be appointed at as early an age as ministers.

But, whether they be young or old, leaders should be better instructed in the work of their office. Many of them need to be told what to leave undone as well as what to do. They should be cautioned against insisting that every member, however timid and inexperienced, should, from the first, be expected to speak in the meeting. It would often be well to read a short portion of God's word at the class-meeting. Leaders should be advised to hold a prayer-meeting at regular intervals, and may be encouraged to use Bible readings occasionally, provided that these are used for the purpose of evoking conversation on Christian experience. But ·strict care should be taken that the meeting shall not become merely a "Bible-class." The proper business of the class-meeting, it must never be forgotten, is spiritual fellowship and conversation.

It is important that leaders be urged to mark the class-books; and, as a general rule, to receive the contribution of the members week by week. They would thus avoid the difficulty which has often, in the case of poor members, discouraged attendance when considerable arrears of contributions had accumulated. In the case of very poor members, the leader should be careful rather to remit these arrears, than allow them to be a difficulty in the way of the member continuing his attendance at class. Above all, the leader should understand that he is not at liberty of his own authority to drop one single name from his book, and in the visitation of the classes each minister should make a careful comparison with the list of the previous quarter, in order to insure that no member's name is dropped, either through inadvertence or for any cause.

VI. An earnest and united effort should be made to restore our ancient discipline as to the showing of tickets at those meetings which, according to our constitution, are intended for the special benefit of the members of our Church. Wherever possible, we should return to our former plan of holding lovefeasts in the afternoon of the Lord's day, allowing no admission except by class or communicant's ticket, or by note from the minister. Where it is necessary to hold them after the evening service, distinct intimation should be given previously that only those persons are entitled to remain who are members of our Church, or who shall have received from the minister a special note of admission. Then the stewards should pass from pew to pew to see the tickets, or in some other way ascertain that only qualified persons are present. This rule should also be strictly observed in reference to the Covenant service, and, so far as practicable, in reference to Society meetings.

Further, it is most important that a united and earnest attempt should be made to secure the presence of all our members, and the showing of tickets at the Lord's Supper. As regards strangers occasionally attending our services, who desire to participate with us, they may reasonably be expected to assure the minister of their fitness by explaining to him that they are members of another Church, or for what reason, not being members of any Church, they desire to be communicants; and such occasional cases can be met by the issue of a special note of admission by the minister. That the table of the Lord should be open to all comers is surely a great discredit and a serious peril to any Church.

VII. The Conference directs that, at the close of each quarterly visitation, those new members to whom tickets of membership have for the first time been given should, wherever possible, be formally recognised as Church members at a suitable service.

Such service might be held in connexion with a special Society meeting, and the administration of the Lord's Supper on a Sunday evening, or, where practicable and convenient, on a week evening. Or, in small and remote places, the public recognition of these new members might be made in connexion with the ordinary administration of the Lord's Supper.

VIII. It appears to be of the greatest possible importance,

for the lessening of the present great loss of members, that a roll of membership shall be kept in every Society. Such a roll should be, in fact, the aggregate of the class-books, and it should be corrected, if possible, quarter by quarter, or at least once a year. While the superintendent must be responsible for seeing that this roll is duly kept, the actual work of correction, from quarter to quarter, might be done by one of his junior colleagues.

APPENDIX B.

THE DISTRICT SYNOD IN METHODISM, ITS DEVELOPMENT AND
PRESENT FUNCTIONS: AN HISTORICAL SKETCH.

THE following extracts are taken from a pamphlet published under the above title in 1894, and which was delivered as an Address to the Annual May Synod of the Second London District, of which the writer was the Chairman:

THE PROBLEM OF 1791.

JOHN WESLEY died in 1791, and with his death came an end of his personal dominion. Then the master was taken away from the Methodist Society, which had grown to be large and widespread, having tens of thousands of adherents. The master was taken away—the living bond of unity was removed—and the pressing question was, How was this unity to be maintained? How was Wesley's influence and authority to be replaced? What substitute could be found for it? What was to hold the circuits and Societies together? What power or presence after his death was to touch them, to guide and encourage them from month to month, from year to year? Wesley indeed had left a Conference—the Conference which he had annually held and consulted for forty years, and which, six years before his death, he had legally constituted. This Conference had been invested with authority to admit, to station, to remove—if need were, to put away—the itinerant preachers; invested with power and authority over chapels and over circuit arrangements. But this Conference could not supply Wesley's place in the continual government of his Society. It only met once a year. It had to choose a President when it first met after his death, and always afterwards when it met. But that President was only the chairman of the Conference, and his authority, as such, lasted only so long as that Conference was assembled. He was not President in successive years, much less did he, or could he, inherit Wesley's powers over his Society. Indeed, the first Conference thought it necessary to say that his powers dropped and terminated when the Conference ended. It is true that the President has had certain powers conferred on him since, but only such powers as the Conference specially gives to do such things as the President is expressly instructed to do. A general power and sway over the Societies no President ever had, and if he had had it, it would only have been for one year. In a succession of Presidents there could have been no continuous sway or true union or unity. Nor could the Conference, meeting once a year, hold the Societies together. It could not encourage and counsel month by month, or as occasion might require. It could not deal with any wrong that might arise, when it needed to be dealt with. How then was Wesley's place to be supplied? How was the whole body to be guided and maintained?

The Problem Solved.

The problem was solved by the creation, at the first Conference after Wesley's death, of District Committees. The power of the central Conference was devolved on these bodies in the interval between Conference and Conference, and around these central bodies the circuits were clustered in Districts duly defined. The preachers and the people of these Districts were placed under the intermediate and provisional authority of the District Meetings. To each District a Chairman was appointed by the Conference, to summon and preside at all official meetings of the District, but also, unlike the President, to have large though limited authority throughout the year. The Chairman of the District was to be the ear and the eye, the hand and mouthpiece, of the District Assembly, and also of the Conference, in dealing with preachers and people, with ministers and circuits.

District Meetings as thus created were styled "Committees of the Conference," and had power accordingly. Their power, though great, was much less than now. At the same time, the power of the Chairman at first was in some respects greater than now, and was more actively used than in later years. The Chairman more frequently visited the circuits, and was more consulted. The Conference, indeed, directed that on all occasions of importance the superintendent minister of a circuit should invite the Chairman to attend his quarterly meetings.[1] It was natural in that early stage of development, when everything had to be shaped and moulded, and when superintendents (then still called assistants) were often young and inexperienced, that Chairmen should have considerable directive power and authority. In the century which has passed since, the District Meetings have undergone an immense development—have acquired many new functions —have had conferred upon them, as to a number of minor points, new and final jurisdiction; and they are now as to various matters more than mere Committees of the Conference. The power of the District Committee is much greater than at the first. The power and authority of the Chairman is in certain respects less. Now, at length, we have been compelled to give these District Meetings a title more justly descriptive of their character than that of District Committees. We call them by the appropriate name of District Synods.

[1] *Minutes of Conference*, vol. i., p. 692, edition of 1862.

A NATURAL DEVELOPMENT.

The development, as I have said, has been immense, but it has been natural, consecutive, inevitable—all arising out of the necessary development of Methodism from a mere religious guild or society, into a great, world-wide, collective Church. What the District Synods are to-day, I repeat—what they have grown to be since District Committees were first created after the death of Wesley—is all a direct and necessary consequence from the changes in the character of the preachers and of the Connexion which followed, and could not but follow, that event.

In Wesley's days, Methodist itinerant preachers both led and fed the Societies. They fed them with saving truth. They were also pastors of the flock—faithful and diligent pastors. But they were not acknowledged as ministers. They were still rated as lay preachers, with the exception of a very few whom Wesley himself had ordained to help him and Dr. Coke[1] in the work of sacramental administration. The death of Wesley led almost immediately to a change in this. The Societies generally demanded the Sacraments from their preachers. Some strong and influential Church Methodists opposed this claim; but the Connexion declared its mind by a powerful majority, and prevailed. Four years after Wesley's death the controversy was over, and whenever Sacraments were called for at the hands of the preachers, they were administered.

This was only one part of a great and peaceful revolution. By this change the preachers ceased to be mere lay assistants and helpers; they became pastors of the Methodist Church. The senior minister in a circuit was soon styled the superintendent—which is the Wesleyan word for the primitive bishop. The junior ministers were pastoral colleagues. But this involved a correlative change

[1] Dr. Coke was a clergyman of the Church of England, whom Wesley had associated with himself in the administration of the Sacraments to his Societies, and had ordained "superintendent"—i.e. bishop—for America.

in the position of the people, the flock, the laity. They had been members of the Church of England, or of Dissenting or Presbyterian Churches. They were now members of the Methodist Church, though, as yet, the Society was seldom called a Church. Leaders' meetings became, in effect, Church councils. Leaders and stewards became Church officers — New Testament deacons, in fact. The leaders and stewards in their meetings became sharers with the ministers in the guidance of the local Churches, and in the guardianship of Church order. This change touched everything. It brought the circuit stewards almost immediately, and one grade after another of principal Church officers after a time, into the District Committees—the "Synods," let us call them. It made natural and necessary the distribution of the Connexional business into Departments, presided over by mixed Committees of ministers and laymen. It resulted, after thirty years had passed, in the grand Committee of Review system, of twenty years ago and more; it finally found a more complete development in the Representative Conference of recent years, and the District Synods as they are to-day. The mighty system of co-operative administration which exists in English Methodism on a scale and with results unrivalled in any other Church in or out of England, has all resulted by direct growth and consequence from the peaceful revolution of the years 1791 to 1797 — by which the Methodism of Wesley became the Wesleyan Methodist Church.

At the beginning of this century the District Committees of Methodism were small and feeble assemblies, which easily did their work in a day or a day and a half, and numbered from ten to thirty ministers, and about half as many circuit stewards, gathered from areas on an average twice as large as our present Districts. To-day, while the number of Districts has doubled, the number of ministers in a District is on the average three or four times as many as at first, while the number of lay members of Synods to-day far exceeds the number of ministers. The special pastoral duties which engaged the attention of the ministers apart then occupied from half a day to a day. Now, they often occupy two or three closely filled days. The business of ministers and stewards at the beginning of the century when they met together in the District Meeting might occupy half a day. Now, if done rightly and thoroughly, it may often fully occupy two days.

THE WORK OF THE SYNOD.

Let us look at the development of the business of District Committees, which we now call District Synods. During Wesley's days all the business of the Connexion of every kind was done at the yearly Conference, over which he presided. The division and rearrangement of circuits, chapel affairs, home missions, help of every kind to circuit and Connexional expenses of every sort (for all which expenses the Yearly Collection was chargeable, so far as its funds would go), all these matters were considered and settled at the Conference.

In 1797, six years after Wesley's death, the Conference was glad to divest itself of all this business, and to be content with the power of saying "no" to an impracticable scheme of finance or circuit arrangement; and "temporal affairs" were relegated to District Meetings in connexion with the circuits and their quarterly meetings. In particular, the District Meetings—informed and instructed by the general or circuit stewards as representing quarterly meetings — were to settle circuit divisions or rearrangements, home mission work, chapel building and chapel relief schemes, and the application of the Yearly Collection raised within the District. This brought the circuit stewards into the District Meeting. Hence the Conference of 1801 instructed the superintendent minister not to fail to invite the general steward of each circuit to be present at the Annual District Meeting during the settlement of everything relating to the finance of the

District; and formally declared accordingly that every circuit steward had the right to be present and to advise in the settlement of all financial matters.[1]

Thus, ten years after Wesley's death, and four years after the Conference had resolved that the financial business and all "temporal affairs" should be discussed in detail, and as far as possible settled, in quarterly meetings and District Meetings, we find an important co-operative lay element organised and established in the District Meetings. The circuit stewards co-operating (in 1801) with the circuit ministers were the nucleus and the root of all the vast lay development which has followed during the century now nearly completed. And the whole progress of the Connexion, spiritual and temporal, was bound up with these temporal matters—these questions of finance, of the division and reorganisation of circuits, the erection of chapels, the hiring of houses for ministers, the maintenance of the ministers—which had to be settled during the presence of the circuit stewards, all such matters of business being, in fact, outward forms of spiritual increase and advance.

MINISTERIAL ALLOWANCES.

The most difficult questions with which the District Meetings were concerned at this period were those relating to the maintenance of ministers. The Connexional system made the difficulty here. Preachers continually revolving, changing from place to place, led to such changes of financial charge upon the circuits as created great difficulties. One year a circuit might have an unmarried but yet senior minister as superintendent (this happened sometimes), or a married minister with no family. The next year there might be a great change

---

[1] As to this point of development, the student of Methodist economics should refer to Myles' *Chronological History of Methodism* (p. 214, fourth edition); an invaluable book for information as to the early stages of our Connexional development.

—the circuit might have a large family besides the minister. This year the circuit could maintain its minister or ministers. Next year it was quite beyond its power to maintain the greatly and suddenly increased burden of ministers and families. The Conference at first left the District Meeting to grapple with these difficulties. It said: "Apply within the District the proceeds of the Yearly Collection" (*i.e.* the Home Mission Fund raised in the classes within the District). "If that is not enough, take extra and supplementary collections or subscriptions, but let the District meet its own need within itself." That was, in substance, the first Conference direction on the subject. But this proved impracticable. There were great inequalities in Districts. Some were small and poor, and others were large and comparatively rich. The necessary conclusion was that the Districts must help each other. But how? The Conference, in stationing the preachers, tried to place the more costly families as far as possible in well-to-do circuits, and the ministers with the smallest families in the poorer circuits; but this was a hard task for the Stationing Committee, and soon proved to be impracticable. It would not work. It was needful to station the preachers where their character and gifts were most useful. And yet wives and families must be provided for. How was that to be done? The only way was to pay them out of common funds, to be raised in all the circuits of the Connexion. There was at first a stationing of wives *pro rata*, so many wives to be provided for by each District, whether there were as many there or not, according to the number of members and the general ability of the circuits. Then the same plan was applied to the children. For the wives, the plan before long came to an end; but the provision for charging the children on a Common Fund has been retained up to the present time—at least in principle. These were cumbrous and complicated methods, but they grew out of the necessities of the itinerancy, and they brought about the result—when the difficulties were fairly mastered—of making all the ministers of our Church to be more equably and equitably, and therefore on an average better and more suitably, maintained than any other body of ministers. It is curious to read in the *Minutes of Conference* of the "salaries paid to wives and children." It is an expression occurring once and again. It was the current and common phrase in 1801. The salary for a wife was £12; for a child £4, which was presently increased to £6. Now for many years this salary for children—or, as it was after a few years called, "allowance"—has been fixed at the minimum of six guineas, and augmented in many circuits to eight or ten guineas per child. There was, in addition, an allowance of £12 for education paid for boys not able to find a place in the Kingswood, or later on in the Woodhouse Grove School. The allowance for girls was £6. These observations will make intelligible a "Minute of Conference" of 1801. "The deficiencies of the preachers' salaries, of the preachers' wives' salaries, and of the preachers' children's salaries, together with the allowances for servants, house rent, coals, and candles, shall be paid at the District Meeting by the means of the Yearly Collection raised in each District respectively; and, as far as is necessary, by extra collections and subscriptions raised throughout each District respectively." In 1804 is found the following, which is an advance in administrative management: "Let the sums necessary to afford the usual allowances to the preachers' children be furnished by the several circuits on a regular and equitable plan; and, in order to this, let the children in future be stationed on the circuits, as well as the wives. Let the stationing of both wives and children be so regulated that the expenses may be equalised in the different Districts in proportion to the numbers in Society." In this Minute the Conference had no doubt adopted some suggestion from District Meetings; but the work was not easy to arrange, and, in fact, was never really accomplished.

Such were some of the methods of Connexional organisation discussed and adopted in the early years of the century. In 1818, after many years of wrestling in the District Meetings with the financial problems of the Connexion, we find the Conference resolving as follows : " In the next District Meetings, at the time of the transaction of the financial business, during which the circuit stewards are to be present, according to our rule, they shall be requested to take into consideration the propriety of making every District responsible for providing within itself, and by its own local resources, the allowances for such a number of preachers' children as would fairly belong to it, according to the principle of proportion to numbers in Society;—leaving it, however, to the preachers and stewards assembled in each District Meeting to modify the application of that general principle, from year to year, according to their discretion, by relieving the more burdened circuits of their own District; so, however, as that the whole quota of each District for children may be always raised within itself. The opinion of the District Meetings on the plan now proposed shall be reported in their Minutes, and brought before the next Conference." That was nearly eighty years ago; but the Minute sounds quite modern, and the principle of adjustment embodied in it has ruled in all subsequent legislation.

So far things had developed during the quarter of a century following the death of Wesley. The circuit stewards continued to be with few exceptions the one class of lay colleagues united with the ministers in the business of the annual District Meetings.

THE GROWTH OF THE FUNDS.

But another line of development had already begun to take form. It had been found necessary to create common funds for the whole Connexion — but more funds than we have had occasion to note. The Children's

Fund was one; the Schools' Fund was another. But a Chapel Fund also was established in the early years of the century. The Yearly Collection was recognised as making provision for Home Mission work and also as providing a "Contingent Fund," and set quite apart from the Foreign Mission Fund, with a special collection of its own, known for many years as the July Collection; and above all, the Foreign Mission Fund was organised as a Fund separate from Home Missions, and our Foreign Missionary Society received between 1813 and 1818 its full Connexional development.[1] All these Funds were placed under Committees of the Conference composed of equal numbers of ministers and laymen. The Missionary Society especially was a masterpiece of conjoint ministerial and lay organisation in all its parts. And all these Funds were represented at the District Meeting, and sustained largely through the influence of the District Meeting. All their District treasurers accordingly were constituted members of the District Meeting, as also were their General or Connexional treasurers. So that, before the first twenty years of the century were completed, the District Meetings consisted, besides ministers, of circuit stewards and Connexional treasurers. The temporal and financial business of the District Meetings was continually increasing in volume and importance. The initial difficulties of Connexional organisation as between the Conference and the circuits had been surmounted largely through the statesmanlike genius of Dr. Bunting. But those larger measures of consolidation and advance which were required in order to the continued progress of the Church were not less necessary to be carried out, especially in connexion with chapel building and Foreign Missions. Here were new fields for organisation and extension. It was found necessary to hold central annual meetings of the managing committees of all the Funds to prepare the

[1] The missionary contributions raised for many years by Dr. Coke had been applied to both Home and Foreign Mission work.

business for review and enactment by the Yearly Conference, which was the legal representative and fountain of authority for all the Districts and circuits of the Connexion. All this progress made the District Meetings more and more important, and gave them more and more business to do.

TWO MEETINGS YEARLY BECOME NECESSARY.

In 1819 it was found necessary to have two District Meetings in the year for the settlement of temporal and financial affairs—besides the full meeting in May to have a special Financial District Meeting in September, to take its instructions and inspiration from the central managing Committees of the various Departments of expenditure and from the Conference "Minutes," and to start the business for the year, the results of which were to be registered at the District Meeting in May. From 1819 accordingly we find in regular working the September Financial District Committee after each Conference, as well as the May District Meeting in preparation for each Conference. After 1820, when the central Annual "Committees of Finance and Administration," as they were called at first—afterwards known as Departmental Committees of Review—had taken their place distinctly in our Connexional system as providing summaries of departmental work in preparation for the Conference, the interest and importance of these Committees of Review, meeting each year before the Conference in the Conference town, continued to increase for half a century or more, till in 1878 they were absorbed in the Representative Conference. To the Connexion they came to be the great annual occasion when the work of the year was set forth and reviewed. From the time of the Centenary celebration in 1839-40, of which the Centenary Fund was the result, the Connexion had learnt to wait and watch for the week of the annual Committees of Review—the proceedings of which came about that time to be duly reported in the newspapers, especially in that valuable newspaper *The*

Watchman. The Committee of Review gatherings were for many years the central annual rendezvous of the Connexional forces from all parts of the country and of the mission field. They were seasons of rejoicing, of mutual encouragement, of festivity, public and social. That period of our history—of which the Centenary Fund was the central event—was the grand period of Methodist increase, unequalled, on the whole, before or since. It was perhaps a period of too great confidence and too much boasting. It represented more than fifty years of advance since the death of Wesley. It contained within itself a prophecy of coming development, of the organised growth of the fifty years that followed.

THE COMMITTEES OF REVIEW BECOME REPRESENTATIVE.

The historian, in looking back, sees in these Committees of Review the promise and root of the United Conference of later years. The principle of District representation, indeed, which has been worked out in our present constitution and organisation, was already coming to be recognised sixty years ago in these Committees. The Districts that were represented, however— about half the total number every year—were selected on account of their convenient nearness to the Conference, and varied from year to year. But in 1835 a distinct and notable step was taken by adding to the General Committee of Management and Review for the Home Mission and Contingent Fund gentlemen chosen from and by *all* the District Committees in England. That was a pregnant movement and the recognition of a master principle. It was not till 1861 that that principle was extended and applied to the other Committees of Review in addition to that of the Home Mission and Contingent Fund. From that time, however, the election in the District Committees of representatives to attend all the Committees of Review became the Connexional rule, till the creation of the United Representative Conference in 1877-8, which, of necessity, did away with the Committees of Review. Thus all the Districts were brought into direct connexion with the great central gathering of Committees which reported annually as to the whole progress of the Connexion, and which, by way of criticism and suggestion, guided the final legislation and moulded the legislative and administrative progress of the Conference and Connexion from year to year.

These Committees of Review sat from day to day for about a week until Conference assembled. The last Committee of Review held each year—on the day before the opening of the Conference and the election of the President — was the great and numerously attended Missionary Committee of Review, which was always interesting, popular, and stimulating, and to which the presence of the minister or ministers suggested privately beforehand as candidates for the office of President lent special interest. It was customary for important resolutions and suggestions of the District Committees as to matters of finance and general administration to receive the notice of the proper Committees of Review before they reached the Conference; and when endorsed by one of these Committees there was little doubt but that the District suggestion would soon become a Minute of the Conference.

Further Developments.

Thus matters advanced and developed at the Connexional centre until the grand development of 1877-8, when the Representative Conference met for the first time at Bradford, and when I had the honour to be elected President. While matters had thus advanced in the centre, important developments had been taking place in the District Meetings, especially in the quarter of a century following 1850. Such developments took place chiefly by means of District Departmental Committees, which were not known during the first sixty years of District organisation.

In 1855-6 the "District Chapel Sub-Committee," as it was then called, was created under the Chapel Fund administration of the late William Kelk and John Bedford, two wise, able, and devoted servants of our Church. Since that period District Sub-Committees—now called Committees of the Synods—have been created for every department of Methodist evangelistic work and mutual Connexional help, so that for years past Chapels, Home Missions, Sunday and Day Schools, Foreign Missions, and Temperance work have all been placed within each District under the charge of District Committees, who report every year to the centre; and all members of these Committees, in addition to circuit stewards and Connexional treasurers, are members of the Synods. Thus the number of lay members in the Synods has continued to increase along the whole line of Connexional development, every important advance of organisation being reflected in a corresponding development in the constitution of our Synods. Taken in connexion with the original and ever-increasing responsibilities of the pastoral work and office, which have advanced and multiplied in full proportion with the whole complex organic growth and development of our Connexional life and work, the functions and responsibilities of the Synods, in relation to the financial and generally administrative business of the Connexion, have continued to grow and develop, until at the present time their volume is immense, and their character and range such as to include every active operation of our Church.

A NEW ELEMENT ADDED TO THE SYNOD.

We have seen that thus far two things have gone together—a natural proportion being maintained between them—*viz.*, the increasing business of the District Synods, and the increasing number of laymen directly associated with the business to be done. The increase in the number of lay members has been dependent upon, and has naturally flowed from, the increase in the variety and volume of business to be done. A few years ago, however, an entirely new principle was brought into play, by which about half as many more laymen were added to the meetings of the Synod than there are circuits in the District, these gentlemen being freely chosen by the quarterly meetings to the number of one or two for each circuit according to the size of the circuit. They are not chosen at all for business reasons—they may or may not in a special sense be business men; they do not represent the financial importance and responsibilities of the circuits from which they come: they are elected because of their high personal character as Christians and members of the Church, and of their just weight of personal influence in the counsels of the circuit. For many years there had been a growing feeling of the desirability of such an element being introduced into our District Meetings, so that, besides the chief business officers of the circuit, they might include a due proportion of circuit representatives chosen on the simple ground of personal character and influence. The matter was looked at in 1876-7, and the introduction into the District Meetings of such a new element was proposed and advocated by more than one member of the Committee that prepared the new proposals for developing and modifying our economy which took effect at the Conference of 1878; but the conclusion arrived at was, that so large an addition at that time to the District Meetings as would be made necessary by adopting such a proposal would prove burdensome and unmanageable. When twelve years, however, had passed away, the proposal, though not without its difficulties, seemed no longer impracticable; in particular, there seemed reason to hope that the increased burden of hospitable entertainment would not now prove to be beyond the power of the circuits which would combine to accommodate the District Synods. It was a great satisfaction to me to have the opportunity in 1890 of taking an active part in bringing into effect an organic extension which I had advocated in 1876. The addition of this new and invaluable element to our District Synods will hereafter be one of the landmarks of Methodist history. It was a great matter when, as already related, the principle of direct District representation to the Conference became a recognised principle in our economy; but it is of no less significance and importance that our circuits should by this new and golden link be brought into closer connexion with our District Synods. It has from the first been necessary that our trusted and honoured, our diligent and faithful circuit and District business officials should have a place in our Synods. It would have been impossible to do business without them; but it is also well—it is eminently beneficial—that besides these there should be joined with us in our Synods chosen brethren from the circuits, whose weight of character and general influence in Church work make them eminently fit to bear a responsible share in the fellowship and Christian counsels of the ministers and lay officials of the District Synod.

A Striking Contrast.

And now what a contrast is seen between the District Committees of 1800 and the District Synods of to-day! Then the District Committees consisted of from eight to thirty ministers, with the general steward from each circuit—*i.e.* three or four to twelve stewards (at that time the custom of having two circuit stewards was not established; such stewards were not easy to find in those days). Now, our Synods, though greatly contracted in geographical boundaries, consist, roughly speaking, on the average, of three times as many ministers, and twelve times as many laymen. A large vestry, if such a vestry could at that time have been found, would, in 1800, have held the members of almost any District Meeting, the laymen being present. Now, the District Synod is often numerous enough to nearly fill the body of a large chapel.

Then, the business of a small District could all be done in a day, and of a large one, in two days, with early morning and evening services, and easy spaces between the meals. Now, in many Districts, the work of the Synod in the sessions when ministers and laymen are united, cannot be thoroughly done in less than two days, while the pastoral enquiries, examinations, and records of ministers occupy other two days, and sometimes more. At that time the special business of ministers in the District Meeting included little more than examinations of each other as to character, doctrine, and abilities, and the obituaries of the deceased brethren, with occasional questions of administration. In the earliest years of the century there was as yet no personal examination at the District Meeting of candidates for the ministry, or of young preachers who were completing their term of probation for the ministry. The financial business of the same period was transacted by the ministers and stewards of a united session, first of all, in the afternoon of the first day, and in later years in the morning of the second day, and consisted partly in considering cases of chapel building and chapel relief, or of the division or rearrangement of circuits, but chiefly of questions of circuit assistance and relief connected with the Yearly Collection, by way of helping in the maintenance of the ministers, especially in the payment of the allowances to preachers' wives and children, or in cases of personal affliction. Now, the chief subjects of enquiry which, by the ministers in their pastoral capacity, must be considered in Pastoral Session, number more than twenty-five, and the number of chief questions with which the United Synod has to deal—laymen being present—is nearly forty.

WHAT THE SYNODS DO WHEN THEY MEET.

In the Pastoral Sessions, which precede and follow the United Sessions of ministers and laymen, the Ministerial Synod passes in review questions of ministerial character and fitness for ministerial service, and the records of deceased ministers. It considers the spiritual condition of the circuits of the District, and the pastoral calls and duties of the ministers. It bestows particular attention upon the question of the religious training of the young. It receives special reports as to Home Mission circuits one by one, and the progress or otherwise of the work. It deals thoroughly with the cases of candidates for the ministry, with the results of their various trials and the recommendations to be founded thereon; and the Synodical examination of each and all of them is conducted in the presence of the assembled ministers. It reviews the results of annual examinations, in various subjects, of probationers for the ministry, especially in regard to their reading and their prescribed studies. It subjects to final examination in theology and doctrine those who are in their last year of probation for the ministry, and who will be presented for ordination at the next Conference. The Synod also, in its pastoral character, considers and reports upon questions of pastoral duty and responsibility referred to it by the Conference, and passes resolutions as to suggestions proposed to be sent to the Conference. And, finally, the Pastoral Session has also to determine which of their number are to attend the next Conference, and on what conditions.

In its United Session, when questions of Connexional finance and of general Church work come under the attention of both ministers and laymen, the Synod has to pass in review the reports of the Committees of the Synod as to the Departmental Funds and the work of the Church generally; as to chapel building and chapel relief; as to the building of schools and ministers' houses; as to the work of Sunday and Day Schools; as to the Home Mission work and needs of the District; as to the Foreign Missionary Department; and as to Temperance work. They have also to receive from their respective treasurers reports as to the Worn-out Ministers' and Ministers' Widows' Fund, and as to the contributions of the District to the Fund for the Maintenance and Education of Ministers' Children, for which Fund there are no District Committees to sit during the year. In our own Synod [1] much time is usefully occupied on the general report, and the special personal statements of our general District missionary. We have had such a missionary in our District for twenty years, besides a considerable number of ministers engaged in our special Home Mission work in the District. Perhaps this is the most interesting part of our proceedings. Our Home Missionary operations in this District cover a very large area in Surrey, Hampshire, Berkshire, and part of Middlesex. All the three London Districts are largely Home Missionary, but this Second London District is more widely Home Missionary than the others. For many years past large special subscriptions have been contributed annually by generous friends of Christian Home Mission work in this District, in order to maintain the special District Fund by which we augment the liberal contributions derived from the general Home Mission Fund of the Connexion for the maintenance of our Home Mission work. All questions of circuit division and arrangement also are considered, and provisionally determined, by the United Session of the Synod. Representatives to Conference are elected, one of these being the minister who is to attend the Stationing Committee which prepares the draft of ministerial appointments for the Conference, and the others laymen who attend the Conference as members of the Representative Session. Laymen are also elected to serve on certain Departmental Committees during the year. Special subjects referred to it by the Conference are considered and dealt with by the United Session. Suggestions also for the Conference may be sent forward from this session. A few years ago this Synod sent forward by a unanimous vote a suggestion that in future these great assemblies should be called District Synods instead of District Committees.

[1] That of the Second London District.

The resolution was immediately adopted by the Conference in Representative Session, and has now for several years been law. But there is one matter of deepest interest, not yet named, that is dealt with in the United Session of the Synod; viz. a general conversation on Christian work in connexion with our circuits and societies. There is, indeed, always a special conversation on the same subject in the Pastoral Session, as could not but be the case, seeing that there are special points affecting ministerial duty and fidelity which require to be dealt with searchingly— perhaps sometimes almost sternly — among ministers with each other; nevertheless, for ministers and laity together, a conversation on the comprehensive subject of Methodist evangelistic duty and work is needed. It is well also for ministers to hear plain talk from their lay brethren, as well as for the laymen to talk to each other, at the District Synod, on points of duty to Christ and souls. A conversation is necessary in both sessions of the Synod, although I have never heard such plain things spoken in the United Session, nor points of duty pressed so faithfully home, as I have sometimes heard in the dealings of ministers with each other. But we also need mutual encouragement—ministers and laymen alike—and all to be impressed and to help to impress each other with the aspects of Christian duty and privilege which belong to the common gospel of Christ alike for all His servants, whatever position they hold in His kingdom.

CONCLUSION.

You see, then, dear brethren, how great is the work to be done at these annual gatherings. To the Financial District Synod which it was found necessary to organise in 1819 I have referred in an earlier part of this address. That is an increasingly important and absolutely necessary meeting of the Synod, which is likely in the future to be less exclusively financial and more directly and largely spiritual than it was formerly. But the May District Synod, of which I have been speaking at length, must always be the great meeting, *the* annual meeting of the District Synod, on the tone, the conduct, the business completeness, the evangelical force of which, from year to year, the evangelical success and progress of the work of the District mainly depends. What I have shown to be the history of the District Synod will illustrate and make good the assertion just made. It will help us to understand that these Synods are the provincial centres of Connexional union and unity, on which the efficiency of our whole Church economy depends—the centres of organic energy and of spiritual vitality and force. Through these Synods the Conference acts upon the Connexion, and through them also, in turn, the Connexion throughout all its circuits, and in particular the whole body of ministers and laymen personally present or represented in the Synods, collectively react on the Conference. It belongs to the Synods—to you, my brethren, as members of the Second London District Synod—to guard and enforce our rules and our Church principles, to preserve our unity, to gather to a focus spiritual feeling and inspiration, to combine the District forces for great enterprises, for the supply of present needs—to take counsel in every way for the extension of the Saviour's kingdom. If the Conference is the governing and inspiring head and centre of the Connexion—of our whole Church—the Synods are the provincial centres; they are as the nerve centres of the human frame to the living man; and through them the whole Church has to be maintained in healthy vigour and in sympathetic and active correspondence, part with part, and all parts with the whole.

I ask your prayers—the prayers of all whom my words may reach—for the Divine blessing on all the counsels and work of our Synod, and your sustained and increased interest in the work of our Church, especially throughout this, our own District, during the whole year, and from year to year.

APPENDIX C.

THE CIRCUIT DEVELOPMENT OF METHODISM.

THE pages which follow contain the substance of an address delivered by the writer in 1895 to the Synod of the Second London District, of which Synod he was the Chairman:

A DISTINCTION must always be recognised between the Methodist Society of Wesley's days and the fully organised Methodist Church which has grown up since his death. Methodism, as such, did not generally make direct provision for the administration of the Sacraments in the lifetime of the Wesleys, though it never overlooked or slighted the duty of sacramental administration. The Wesleys themselves administered the Sacraments when and where they itinerated, and kept up the regular administration of them in the model and chief congregations, as, *e.g.*, in London and Bristol, of which they themselves had immediate pastoral charge. In other places, their "assistants" and "helpers," the travelling preachers whom they called out, were required to insist upon the members observing the sacramental ordinances of Christianity in connexion either with their parish churches, or, if Dissenters, with their meeting-houses. After the death of Wesley no time was lost in meeting the wishes of the Methodist Societies, which desired the Sacraments to be administered by their own pastors and teachers.

From the beginning, indeed, the travelling preachers

were the true pastors of the Methodists. They preached to them the gospel which became the power of God to their salvation; they expounded to them the privileges and duties of the Christian life; they watched over their souls as those who must give account to the great Shepherd of souls. They performed the two parts of the office of a shepherd— they led and they fed the flock; they admitted them into the fold and guarded them from straying; they sought out and they guided them into green and good pastures; they went after the stray sheep and healed the wounded; they gathered the lambs and kept them with the flock.

The spiritual discipline of Methodism, in its main features, was marked out in Wesley's days, and, under providential leading, by Wesley's own hand. In its heart and centre the spiritual Church organisation of Methodism to-day remains what it was in Wesley's lifetime. The organised fellowship of the Church is its life-tissue now as it was then. It is a web of fellowship meetings, called class-meetings, each with its leader at its head, now as it was then. It has always been—it still is—the duty of the pastor to visit these class-meetings in turn, conversing spiritually with the members, one by one. The leaders of these classes, now, as then, form the chief part of the pastors' council. At the leaders' meeting it has been always, and is to-day, the business of the Church pastor to learn from the leaders, and the leaders' class-books, what is the spiritual condition of each flock, or, as we say, each Society, and which of the members he is specially called upon to visit pastorally, as being in need of spiritual direction or of human and brotherly sympathy.

With the leaders in the pastoral council, which is named the leaders' meeting, are also joined what we call stewards, who are a sort of deacon distinctly appointed to take charge of the offerings of the Church members in their classes, and also of the contributions for the poor given in the congregations meeting in the sanctuary. Of these stewards or deacons there are two kinds: the Society stewards, who receive what the members of the Society or local flock give for the Lord's cause in their classes; and the stewards for the poor, who receive the contributions given in the Lord's house for the poor. In small Societies there is one steward of each kind; in larger there are two. The leaders and stewards together formed, in the days of Wesley, the pastors' council for each Society. The same is the case to-day. Some other special and occasional duties of great importance have, since Wesley's days, been added to those assigned to the leaders' meetings. But their fundamental duties and their ordinary responsibilities are still what they were then. The development of Wesley's Methodist Society into a fully organised Church, with world-wide branches, has added dignity and importance to the leaders' meeting—that meeting has developed into a pastoral council, which is also, when occasion demands, a court of spiritual discipline for the Church; but this has not obscured its fundamental character, or changed its original constitution. The type is the same, although new faculties have been developed.

Original Methodism, like the primitive Church, developed naturally according to need and opportunity. Each function added, each organ developed, answered to some proved and manifest necessity. Not seldom the work had come to be done—a custom of doing it had grown up—before the fitness and the need of expecting or requiring it so to be done had come to be formally recognised and provided for. It was so with the leaders' meeting and its functions. There were leaders before there were leaders' meetings. In the creation of new Societies, the first few converts needed, at the earliest possible period, to have one placed at their head and made responsible for their gathering together in mutual fellowship, according to the rules of Wesley's Societies. After a while a second leader would be required, because it was found necessary to form a second class; and so, presently, with a third. Two or three leaders and two stewards would constitute a minimum for a leaders' meeting. Till two or three leaders had been appointed there could be no leaders' meeting. It was necessary, accordingly, that a pioneer Methodist itinerant evangelist should, like Titus or Timothy, have power, without reference in the first instance to any local authority, to appoint leaders and also stewards, thus constituting or creating a leaders' meeting. It must also be so to-day in regions of the country where Methodism as yet has had no existence, but where a missionary minister has the privilege of laying the first foundation of a local Methodist Church. The pioneer minister is explorer and discoverer, is captain, is generalissimo; he is, for the time being, clothed with all authority, for, under God, he creates the Church. It could not be otherwise. Of necessity this was almost always the case with the Methodist travelling preachers in the early days of Wesley's Methodism. Hence Wesley insisted upon the unfettered prerogative of the preacher, his "assistant," as he called him, in the organisation of the infant Churches. But he was too wise a man not to recognise that, in a settled Society or local Church, a different state of things must presently supervene. In 1771, referring to Dublin, where the development of Methodism was still in its early infancy, he vindicates for his assistants very high—indeed, unlimited and absolute—prerogative in the appointment of leaders and the organisation of the Society. But he closes his statement of their authority with these characteristic words: " It is common for the assistant, in any place where several leaders are met together, to ask their advice as to anything that concerns either the temporal or spiritual welfare of the Society." So wide was the latitude of care and counsel allowed to the leaders' meeting where even a small leaders' meeting had been organised. Wesley, however, with the caution of which much and sometimes painful experience had taught him the necessity, adds the words: " This he may or he may not do, as he sees best."

This was in 1771, and in Ireland, where Methodism was

at this time far behind England in development. Five and twenty years later, when Wesley's Society had become the Methodist Church, when, if the preachers had become in the fullest sense Church pastors, the laity also had obtained a distinct charter of rights as members of the Church, that which in 1771 was but a *custom* obtained recognition as a *right*. It was enacted in 1795 that when the question of sacramental administration was raised in any Society, it should be determined by the concurrence of the trustees and the leaders' meeting — the trustees as a local authority of one kind, recognised in those days almost more than to-day as of high importance, and the leaders' meeting, as representing especially and with peculiar fitness the spiritual claims and convictions of the Society. So, again, in regard to another point of discipline or administration in connexion with the leaders' meeting, the Conference in 1795 says: " It has been our general *custom* never to appoint or remove a leader or steward without first consulting the leaders and stewards of the Society; and we are resolved to walk by the same *rule*." Here we see how a custom had grown up out of a generally felt sense of fitness and propriety—grown up as the organisation of leaders' meetings became generally mature and efficient—and how that custom is now recognised as a *rule*. In the following year, without any qualifying phrase as to general custom, the Conference affirms a corresponding rule—a rule absolute—as to this point. And in 1797 the rule was finally formulated which has been observed and upheld ever since : " No person shall be appointed a leader or steward, or be removed from his office, but in conjunction with the leaders' meeting ; the nomination to be in the superintendent, and the approbation or disapprobation in the leaders' meeting." In the same year, 1797, the leaders' meeting was first invested with the important responsibility of acting as a jury for the trial of any member accused of immorality.

I am not pretending to give a history, even in barest

outline; but I am giving instances to show how the leaders' meeting came to be organised, and how its functions naturally developed, and were finally fixed at the period when Methodism became an organised Church in the full sense, and when, alike for the pastors and the flock, for the ministers and the Societies, mutual rights, duties, and responsibilities were agreed upon and settled—settled, thank God! for all the generations which have followed.

One lesson, I think, all ministers, in particular, may learn from the instances given and the extracts quoted. If but a few years after the founding of Methodism, —and even in the case of small Societies and leaders' meetings,—it was the custom of Wesley and his assistants to "ask the advice of the leaders as to anything that concerns either the temporal or spiritual welfare of the Society,"—and if, in 1795, four years after Wesley's death, the Conference enacted that the sacrament of the Lord's Supper should not be administered in any chapel without the consent of "the majority of the stewards and leaders belonging to that chapel, as the best qualified to give the sense of the people," how emphatically necessary must it be at the present time that, as to matters of any importance affecting the minds or the feelings—even the prejudices—of the Societies, the superintendent ministers should regard it as their duty, not only to consult, but to take with them the concurrence of, the leaders' meeting! Yet at the same time, how sacred a duty is it for the leaders and stewards, assembled in their meeting, to study, without passion or prejudice, in a large and enlightened way, what in Church arrangements and Church work is most likely to be for the salvation of men and the glory of God! Ministers have their prerogative and responsibility—Church officers their rights and their responsibilities; but all must be for the building up, in truth and holiness, of the Church which is Christ's body. If it is the duty of ministers to regard with religious respect the convictions and feelings of the flock over which they are placed in office, it is also their duty to lay clearly and earnestly before their official helpers and counsellors what they regard as principles, plans, methods necessary for the effectual carrying on of the Lord's work. Ministers are not to be despots, they are not clothed with absolute power; but chief leaders they are to be, initiating plans and leading forward in enterprises for the spread of gospel truth and gospel influence. If they never initiate or lead, or guide, or convince and persuade, or bear strong witness for high principle, but do only what others urge or suggest, allowing routine to rule, and are the mere agents of accidental majorities, then they cannot justly be regarded as ministers of Christ, or stewards of the Divine counsel and will. They do not, indeed, preach themselves, but neither do they preach Christ Jesus the Lord; they are not truly the servants of either Christ or His Church, but are the passive servants of circumstance. On the other hand, without due consultation of their helpers and co-workers, to attempt to force new methods in Church services or Church work, or to set on foot novel schemes or enterprises, would be inexcusable in a Christian pastor, and opposed to the principles and usages of the Methodist Church from its earliest beginning till now.

Methodism can never be understood unless it is borne in mind that it is essentially a missionary organisation. Not only to enter open doors, but, when need demands, to force a way for the gospel against whatever barriers or difficulties, was the spirit of early Methodism; and this spirit ought still to live in modern Methodism. A missionary inspiration should govern the whole working of our Church, whether abroad or at home, in country or in town. When this inspiration has died out—God forbid that it ever should !—when Methodism has come to be a mere aggregate of routine Churches, locally centred and settled, its glory will have finally departed—its character will be lost; settled on its lees, it will become stagnant and corrupt.

The spirit of primitive Christianity alone can avail to perpetuate true Methodism. The persecuted and scattered refugees from Jerusalem came to Antioch—mere laymen, no apostle or elder or official evangelist among them; but they "preached the word," and founded, in the face of obloquy and opposition, alike from Jew and Gentile, the great Christian Church of Antioch, the mother Church of Gentile Christianity. Such a spirit of witness-bearing, of preaching in the true sense, should animate every member of the Church wherever he goes, whether in town or country, whether among cultured people or the homeliest or even lowest classes of society.

I have spoken of the local Society, with its living, practical fellowship, linking together all the members of the Church, with its leaders and stewards,—and with its leaders' meeting, in which the minister meets in council his chief Church helpers,—as the unit of Methodism. Each such unit, however, is a composite unit; the class-meeting is the germ-cell in the life-tissue of Methodism; and each Society is a group of such germ-cells. The Connexional principle rules throughout the entire system. Each Circuit is made up of Societies—is, I may say, a Connexion of Societies. Each province or District of Methodism is a Connexion of Circuits. The entire Methodist Church is a Connexion of Districts, Circuits, and Societies. All these obey the same rules, are under the charge of the same united though itinerant—united because itinerant—pastorate, are all governed by the same yearly Conference.

How the Society unit stands related to the circuit is the point on which I must now touch. The leaders' meeting represents the Society; the circuit meeting, held once a quarter, and known as the Quarterly Meeting, represents the circuit. For many years the quarterly meeting, representing the whole circuit, was in effect an aggregate assembly of all the leaders' meetings in the circuit, and thus was naturally representative of all the Societies included in the circuit, which itself was little else than an aggregate of all the Societies. This was a very natural, and at first apparently an adequate, arrangement; nevertheless, it was not really complete, and now for forty years past the quarterly meeting has been much more than a mere aggregate of the leaders' meetings in the circuit; such, however, and no more, it was, as I have said, for many years. It was never, indeed, defined until the year 1852—that great year in the constitutional development of our Church. The quarterly meetings grew into form by natural laws of working, and the form came, after a while, more or less to vary—more elements being included in them in some circuits than in others—so that it became necessary for the unity and well-working of the Connexion that the meeting should be constitutionally defined. In some quarterly meetings, local preachers had been allowed the right to attend; in many this was not the case. In some, trustees of chapels claimed and were allowed a place—trustees, that is, of principal chapels. In many, trustees had no place. Indeed, it was not in all circuits the rule or usage even for all leaders to attend the quarterly meeting. At first, only the leaders of the principal chapels attended. At the very first, indeed, in most circuits not even these, but only the Society stewards and the general steward—as the circuit steward was originally called; and at first there was but one such general steward in each circuit. That is to say, in the earliest stage of Methodism the quarterly meeting was a meeting of travelling preachers and stewards exclusively.

The necessity from the first for some periodical meeting —and, in conformity with English habits of business, for some quarterly meeting—of at least the Society stewards for their respective Societies and the general steward for the circuit, is obvious. The income of the circuit for the support of the work of Christ—on which the maintenance of the itinerant preachers, though the principal, was not by any means the only charge—needed to be regularly collected. The Society stewards had charge of the income for the respective Societies. The general steward in each circuit received the whole and disbursed the whole, on account of the circuit. It was at first disbursed or distributed according to the requirements and rules of Mr. Wesley personally; after a while, not of Mr. Wesley merely, but of the Conference which he was led to organise; hence, each quarter, it was necessary that the general steward should see the books and receive the contributions of the Society stewards. Here we have the germ of the Quarterly Meeting, the nucleus of what is now so numerous and comprehensive a gathering. When, however, at these quarterly meetings the itinerant preachers met the stewards at the circuit centre, or one of the chief places of the circuit, such leaders of the Society at the place where they met as were able and willing to attend would be naturally welcomed; and as these meetings were also of necessity, more or less, meetings for consultation as to the needs of the circuit, spiritual as well as temporal, the presence of such leaders would be a valuable addition to the gathering. At a period, however, when nearly all the officers of the Society, all the leaders, as well as the members, and all the stewards also, with rare exceptions, were labouring men, not their own masters, and to whom, besides, a day's work was precious, it will be understood that the primitive quarterly meetings of Methodism were very small in numbers, and that business was briefly and speedily disposed of. As years passed, and many of the Church officers came to be in better circumstances, by a natural process the quarterly meetings became larger and their business occupied more time. Not long after the death of Wesley, it became the rule to have in each circuit two general or circuit stewards; in many circuits it grew to be the usage and came to be regarded as a matter of right that all leaders should have a place in the quarterly meeting. Where it was the custom for the local preachers—of whom more must be said presently—to hold their quarterly meetings at the same place and at nearly the same time as the circuit quarterly meeting, the local preachers were often drawn into the circuit quarterly meeting, and, after a time, came to be recognised as members of that meeting. This, however, was nothing more than a local custom till 1852, when the composition of the quarterly meeting was, at length, defined by the Conference.

In that year, on the recommendation of the special committee for the revision of the constitutional rules of our Church, of which the Rev. William Arthur and myself are now the only surviving members, the quarterly meeting received a definition which was not modified for nearly forty years, and which was intended to make it representative of all the official elements of power or influence essential to the circuit, including not only all stewards and leaders, but all trustees being also members of the Church, all local preachers, and certain officers appointed by the meeting.

It may surprise you when I say that in 1852 there was considerable objection on the part of laymen as well as ministers to what was regarded as a sudden and more or less dangerous enlargement of the representative circuit meeting. More than a few objected to the admission of local preachers, some even objected to giving all leaders a necessary and official place in the meeting. In Cornwall, in particular, there was a considerable objection to this point on the part of some able and loyal men. It had not been the custom in that county for the leaders from small and remote country places to attend the quarterly meeting. In this respect primitive conditions and primitive customs had continued there to prevail. Indeed, I have often heard leading Cornish gentlemen tell how the Rev. Samuel Dunn, himself a Cornishman, not without the support of some of his stewards, had refused to recognise any other quarterly meeting than one composed exclusively of stewards, and had enforced his determination effectually. This minister, however, having soon afterwards tried the same thing in a leading circuit of the rough and strong " Black

Country," his daring and strong-willed attempt led to an historical case, which issued in the Conference, ten years before any formal definition of the quarterly meeting, passing a judicial resolution which deserves mention in this sketch of the development of the quarterly meeting. The superintendent minister in question maintained in Dudley what he had maintained in Camborne, declaring that he stood upon the ground of John Wesley's own Methodism. Mr. Cox, the father of three sons in the ministry, of whom two still survive, himself a loyal as well as an influential Methodist, appealed to the Birmingham District Meeting, against his superintendent. The District Meeting condemned the action of the superintendent, and overruled his decision. The Conference confirmed the judgment of the District Meeting. Thus, indirectly and by a special decision in the case, the Conference was led to anticipate by several years the legislation of 1852, at least in regard to all circuits where leaders or local preachers had gained a customary title to attend the quarterly meeting. What was done in 1852 was, however, more than this. The right was made universal, and, as I have said, such an extension as this was not approved by all. The laymen who demurred were wise and liberal as well as loyal men, who were influenced by local circumstances and feeling, and whose objection was limited to making the right necessary and universal. I have referred to this case and the minister in question as necessary elements in a history of circuit constitutional development. Before the year 1852 Mr. Dunn had ceased to belong to our Church.

No change was made in the definition of the quarterly meeting after 1852 till 1894, when, for the first time, direct representatives of Sunday schools were admitted to the circuit meeting. This subject had been long under consideration. Twenty years earlier, the Education Committee had recommended the principle to the adoption of the Conference. But the Sunday-school constituency was so immense, that the difficulty was to give any representation at all to the schools without making the quarterly meetings unmanageably large. Besides which, as many of the Sunday-school teachers and officers were otherwise qualified as members of the quarterly meeting and actually attended that meeting, and as the affairs of all the schools were brought up by separate schedule and report every year at the spring quarterly meeting, it was argued that Sunday-school affairs were already well represented at the quarterly meeting. At last, however, after many plans had been discussed and found impracticable, in 1893 a plan of representation was finally adopted by the Conference.

At first, for reasons which are sufficiently obvious, the business of the quarterly meetings was confined to the limits of the necessary minimum. That business, however, was never, as some have imagined—it was not even in the earliest times—merely financial. It is doubtful, indeed, whether the business of any meeting in our Church, except some strictly limited sub-committee, whether even the ordinary business of a trustees' meeting, can be held to be strictly and barely financial. Spiritual uses and objects underlie all the business of Methodism. Circuit funds are for spiritual objects — and only for such objects. Stewards, in making up circuit accounts, or, at any rate, in calculating circuit needs and expenses, cannot but keep spiritual objects and needs in view, as the ground of all their business. The two aspects of our business, the financial and the spiritual, are inseparable. There is an important, a necessary, an indispensable financial side to the class-leader's work as well as to the steward's. The leader is himself steward for the moneys of his class. And he is a very defective leader who ignores or neglects his financial duty. Thus, at the quarterly meeting, from the first, the reports as to Church membership and as to Church funds stood alike to the front as inseparably allied subjects for the attention of the meeting. Every steward, no less than every leader, ought, like the deacons of apostolic times, to be full of the Holy Ghost as well as of wisdom. If their functions, in their outward aspects, are secular, they have, at the same time, a spiritual meaning and reference ; and it is a great evil when the stewards of a circuit or of a Society are mere men of business, are men of merely secular minds.

The quarterly meeting, indeed, is the centre, and I might almost say the sum, of the spiritual forces of the circuit for carrying on the work of Christ and His Church. The spiritual condition of the different Societies, with their increase or decrease in Church members, the prosecution of circuit missions, the building of new places of worship, the efficiency or otherwise of the Sunday schools and day schools of the circuit, the provision of pastors for the Churches, the support of the Connexional, or of the special District, Home Mission work, the support of Foreign Missions—all these subjects are under the charge and direction of the quarterly meeting, which is the common council of all the local branch Churches that make up the circuit. Nor is this all. It is from the circuit quarterly meeting that candidates for the work of the sacred ministry have to obtain their first credentials of character, before they can be admitted to any examination as to gifts and calling for the pastoral office. Is it possible, then, to exaggerate the spiritual responsibility or to insist too strongly on the spiritual character of the quarterly meeting? The superintendent and his colleagues standing in the midst of such a council of Church officers, every one of whom is entrusted with special work and responsibility on behalf of Christ and His kingdom, are placed at the centre of an aggregate of great Christian forces. What a post of vantage! what need of wisdom, grace, divine inspiration for all ministers so placed, and also for those who are called to be their fellow helpers! A circuit with five hundred members and two ministers may, not unlikely, have a quarterly meeting of not less than one hundred members. Many circuits have much larger common councils than this :

some not less than two hundred, if all attended that had the right; while scarcely any, even in small and feeble circuits, have as few as thirty; so popular a system is our Methodist circuit organisation. And yet how harmoniously are these meetings conducted, how seldom do we hear of serious divisions of opinion, much less of disturbances! The principle that, in the appointment of circuit or Society officers, those chosen must have the confidence equally of the superintendent minister and of the members of the meeting into which they are to be introduced, is, no doubt, to a considerable extent, the secret of the order, the harmony, the good feeling which so generally—almost universally—prevails. But a gracious Providence has ruled in the ordering of the whole.

With a few words as to local preachers I shall conclude this address. Our lay helpers in preaching work—called local preachers in contradistinction from the itinerant preachers—were not organised into definite bands with their regular quarterly meetings till after the days of Wesley. At first the number of such preachers was, of necessity, very small. They were allowed to help in preaching at the call of the assistant—Wesley's itinerant helper—who often employed casually, under stress of demand, those whom it would not have been wise to employ regularly. The best of them at first were soon reported as such to Wesley, and if he approved, and they were willing to bear the cost and burden, were sent forth as itinerants. A list was kept by the assistant, where such a list could be formed, and handed on to his successor; but all was in a condition of continual flux. Towards the close of Wesley's life, in some of the larger and older circuits, the number became considerable, and there was some continuity in the company of preachers, so that local preachers' meetings began to be called and held with something like regularity. A natural consequence was that about the year 1796 it became a rule that local preachers should not be placed on the plan or officially recognised without having been approved at the local preachers' meeting. Local preachers' meetings thus grew up, at first only in the best organised circuits, but afterwards in all. These local preachers' quarterly meetings, of course, were altogether independent and apart from the circuit quarterly meetings. Nor was there any obvious link of connexion between the work and charge of a local preacher and the business of the quarterly meeting in the earlier years of its history and development. It was, as we have seen, the accident of holding the local preachers' meeting in some large and important circuits at the same place and nearly at the same time, of holding it in a sort of business contiguity, with the circuit quarterly meeting, which led to the admission, in the first instance, rather in the way of brotherly courtesy than of business, of the local preachers into the quarterly meetings. Nevertheless it was a wise and statesmanlike, as well as a large and broad, provision which led the Conference, in 1852, to give local preachers as such an official place in the quarterly meetings. It united in the common council of the circuit an important and popular class of Christian workers; and it served to mark the broad spiritual field and range of the quarterly meeting's responsibility.

Such is a condensed outline of circuit development in Methodism—embracing the class-meeting, the leaders' meeting, the circuit quarterly meeting, and the local preachers' meeting; including also the respective responsibilities and duties of ministers and circuit officers in their different spheres. This development covers a century and a half of growth and advancement, from stage to stage, under the pressure of need, the incentive of opportunity, the light of New Testament teaching and apostolic precedent, and the guidance of Divine Providence.

GENERAL INDEX

A

ACT OF UNFORMITY, 65.
AMERICAN EPISCOPAL METHODISM: outline of its origin and development, 262-266; first General Conference (1784), Delegated Conference (1812), laymen admitted (1872), 266-267; Wesley's "bishops" and their powers, 268; the "presiding elder" in his duties and prerogatives, 269-274; the "preacher in charge" and leaders' meetings, 274; varieties of local preachers in, 275; peculiarities and development of, 276; rights of the laity in (secession of Methodist Protestant Church, 1830), 277; compared with Independency, 279; strain on the presiding eldership, and the principle of lay delegation in, 280-284; development of constitutional lay authority in, 285, 286; plan of lay delegation adopted, 287-290; scene at Brooklyn Conference (1868), 290, 291; alternative suggestions by Dr. Perrine and others, 292, 293; over-pressure of business in the General Conference, 294; comparison of, with English Methodism, 296-298; secessions from (Methodist Episcopal Church South, 1844), and statistics, 298, 299.
AMERICAN STATES, The, and Disestablishment, 107, 108.
ANGEL OF THE CHURCH, The, in the Apocalypse, 41.
ANGLICAN CHURCH: its appeal for authority, 3, 25, 26; Puritanism cast out of, 16; does it provide adequate fellowship? 18, 21, 22; its claim to be primitive and apostolic, 49-54, 69, 72, 73; other exaggerated assumptions and invention of the theory, 49, 74-78; effect of the *Reformation* on the, and its position during the *Tudor period*, 49-66; its need of apology, 51; its relation to other churches, 51, 52, 56, 80; monarchical head of, 52; loss of primitive fellowship in, 54, 59, 65, 70, 71; 89-92, 99, 103; disabilities of the laity, 53, 55, 91, 93, 98, 102, 107; private brotherhoods within the, 57; Erastianism and the, 59-61, 70; effect of the Spanish Armada on, 64; its unevangelical character, 66, 70; Latitudinarianism of, 68, 76; recent provision for lay fellowship, 104; its position during the *Stuart period*, 67; changes within the, 68; its Romanised ritual, 69; its form of government, 72; revival of Stuart-Reformation claims, 76; social effect of theory of apostolical succession, 85; its relation to the unity and continuity of the Christian Church, 81; its Articles, 62, 64, 83; controversy on *Church Reform* in, 87-114; its threefold ministry and diocesan authority, 87-90; its defect in the matter of lay diaconate, and believers' fellowship, 90-96; University addresses (1885) and other discussions on reform of, 96-104; anomalies as to membership in, 97-104; the Guild movement in, 104, 105; Disestablishment and the, 107, 110; Popish principles and rationalism in the,

110; intolerance of its clergy, 111; its perils and possibilities, 114.

APOSTOLICAL SUCCESSION: The theory of, exaggerated claims of Anglican Church, 49-54, 69, 72; a "fable," 73; invention of the theory, 74, 75; its incredibility, and the contradictions it involves, 76-78; incongruity of the claim; and relation of the theory to Roman Catholic Greek Churches, 80; social effect of the theory, 85.

Appendices.—The Class-meeting in Wesleyan Methodism, 345-354; the District Synod in Methodism, 355-376; the Circuit development of Methodism, 377-392.

ARNOLD, DR., on the laity of the Church, 54, 95, 96.

ARTICLES, THIRTY-NINE, The, their definition and adoption, 62, 64; the nineteenth article, 83.

ASSOCIATION, WESLEYAN METHODIST (1836): Principles and statistics of, and absorption of Protestant Methodists, 311; amalgamation of, with "Reformers," forming United Methodist Free Churches (1857), 313.

B

BANCROFT, DR.: his Anglo-Catholic theory of orders, 63; his teaching as to the divine right of bishops, 74, 75.

BIBLE CHRISTIAN CHURCH, Origin of, 315-317; article by Rev. John S. Simon quoted, 318-322.

"BRETHREN," The: their ideas as to Church organisation, 4, 7; their fellowship and brotherhood, 21, 22.

C

CALVINISM: personal influence of Calvin, 118, 119; its stern logical system, 120; instructive rather than experimental, 121; features of modern, 123; influence of, upon Protestant churches, 124.

CIRCUIT DEVELOPMENT of Methodism, 377-392.

CLASS MEETING in Methodism, The, 345-354.

CLEMENT OF ROME, 36.

CONGREGATIONALISM: an historical study of the principles and working of Independency till recent years, 153-169; an examination of the principles of Congregational Independency, 170-203; its basis of membership, 154; a point of fundamental difference from Episcopalianism and Presbyterianism, 154; early Independency and "free" prophecy, 155, 156; subsequent sterility, 157; influence of Evangelical revival on, 157, 158, 160-162; political and religious activity in, 159, 162; success in the great cities, 158, 161; its three leading principles, 162, 163; its politico-ecclesiastical theories, 163-169, 172; its limited provision for fellowship, 166-169; its fundamental theoretical error, 171, 175; the position of the pastor in, 172-174; its non-aggressive tendency, 176, 185; practical dangers of its theories illustrated, 177, 182; its lack of ministerial unity, 179, 183, 184; lay preaching in, 184; its derivation of ministerial authority compared with Scripture teaching, 187-192; its discipline in the light of the apostolic churches, 192, 194; an analogy from worldly commonwealths, and a suggestion, 195, 196; its power of adaptability, 196-198; the relation of Methodism to, 198-200; *Note* on membership in, 201-203.

CONTINENTAL PROTESTANTISM: Lack of mutual fellowship in, 15; comparison with Roman Church, 16; influence of, at Reformation, 62.

CURTEIS, CANON: his threefold division of Christendom, 49, 50; his proposed equivalent for the primitive fellowship, 100; other references to, 69, 73, 81, 94.

D

DALE, DR.: his views on Church organisation, 34; his Manual of Congregational Principles, 162.

DEACONS: Earliest appointment of, 28; other references to, 36, 39-41, 193.

DEED OF DECLARATION, Wesley's (1784), 225, 231.

GENERAL INDEX

DISESTABLISHMENT: The Anglican Church and, 107, 110; the American States and, 107, 108.
DISRUPTION, The, 120, 146.
DIVINE RIGHT OF KINGS, 67, 68.

E

ELDERS (presbyter-bishops): First appointment of, 28; nature of office of, 31; eldership included teaching as well as governing, 31; the ruling eldership in Presbyterianism, 125-132.
ERASMUS, Effect of writings of, on the Reformation, 58.
ERASTIANISM: definition of, 59 (*note*); the Anglican Church and, at the Reformation, 59-61, 70; Presbyterianism and, 118, 120.
EVANGELICAL ORTHODOXY, the essential doctrines of, 10.

F

FELLOWSHIP, CHRISTIAN: its vital elements, 8, 9; necessity for its provision, 11; consequences of absent or impaired, 14; substitutes for, in Roman Church, 17; its reproduction in Methodism, 18; place of, in Anglican Church, 18; in Scotch Presbyterian Churches, 19; in Congregationalist bodies, 20; among the "Brethren," 21, 22; absence of equivalent for primitive, its vital defect in any Church system, 300; see also references to, under various Church organisations.

G

GENEVAN CALVINISM, 60, 62, 63, 66.
GORE, CANON, his views on apostolical succession, 73, 76.
GROSSETESTE, his influence on the Reformation, 56.

H

HARE, ARCHDEACON: on Anglican claims, 50; the laity of the Church, 94-96.

HATCH, DR.: his views respecting elders, 31, 41; fellowship, 106 (*note*).

I

IGNATIAN EPISTLES, The, 41-43, 88, 128.
IRISH CHURCH, The, 109.

J

JACOB, DR., his "Ecclesiastical Polity of the New Testament," 50.

K

KEBLE, JOHN, his view of Nonconformists as "heretics," 85.
KILHAM, ALEXANDER, leader of 1797 secession, 252, 306, 307.
KNOX, JOHN, the *First Book of Discipline*, 133.

L

LIDDON, CANON, on Anglican claims, 49, 69, 73, 87-89.
LIGHTFOOT, BISHOP: his views as to Epistle to Ephesians, 35; Ignatian Epistle, 43; Episcopate in early Church, 43.
LUTHERANISM: Effect of Erastianism, 60; Luther's influence on the Reformation, 58.

M

MINISTRY: Varieties of, in the early Church, apostolic witness to, 27-37; other witness to, 37-44; the threefold ministry in Anglicanism, 87, 89.
MODERATISM in the Presbyterian Church, 19, 120.
MONASTERIES, Dissolution of the, 57.
MORAVIANS, their maintenance of the primitive fellowship, 16.

N

NEANDER, the election of Church officers, 195.

NEW CONNEXION CHURCH (1797): Principles of, and statistics, 305–308; article by Rev. John S. Simon quoted, 307.
NONCONFORMITY, its part in maintaining primitive doctrine, 16, 20.

O

ORDINATION OF MINISTERS, in Wesleyan Methodism, 310.
ORGANISATIONS, CHURCH: the Primitive Church, 24–45; Anglicanism, 49–114; Presbyterianism, 117–150; Congregationalism, 153–203; Wesleyan Methodism, 207–301; other Methodist bodies, 305–342; the essential attributes of, 3; incomplete if fellowship not provided for, 14; New Testament only gives principles as to, 24, 26; simplicity of original, and stages of development, 27–31; the apostolic brotherhood, 27; appointment of deacons, 28; elders, 28; incidental character of New Testament references to these appointments, 29; no fuller information as to, in Gentile Churches, 29, 30; nature of the elder's office, 31; considerable difference in apostolic, 32; illustrated in Epistles to Romans, Corinthians, Ephesians, 32–36; witness of the *Teaching of the Apostles*, etc., as to variations and developments of, 37–44; adaptation and development of, according to circumstances, 44, 45; the true mean as to, midway between Episcopalian theory and Congregational Independency, 186; review of, in apostolic times, 187–195.

P

PIETISTS, The, their maintenance of primitive doctrine, 16, 17.
PRESBYTERIANISM: its first principles, 117–137; its later character, 138–150; anomalies of early, 117–120, 134; Erastianism and blending of Church and State in, 118–120; defective as to fellowship, 19, 117; its special difficulties in relation to spiritual experiences, 136–139; influence of the Disruption on, 120; modern character of, 124, 125, 140; displacement of "deacons" in, 128, 129, 131; "lay elder" a misnomer, 130; the "ruling eldership" in, 60, 125–132; its approach to Ignatian Episcopacy, 128; the spiritual lay element in, 132–135; its promotion of evangelical family life, 135, 136; influence of the Methodist spirit on, 139–142; a masterpiece of organisation, 141, 142; its anti-popery influence, 135, 136, 141, 143; its position in America, 142, 149; in other countries, 143–145; modern external changes, 146–148; its future, 150; Calvinism, etc., 118–124.
PRIMITIVE CHURCH: its fellowship, 3–23; its organisation (30–130 A.D.), 24–45; appeal of Anglicans, "Brethren," Presbyterians, Congregationalists, to, 3–5; nature of Wesleyan appeal to, 24; its fellowship a brotherhood, 11; apostolic witness to varieties of ministry and Church organisation in, 27–37; other witnesses, 37–44; authority of apostolic brotherhood, 27; appointment of deacons, 28; elders (presbyter-bishops), 28, 31; incidental character of New Testament references to these appointments, 29; nature of the elder's office, 31; adaptation and development of organisation in, according to circumstances, 44, 45; review of the organisation of the, in apostolic times, 187–195.
PRIMITIVE METHODIST CHURCH: Origin of, 315–317; article by Rev. John S. Simon, quoted, 318–322.
PROTESTANT METHODISTS (1828): Origin of, 310; coalesced with Wesleyan Methodist Association (1836), 311.
PURITANISM: its savour of fellowship, 16; beginning of the Puritan controversy, 65–68; its insistence on the divine right of the Presbyterian platform, as opposed to prelatic episcopacy, 74, 75; decay of, 76.

R

REFORMATION, The: its effect on the

GENERAL INDEX 397

Church of England, 49; its incomplete character, 53, 56; Reformers before the, 57; preparation for the, 58; personal and political motives in the, 59; not an evangelical reform, 59; Erastian and Episcopal elements in the, 59, 61, 67; its real but slow advance, 62-64; effect of Spanish Armada on, 64; influence of Elizabeth on, 65.
REFORMERS, WESLEYAN METHODIST (1850), amalgamated with "Association," thus forming United Methodist Free Churches (1857), 313.
ROBINSON, JOHN, of Leyden, 155, 156, 165.
ROMAN CATHOLICISM: Loss of primitive fellowship in, 16, 17; monasticism and the confessional, 16, 17; its absolute claim to divine origin and direction, 25; the Anglican Church and, 49; despotism of, 56; reaction against, 63.

S

SACRAMENTS, the two, 10.
SCOTLAND, Free Church movement in, 61.
SECESSIONS, METHODIST: General remarks upon, 243, 244; *New Connexion* (1797), 305, 308; *Protestant Methodists* (1828), 310; *Wesleyan Methodist Reformers* (1850), 313; *United Methodist Free Churches* (1857), 313; amalgamation between "Association" and "Reformers" (1857), 313; *Primitive Methodists* and *Bible Christians* (offshoots rather than secessions), 315-317.
SEPARATISTS, THE, their protest against early Presbyterian principles, 134, 135.
SIDMOUTH'S, LORD, Bill, 159.
SPANISH ARMADA, Effect of the, on the Reformation, 64.
SPURGEON, MR., his influence on Baptist Churches, 21, 144.
STANLEY, DEAN, on Anglican claims, 50, 73.
SYNOD, DISTRICT, in Methodism, 355-376.

T

TEACHING OF THE APOSTLES, The

light thrown on questions of Church organisation and discipline by, 14, 23, 37-43, 88, 129.
THEOLOGICAL INSTITUTION, formation of, 309, 310.

U

UNION, METHODIST: General considerations involved in the question of, 322; the rights of "societies" as well as Conference, 323; the inwardness of the question of, 324; difficulties involved as to ministers, 325; trust-estates, 325; leaders' meetings, 325; doctrine, 326; New Connexion and, 326; United Methodist Free Churches and, 327; Primitive Methodists and Bible Christians and, 328-331; no ripeness for, 331; advantages of variety, 332-334; the case of Irish Methodism and, 335-337; the case of Canadian Methodism and, 337-340; dangers of premature action in the direction of, 340; Methodist fraternity illustrated at Westminster and Southlands, 341; combination of Methodist Churches for practical purposes, 342.
UNITED METHODIST FREE CHURCHES (1857): an amalgamation of "Association" (1836) and "Reformers" (1850); principles and statistics, 313-315.

W

WARREN, DR., leader of "Association" secession, 311.
WESLEY, JOHN, apostolical succession "a fable," 73.
WESLEYAN METHODISM: *its early history and characteristics*, 207-220; reproduction of principle of fellowship in, 18, 211-213; its influence on other churches, 20; its appeal to the primitive Church; 24; erection of organs in chapels of, 143; the revival of primitive doctrine and fellowship in, 207; its doctrinal combat with sacramental superstition and Calvinism, 208-211; its earliest organisation, 214; maintenance of living fellowship essential to evangelical

doctrine, 215 ; a training-ground for service and authority, 216 ; its experimental character: preaching should be extempore, 217–220 ; *its ecclesiastical organisation*, 221–234 ; harmony of, with apostolic Christianity, 221–223 ; growth of lay element in : leaders, stewards, local preachers, 223, 224 ; its administration : local bodies, the annual Conference, District Synods, 224–228 ; its organisation a growth, 228 ; itinerancy of its ministers, 229–234 ; *its distinctive principles*, 235–261 ; the balance of forces in, 235 ; comparison of, with Presbyterianism (letter from John Wesley, 261), 236–242 ; its distinctness from more democratic bodies, 243, 244 ; political analogies misleading, 244, 245 ; the pastoral office (Richard Watson quoted), 244–249 ; ministers and leaders' meetings in (William Arthur quoted), 249–253 ; union of ministers and laity in, 254–261 ; ministers of, first officially styled " Reverend " (1818), 309 ; Theological Institution established (1834), 310 ; ordination by imposition of hands (1836), 310 ; effect of secessions on, 311, 312 ; Class-meeting in, 345–354 ; District Synod in, 355–376 ; the circuit development of, 377–392.

WESTMINSTER CONFESSION, The, 123.

WICLIF, his influence on the Reformation, 56, 58.

www.ingramcontent.com/pod-product-compliance
Lightning Source LLC
Chambersburg PA
CBHW022110290426
44112CB00008B/619